MW01148570

SET APART

THE NATURE & IMPORTANCE OF BIBLICAL SEPARATION

MARK SIDWELL

JOURNEYFORTH
ACADEMIC

GREENVILLE, SOUTH CAROLINA

Library of Congress Cataloging-in-Publication Data

Names: Sidwell, Mark, 1958- author.
Title: Set apart : the nature and importance of biblical separation / Mark
    Sidwell.
Other titles: Dividing line
Description: Greenville : JourneyForth Academic, 2016. | Previous edition:
    The Dividing Line. Greenville, SC : Bob Jones University Press, 1998. |
    Includes bibliographical references and index.
Identifiers: LCCN 2016011894 (print) | LCCN 2016012733 (ebook) | ISBN
    9781628562583 (perfect bound pbk. : alk. paper) | ISBN 9781628562590
    (ebook)
Subjects: LCSH: Fundamentalism. | Separation from sin--Christianity. |
    Fundamentalist churches--Doctrines. | Separation from sin--Biblical
    teaching.
Classification: LCC BT82.2 .S53 2016 (print) | LCC BT82.2 (ebook) | DDC
    270.8/2--dc23
LC record available at http://lccn.loc.gov/2016011894

All Scripture quotations are from the King James Version (KJV) unless otherwise
noted.

Set Apart: The Nature and Importance of Biblical Separation
Mark Sidwell, PhD

Cover design by Nathan Hutcheon
Page layout by Michael Boone
The first edition of this book was published in 1998 as
The Dividing Line: Understanding and Applying Biblical Separation.

©2016 BJU Press
Greenville, South Carolina 29614
JourneyForth Academic is a division of BJU Press.

Printed in the United States of America
All rights reserved

ISBN 978-1-62856-258-3

15   14   13   12   11   10   9   8   7   6   5   4   3   2   1

CONTENTS

PREFACE

It encourages a writer when there is enough interest in something he has written to merit a new edition. I am happy and humbled to be asked to provide an updated second edition of *The Dividing Line*. I will allow the preface to the first edition (reprinted on the following pages) to introduce my theme and purpose since my overall focus has not changed. I will limit this note to explaining what is different in this edition and expressing appreciation for several people who contributed to the revision. I mention first of all that the publisher has suggested the new title for this edition: *Set Apart: The Nature and Importance of Biblical Separation*. I heartily endorse this change because it highlights a key element of my argument. The Christian doctrine of sanctification means being "set apart" by Christ, and sanctification is a major motive in the practice of separation.

The text is substantially the same. I have taken the opportunity to clear up some ambiguities, expand on thoughts that needed clarification, and to update illustrations. The purpose of an illustration is to make a point more obvious, which does not happen when the illustration has become so dated as to be obscure. For example, while working on this revision, I mentioned to my family that I had dropped the reference to Promise Keepers, a group so much in the news among Christians in 1998. My college-aged son asked, "What are the Promise Keepers?" He made my point for me.

There are only three sections where there is any significant difference. In Chapter 6 on fundamentalism, I have expanded the discussion of the more recent period in order to show how there are ongoing questions about the practice of separation even within the movement. Chapter 9 of the first edition, "The New Evangelicalism," is now simply "Evangelicalism." Rather than focus on just the movement that challenged fundamentalism over the separation question, I wanted to deal with the whole evangelical movement and discuss questions that have arisen since the first edition. Chapter 12, "Examples of Separation in History," is the only entirely new chapter. Its purpose is to reinforce a lesson I have tried to emphasize, that separation is not simply the practice of a contemporary group that arises from its historical situation. Rather, Christians throughout history have seen and obeyed the imperative to defend the Christian faith, even to the point of separation.

The preface to the first edition contains notes of thanks to many who originally contributed to this work. For the second edition, I want to add several more acknowledgements. First, I would like to thank Dr. Stephen Hankins who provided for this revision under the writing endowment of Bob Jones University Seminary and Graduate School of Religion. I also want to thank friends and colleagues from the university who read and commented on the manuscript: Dr. John Matzko, Dr. Gerald Priest, and Dr. Sam Schnaiter. Thanks also goes to Patrick Robbins and others on the library staff at BJU for helping dig out research materials. I thank all of these folks for their help, but of course any errors that remain in the book are entirely my responsibility.

Mark Sidwell
March 2016

PREFACE TO THE DIVIDING LINE

An unusually large number of books on Fundamentalism written by Fundamentalists have been published since 1990. I personally have had the pleasure of serving as editor for two such books (*"Be Ye Holy": The Call to Christian Separation* by Fred Moritz and *The Tragedy of Compromise: The Origin and Impact of the New Evangelicalism* by Ernest Pickering). The question will probably be asked, in light of these and other works,[1] why yet another book on separation?

The purpose of this book is to supplement, not to supplant, other studies. One of my goals is to present an introductory work on the topic that laymen can profitably use. I was surprised how many works on separation assume that readers already know basically what separation is and what terms such as "personal separation" and "ecclesiastical separation" mean. But I do not want to limit this work just to laymen. I hope that pastors, missionaries, Bible teachers, and others involved in Christian ministries may profit as well from its brief discussions.

I also want to help Christians see how separation applies to trends and movements in history and even more in today's religious scene. Perhaps it is my own background in church history, but I have often found my own understanding of biblical teaching deepened as I have seen such teachings worked out and applied in history. I hope, therefore, that the chapters on Fundamentalism, liberalism, Neo-orthodoxy, the New Evangelicalism, the Charismatic movement, and Roman Catholicism will help Christians understand how separation should be applied and practiced.

This book is written from an unashamedly Fundamentalist viewpoint. That fact will be obvious as the reader proceeds. It is not written as a justification of the Fundamentalist position, however, as much as it is a defense of a biblical teaching that Fundamentalists affirm. My goal is to explain and apply the biblical teaching of separation. I wholeheartedly believe that of all contemporary religious movements, Fundamentalism most closely follows the biblical pattern for separation. But I am more concerned that readers practice separation in a biblical manner than I am whether they bear the label *Fundamentalist*.

This book is titled *The Dividing Line*. As certainly as Christ separates the sheep from the goats (Matt. 25:32–33), so there is a divide between truth and error. Separation involves discerning that line and taking a stand on the right side of that line. In order to echo Moses' call, "Who is on the Lord's side?" (Exod. 32:26), Christians need to know what the sides are and which of the sides is the Lord's. These questions can be answered only through searching the Scripture.

The issues involved in biblical separation are not minor ones. Just before God brought judgment on Korah and his rebellious followers, Moses said to the children of Israel, "Depart, I pray you, from the tents of these wicked men, and touch nothing of theirs, lest ye be consumed in all their sins" (Num. 16:26). Fundamentalists view the dividing line of scriptural separation with that same seriousness. I recognize that some critics of Fundamentalism view statements such as these as a return to Manichaeism, the ancient dualistic heresy that viewed history as the eternal struggle between spiritual forces of light and darkness.[2] Supposedly, this dualistic point of view causes Christians to be too absolutist in their outlook toward life and toward other people. Also implied in this criticism is that Fundamentalists have too small a view of God. The sovereign God who controls our destinies and comforts our hearts is replaced by a limited deity who needs our aid in a conflict whose outcome is in doubt.

Christians must see the reality of this present spiritual struggle, and it is no favor to anyone—Christian or non-Christian—to pretend that this conflict does not exist. But the fact that this struggle is presently occurring does not mean it is an eternal warfare. One of my former teachers, Edward Panosian, has written, "One who reads the Bible is conscious of a universal struggle between two powers: God and Satan, good and evil, truth and error. This conflict pervades the ages and all the institutions of life, even life itself." But he does not stop there: "While universal, it is not eternal. The Bible assures us that God is Victor, good is triumphant, Truth will be enthroned. This assurance is not only a hoped-for expectation; it is a present reality—not yet realized but no less real."[3] It is with a view toward that inevitable victory that this book is written.

*   *   *   *

In any published work there is always a need to acknowledge the debts to many people who have helped in its preparation and production. Let me first express my deep gratitude to the Bible faculty of Bob Jones University, whose little pamphlet *Biblical Separation* (1980) laid the basis for Chapters 3–5 of this book. Although the content has been expanded, the basic outline and approach still follow that of the original pamphlet. It helped my confidence in writing those chapters to know that I was drawing on the work of men devoted to both sound biblical scholarship and the pursuit of godliness.

Recognition is also due to Dr. Randy Leedy of the graduate religion faculty at BJU, who did the initial work on this project. His contribution is largest in Chapter 2, and his research on liberalism greatly facilitated the writing of Chapter 7. Likewise, I was guided in the later chapters by Dr. David Beale's syllabus "Fundamentalism and Its Foes: Recent and Current Trends in Religion."

My thanks also goes to Dr. Philip Smith, provost of Bob Jones University, for initiating this project. A special word of gratitude is also due to several others who read all or part of the manuscript: Dr. Bob Jones III, president of BJU; Dr. Thurman Wisdom, dean of the School of Religion; Dr. Dan Olinger of the staff at Bob Jones University Press; and several members of the University's Bible and history faculties: Mr. Richard Gray, Dr. David Beale, Dr. Terry Rude, Dr. Sam Schnaiter, Dr. Randy Jaeggli, Dr. Carl Abrams, Dr. John Matzko, and Dr. Edward Panosian. I appreciate their time and their many valuable suggestions.

And finally, let me say a special word of thanks to my former colleagues at Bob Jones University Press. All I can say is that they have performed at their usual high levels of professionalism, excellence, and Christian dedication. Seeing the results of their labor in print will always remind me how much I owe them and how much I miss working with them.

Mark Sidwell
September 1998

CHAPTER ONE
DEFINING OUR TERMS

Depending on your background, as you pick up this book, the words *biblical separation* may interest you, offend you, or mystify you. Some Christians have grown up in churches with balanced teaching on the idea of separation, and for them it is as much a part of their system of belief as the deity of Christ or the inspiration of the Bible. Others come from situations in which the term seemed to be an excuse for quarrels, antagonism, and hostility. Still others may have been Christians for years and have never heard the term.

Let us say first, then, that the teaching of separation is not just some offbeat idea dreamed up by American fundamentalists during the twentieth century to justify their practices. Rather, it is a concept taught in the pages of Scripture. That some Christians have not heard of the concept or that others have abused it does not change the fact that separation is a biblical concept Christians should pay close attention to.

What is biblical separation? The basic idea is that Christians should strive to be free from sin. More specifically, they are to be separated *to* God and *from* sin. There are many ramifications to this idea. You may hear of "personal separation" and "ecclesiastical separation," for example. We will discuss these and other concepts as we go on, but the main point to keep in mind is that Jesus Christ died so that believers would be free from sin. A popular way of summarizing this deliverance is to say that Jesus delivers sinners from the penalty of sin (the punishment in hell due for their sin), the power of sin (the corrupt habit of sin in the life as a result of natural corruption from Adam), and ultimately the presence of sin (in heaven, where believers will suffer neither inner sinfulness nor association with the sins of others). The practice of separation from sin in this life is one aspect of this deliverance from sin.

SEPARATION AND SANCTIFICATION

A good place to start in discussing this concept is its location in theology. When you study theology, you find that theologians divide the subject into different headings. Bibliology is the doctrine of Scripture. Christology is the study of doctrines concerning the person and work of Jesus Christ. Separation fits into this scheme as well. Generally, we look at separation as an expression of sanctification. Sanctification, in turn, is usually discussed as a part of soteriology, the doctrines concerning salvation. (*Soteriology* is from the Greek *soteria*, meaning "salvation.")

Soteriology includes a number of topics: biblical teachings such as justification, redemption, propitiation, and adoption. Sanctification is one of these teachings and a very important one. There are two aspects to sanctification, sometimes called positional and progressive sanctification. When a person is born again by the work of the Holy Spirit and converted, he or she is "set apart" (which is basically what *sanctify* means). The believer is positionally "in Christ" and therefore set apart to God. The holiness of Christ is credited to the Christian so that God views the believer as holy (1 Cor. 1:30). In this

THE TEACHING OF SEPARATION IS NOT JUST SOME OFFBEAT IDEA DREAMED UP BY AMERICAN FUNDAMENTALISTS.

aspect, sanctification is closely connected to justification, in which God declares the sinner righteous by imputing (or crediting) to that person the righteousness of Christ.

At the same time, newly converted Christians are far from mature. They will undergo a process of learning more about Christ and about God's Word. Through the power of the Holy Spirit and on the basis of Christ's atonement, believers will by degrees triumph over the power of sin in their lives. In short, believers will, as Peter puts it, "grow in grace, and in the knowledge of our Lord and Saviour Jesus Christ" (2 Pet. 3:18). This is progressive sanctification. Paul illustrates these two aspects in 1 Corinthians. He tells the Corinthians, "Ye are sanctified" (6:11). Yet he says earlier, "Ye are yet carnal" (or "fleshly"; 3:3). The Corinthians were sanctified in Christ (positionally), but they had not yet achieved holiness in this life (progressively). Later, Paul beautifully describes progressive sanctification for the Corinthians: "But we all, with open face beholding as in a glass the glory of the Lord, are changed into the same image from glory to glory, even as by the Spirit of the Lord" (2 Cor. 3:18).

Look at it this way. When a person is converted, God views that individual as being as righteous and holy as Jesus Christ because his or her sin has been covered by the atonement of Christ. In everyday experience, that person is becoming more like Jesus Christ. God sets the goal, and the believer progressively approaches that goal through God's grace. Paul expresses this thought when he says, "Not as though I had already attained, either were already perfect: but I follow after, if that I may apprehend that for which also I am apprehended of Christ Jesus" (Phil. 3:12).

Perhaps you can already see how the idea of separation fits into the doctrine of sanctification. If a Christian is delivered from sin as a result of being "in Christ" and is being progressively delivered from sin in this life, then striving to be separate from sin is only logical. We will look more fully at the theological context of separation in Chapter 2, particularly the important relationship of holiness to separation.

Please keep another thought in mind. The goal of sanctification is "to be conformed to the image" of Jesus Christ (Rom. 8:29), that is, to become more like Christ in thought, action, and all manner of life. Since separation is a part of the doctrine of sanctification, then the goal of separation is to become more like Christ.

We should mention that we can (and will) discuss separation in connection with other doctrines. As we will see, ecclesiology (the doctrine of the church) is an important arena for the practice of separation. Church discipline in particular will take a large place in this discussion, but we do not want to lose our focus on Christlikeness. Even the church, Paul says, is to be sanctified by Christ "that he might present it to himself a glorious church, not having spot, or wrinkle, or any such thing; but that it should be holy and without blemish" (Eph. 5:27).

SET APART

ASPECTS OF SEPARATION

As we said before, you often hear about what sound like different kinds of separation. Actually, all of these are simply different aspects of the same teaching. Two common terms are *personal* and *ecclesiastical* separation.

Personal separation is the practice of individual sanctification, a refusal to follow the world's philosophy in thought and action. A general supplication in the *Book of Common Prayer* contains this plea: "From all inordinate and sinful affections; and from all the deceits of the world, the flesh and the devil; *Good Lord, deliver us*." Personal separation is the working out of a Christian's deliverance from "the world, the flesh, and the devil" in daily life.

We sometimes think of worldliness in terms of certain actions (e.g., drinking, smoking, or style of dress). Like any other spiritual problem, however, worldliness begins in the heart, and these actions are the outward expression of the heart. Rolland McCune notes,

> So what is *worldliness*? People often define it in terms of some of its outward activities, but actually it goes much deeper than that. We can define *worldliness* as an affection for and an attachment to some aspect of the present arrangement of things. This attachment includes the world's thought patterns, amusements, fads, habits, philosophies, goals, friendships, practices and life-styles. Worldliness is a matter of inward attitudes, motives and yearnings as well as outward activities.[1]

Such is Paul's meaning when he tells Christians, "Be not conformed to this world: but be ye transformed by the renewing of your mind" (Rom. 12:2). In Chapter 3, we will examine how Scripture addresses this problem of worldliness.

Ecclesiastical separation is in many ways simply an extension of the principles of personal separation. The difference is that it is not practiced on the individual level but on the corporate church level. The main idea is that Christians refuse to align themselves with false doctrine or unbelief and that they reject the willful practice of disobedience. In the case of theological error, Christians expose false teachings and warn other Christians against them. In the case of willful disobedience, Christians separate from the disobedient believer to preserve the purity of the church and to restore the erring Christian to full fellowship through discipline. Ecclesiastical separation

4

may involve a church, a group of churches, or even an individual Christian. It might involve a local church leaving a denomination that has become dominated by unbelief or a denomination expelling churches or teachers who hold to false doctrine. It might be as simple as a church disciplining an unrepentant member who has fallen into sin or an individual Christian removing his or her membership from a church that has departed from the truth.

This form of separation involves not only separation from false teaching but also from unregenerate false teachers who, like wolves "in sheep's clothing" (Matt. 7:15), pose as Christians but are actually "false prophets" who teach "damnable heresies" (2 Pet. 2:1). Fundamentalists generally consider separation from disobedient Christians as a form of ecclesiastical separation, but some others treat this as a separate category.[2]

Some other terms you may hear are *first-degree* and *second-degree* separation (or sometimes *primary* and *secondary* separation). Usually, writers or preachers use these in reference to ecclesiastical separation. *First-degree separation* is the term for refusing to cooperate with false teachers in religious activities. *Second-degree separation* is refusing to have fellowship with anyone who does not practice first-degree separation. Some writers who use this first- and second-degree distinction argue that although primary separation is right, secondary separation is wrong.[3] Others who use the terminology believe that both are forms of separation that the Christian should practice.[4]

We must deal carefully with this first- and second-degree designation, depending on the motivation of the person making such a distinction. The question of separation is not how close or how far you are to or from a sin. Instead, it is a matter of obeying what the Bible says. If Scripture commands personal separation from the world, separation from false teachers, and separation from fellow Christians who are willfully practicing disobedience, then in one sense there are no "degrees" about it. "Separation does not really admit of degrees: It is directed to the other person because of *his* deviation from Scripture in whatever ways he may express them. If he runs with the wrong crowd, separation at this point is from him and not from the crowd he runs with."[5] In another sense, if someone wants simply to distinguish two forms of necessary separation with differing circumstances and requirements (such as the goal of restoring an erring Christian), then the distinction is helpful.

Two other terms you sometimes hear in connection with separation are *exclusivism* and *inclusivism*. Simply put, exclusivism is the separatist position, and inclusivism is the nonseparatist position. The Fundamentalist-Modernist Controversy of the 1920s illustrates these terms. The fundamentalists sought to exclude liberals from their denominations—their churches, schools, mission boards, and other agencies. The modernists (the liberal party), however, did not seek to exclude the fundamentalists. Rather, they wanted to include all shades of belief within the denominations, everything from fundamentalism to outright liberalism. For the separatist, the exclusion of false teaching is necessary, and the inclusion of such teaching in a religious fellowship is a violation of God's Word.

Other issues could be discussed under this topic of separation. For instance, some view separation of church and state as another expression of biblical separation.[6] In this book, however, we will focus on three issues in separation—separation from the world, separation from false teachers, and separation from disobedient fellow Christians. We will not exhaust the topic of separation, but we will at least introduce you to the main concepts and their biblical bases.

CONSIDERING SEPARATION IN HISTORY

Although discussions of biblical separation seem to focus on American churches during the twentieth and twenty-first centuries, the idea of separation has a long history and is not a new idea invented by American fundamentalists. Nevertheless, history is not the test of truth. We do not judge the rightness of separation by whether it has historical precedent but by whether it accords with the Bible. Still, historical precedent helps us understand the nature of separation and gives us some idea of how it has been practiced in the past.

PERSONAL SEPARATION IN HISTORY

Throughout history, the idea of personal separation from worldliness has usually not been questioned, although there have been lively debates about what constitutes worldliness. Such separation has long been considered one of the marks of a Christian. In the second century, the anonymous *Epistle to Diognetus* describes in what way

Christians are "distinguished from the rest of mankind." Among other qualities, the author says, "Every foreign country is a fatherland to them, and every fatherland is foreign. They marry like all other men and they beget children; but they do not cast away their off-spring. They have their meals in common, but not their wives. They find themselves in the flesh, and yet they live not after the flesh. Their existence is on earth, but their citizenship is in heaven."[7]

In the third century, Tertullian of North Africa warned against the bloodshed and pervasive immorality of Roman "spectacles" (gladi-atorial competitions, chariot races, and the theater). "What concord can the Holy Spirit have with spectacles?" he asks.[8] "For what sort of behavior is it to go from the assembly of God to the assembly of the Devil, from sky to sty, as the saying goes? Those hands which you have uplifted to God, to tire them out afterwards applauding an actor? To cheer a gladiator with the same lips with which you have said 'Amen' over the Most Holy?"[9]

> **PERSONAL SEPARATION FROM WORLDLINESS . . . HAS LONG BEEN CONSIDERED ONE OF THE MARKS OF A CHRISTIAN.**

The practice of monasticism in Roman Catholic and Orthodox churches is an exaggeration of the principle of separation. In response to the growing worldliness of the church, some Christians lived apart as hermits or in monastic communities. The monks sought to be separate from the corruption of the world and devote themselves to service for God. They were right in their desire to be free from worldly corruption, but in their zeal they identified isolation with separation. Paul warns the Corinthians that they could not avoid contact with unregenerate sinners: "Then must ye needs go out of the world" (1 Cor. 5:10; cf. John 17:15). Monks also tended to see the discipline of monasticism as a means to greater holiness. But Scripture presents discipline as the outgrowth of the work of God's grace in the Christian's heart. Monasticism provides a historical example of the importance of grounding separation in the teaching of Scripture and not simply applying the principle according to one's own viewpoint or desires.

We usually associate the Puritans and the Separatists (such as the Pilgrims of Plymouth Colony) of England and New England with ecclesiastical separation. These believers advocated either the cleansing of the Church of England or outright separation from it, but alongside that desire for a pure church was a desire for pure lives. The word *puritan* is sometimes used as an insult for someone who has strict moral standards, the critics caricaturing the desire for holiness that characterized the Puritans. In fact, the Pilgrims came to New England partly because they were concerned about the worldly lifestyles that their children had learned in the Netherlands.

A more modern example of the stress on personal separation is the Holiness Movement that arose within Methodism in the 1800s. For example, some of the most conservative Holiness Christians oppose the wearing of jewelry, even wedding rings. Others hold that Christians should not own televisions because of the worldly influences they introduce into the home. These outward practices are visible expressions of the Holiness Christians' desire to separate from the world and be conformed to Christ. They ask, as did John Wesley, "Who is he that will open his mouth against being cleansed from all pollution both of flesh and spirit; or against having all the mind that was in Christ, and walking in all things as Christ walked?"[10]

ECCLESIASTICAL SEPARATION IN HISTORY

Ecclesiastical separation is likewise no new idea, although the practice has varied through the centuries. Chapter 12 will consider in more detail some major separatist controversies. In early church history, separation was often practiced by expelling false teachers or flagrantly immoral members. In the second century, the church at Rome was quite impressed with the charm and eloquence of a teacher named Marcion. But then the church discovered he was teaching that the God of the Old Testament was evil whereas the God of the New Testament was good and that only certain books of the Bible (mostly Paul's epistles and an abridged version of the Gospel of Luke) were inspired. The church expelled him for teaching these heresies.

Likewise in the fourth century, the Councils of Nicea (325) and Constantinople (381) condemned the teaching of Arius, who believed that Christ was not God but only a great created being (a teaching similar to that of the Jehovah's Witnesses today). The church excluded the Arians for their error. The early church councils were not designed to promote unity at all costs, as is commonly thought, but to draw clearly the line between truth and error.[11]

Several groups also separated from the institutional church in the Middle Ages. The Waldenses (dating from the eleventh century) were persecuted for their desire to translate and preach the Word of God without ordination and their rejection of immoral priests. Most other separatist medieval groups, however, held heretical views on major points of doctrine and do not provide the best model of separatism.[12]

The Reformation is one of the clearest examples of ecclesiastical separation. Protestant reformers such as Martin Luther, John Calvin, Ulrich Zwingli, and John Knox opposed the false teachings that had emerged in the Roman Catholic Church. The reformers insisted that Christians are bound only by the authority of Scripture (not Scripture *and* church tradition) and are justified by faith alone (not faith *and* good works). These and other teachings caused the reformers to separate from Rome and form their own churches. (Chapter 12 will look more closely at the Reformers' arguments.) The Anabaptists, one of the Protestant groups, even went so far as to advocate an early form of the separation of church and state.

CONCLUSION

The chapters that follow develop and illustrate the idea of biblical separation and discuss how the Scriptures teach this important principle. Do not lose sight of the basic idea that Christians should strive to be free from sin. As the apostle Paul wrote, "Abhor that which is evil; cleave to that which is good" (Rom. 12:9).

CHAPTER TWO
SEPARATION IN THEOLOGICAL CONTEXT

It may have occurred to you that if separation is simply striving to be free from sin, why would any Christian question the practice? Virtually no professing believer argues that a Christian should not seek to be free from sin. For a "Christian" objection to separation to be credible, it needs at least to appear to have some biblical basis. One tactic is to argue about Bible passages that separatists cite, attempting to prove they do not actually teach the sort of separation that separatists practice. We will deal with this criticism in Chapters 3–5, where we discuss the biblical basis for separation.

Another common tactic used to argue against separation is to set it against another biblical teaching. In other words, opponents of separation formulate dichotomies. A dichotomy is a statement of two mutually exclusive ideas. The cliché "You can't have your cake and eat it too" expresses a dichotomy. You cannot eat a piece of cake and simultaneously save it for later. The problem, as we will see, is that critics of separation use false dichotomies, setting biblical ideas in opposition to separation that do not really exclude it.[1]

Those who argue by dichotomies nonetheless have a point. One of the dangers in arguing an important point of doctrine and practice is the possibility of imbalance. A long-distance runner strives for the optimal balance between speed and energy conservation. If he errs too far in either direction, he will finish poorly—if at all. A dietitian may tout the nutritional value of certain foods, but she would never recommend a diet of just one food. Foods highly beneficial in proper proportion can do damage when consumed in excessive quantities. Students of Scripture must likewise develop a sense of balance. Theology deals with many issues that cannot be reduced to a single fact that is demonstrably true and whose opposite is a single fact that is demonstrably false. Instead, Christians must hold opposing pairs of truths in proper balance.

Some issues in life are simple. A mathematician knows that $2 \times 3 = 6$ is true and that $2 \times 3 \neq 6$ is false. But consider a theological proposition: God is one. This statement is consistent with biblical teaching and is therefore true. However, the opposite, that God is more than one (Father, Son, and Holy Spirit), is also true in a sense. (To be more precise, we should say, "God is in three.") Theologians must constantly balance truths that operate in tension with each other. (Everyone is a theologian, at least informally, because everyone believes *something* about God.) Just like the runner balancing speed and endurance in setting his pace, theologians must pay attention to contrasting biblical emphases. They must formulate an understanding of truth in a way that adequately accounts for both. In the case of the oneness of God, a careful study of Scripture uncovers the doctrine of the Trinity: God is a single essence comprising three persons.

What teachings do critics offer to offset separation? Christian unity is an obvious one. The Bible's warning against the sin of schism is another. Likewise the scriptural commands for association with others (for evangelism and witness) present an apparent contrast to separation. We will look at each of these dichotomies in turn as well as the most important, the alleged tension between holiness and love.

CHRISTIAN UNITY VERSUS SEPARATION

The Bible unquestionably issues a call to Christian unity in tension with the call to separation. "Behold," says David, "how good and how pleasant it is for brethren to dwell together in unity!" (Ps. 133:1). John 17:20–23, where Jesus prays "that they all may be one," and Ephesians 4:1–16, where Paul tells believers "to keep the unity of the Spirit in the bond of peace," are two major passages that reflect God's desire for His people to maintain spiritual unity. In the 1950s and 1960s, when Bible expositor D. Martyn Lloyd-Jones was confronted with the call for uniting churches in Great Britain at the expense of truth, he carefully reviewed these two passages and concluded that neither passage supported the idea of unity apart from the truth.[2]

Lloyd-Jones points out that the unity Christ prays for in John 17 is restricted to believers ("them which thou hast given me"). Lloyd-Jones notes that "we must emphasize the element of separation and distinction. Our Lord does not pray for the world; He prays only for these people who have been given to Him."[3] Second, Lloyd-Jones says the origin of unity is in the work of God. Christians *maintain* the unity God has given and do not *create* unity. "Our Lord is not dealing with something at which we should aim. . . . It is a prayer to God to keep the unity that He, through His preaching, has already brought into existence among these people."[4] Third, he says the unity commanded in John 17 must be of the same nature as the unity between the Father and the Son: "that they may be one, even as we are one." Only those regenerated by the Holy Spirit and brought into union with the Father through Christ can enjoy this kind of unity.

In dealing with Ephesians 4, Lloyd-Jones points out that Ephesians 1–3 shows that this passage relates to those who are already "in Christ," who are already saved. He mentions that again the idea is to maintain, not create, unity because unity is "of the Spirit"—created by the Holy Spirit. Lloyd-Jones says that in both John 17 and Ephesians 4, "the question of unity must never be put first. We must never start with it, but always remember the order stated so clearly in Acts 2:42, where fellowship follows doctrine: 'They continued stedfastly in the apostles' doctrine and fellowship, and in breaking of bread, and in prayers.'"[5]

Therefore, objections based on the Bible's teaching about unity among Christians are fairly easy for the separatist to answer because the Bible teaches that spiritual unity assumes a common commitment to God and His truth. Jesus prayed that believers would be one as He and His Father are one, and the Father and the Son do not disagree on the fundamentals! Where there is no Christian unity, there can be no sin in separating. Although fundamentalists cannot ignore God's commands for unity, "the starting point in considering the question of unity must always be regeneration and belief of the truth."[6]

SCHISM VERSUS SEPARATION

Another danger the Christian must balance against separation is the sin of schism. Lloyd-Jones defines schism as "division in the true visible church about matters that are not sufficient to justify division or separation."[7] The Bible often warns against schisms (divisions) in the church (1 Cor. 12:25; Rom. 16:17; Gal. 5:20). We use the word *heresy* to describe a dangerously false teaching, but in Scripture the word often has the meaning of "division" (1 Cor. 11:19; Gal. 5:20). *Heresy* came to mean "false doctrine" probably because false teachings create divisions (cf. 2 Pet. 2:1).

The fullest teaching against schism is found in 1 Corinthians. "I beseech you, brethren," the apostle Paul says to the Corinthian believers, "that ye all speak the same thing, and that there be no divisions among you; but that ye be perfectly joined together in the same mind and in the same judgment" (1:10). He reports how he has heard that they are divided into factions saying, "I am of Paul; and I of Apollos; and I of Cephas; and I of Christ" (1:12). "Is Christ divided?" he asks. "Was Paul crucified for you?" (1:13). Later Paul condemns these divisions as desecrating the celebration of the Lord's Supper (11:17–22). The church is a body, he says, and there should be no divisions within the body (12:12–25, especially v. 25).

Schism is a sin, but separation is not necessarily the same thing as schism. Schism can exist without separation. Lloyd-Jones points out that the Corinthian church suffered from schism, but it had not actually broken into separate churches.[8] More importantly, as we will see in the following chapters, God commands separation in certain circumstances. Obeying God's commands from a pure heart can never be a sin, and God's Word does not

WHERE THERE IS NO CHRISTIAN UNITY, THERE CAN BE NO SIN IN SEPARATING.

contradict itself. "Any separation which is made in obedience to the clear command of Scripture (because of opposition to false doctrine or some other serious error) cannot possibly be the sin of schism."[9] As in the case of Christian unity, we cannot dismiss a major biblical teaching to accommodate separation, but likewise we cannot dismiss separation because of an improper fear of schism.[10]

ASSOCIATION VERSUS SEPARATION

A third argument made by critics of separation is an appeal to the biblical command to associate with sinners in order to witness to them of salvation through Christ. For instance, L. Nelson Bell says that "the 'doctrine of separation' can lead people to abandon the opportunity for witness where it is most greatly needed. The Bible teaches that we should be separated from sin, but not from the sinner."[11]

Obviously separation from unbelievers cannot be absolute because, as Paul says, "then must ye needs go out of the world" (1 Cor. 5:10). A believer's total isolation from the world is not only impossible but also undesirable. Jesus has left us "in the world" (John 17:11) so that He can send us "into the world" (John 17:18). Furthermore, the sinless Son of God Himself is our example of living in a sinful world. The verse just cited, along with eight other verses in John, refers to Jesus' having been sent into the world.[12] The only way God can save sinners is to come into contact with them, and if God Himself does this, His servants must also. There is indeed a necessary association of the saved with the unsaved.

But it is a mistake to believe that necessary Christian association with those who are not right with God justifies Christians patterning themselves after sinners and sharing their sinful lifestyles. With Jesus as our pattern, we can be certain that it is God's will for us while we are "in the world" (John 17:11) not to be "of the world" (John 17:14, 16). Just as Jesus lived and moved among sinners in order to minister to them without ever sinning Himself, so believers must aim to remain free from any taint of evil as they serve God among the ungodly. Jesus prayed for us to this end: "I pray not that thou shouldest take them out of the world, but that thou shouldest keep them from the evil" (John 17:15). Jude tells us, "Others save with fear, pulling them out of the fire," but warns that, while doing so, we must hate "even the garment spotted by the flesh" (Jude 1:23).[13]

Believers should not expect evil people to understand or appreciate their posture toward them. Jesus says, "The world hath hated them, because they are not of the world, even as I am not of the world" (John 17:14). The world that crucified Jesus opposes His people in every age for the same reason that they killed Him. It is not surprising, then, to find the world objecting to practice of separation.

HOLINESS VERSUS LOVE

The nonseparatist tends to see love as transcending other teachings of Scripture, modifying biblical commands to separate. There is no denying the fact that Jesus identifies love for God and neighbor as the two greatest commandments (Matt. 22:36–40) and that the apostles reinforce this assessment (Rom. 13:9; Gal. 5:14; James 2:8). The nonseparatist argues that separation, as fundamentalists practice it, is a violation of love and is therefore unbiblical. Ronald Nash, for example, charges fundamentalism with "sectarianism, separatism and total ignoring of the law of love."[14]

Separatists, on the other hand, find firm ground in the Bible's pervasive emphasis on holiness. They separate from evil because God is separate from evil and because He calls His people to imitate Him on that point: "Be ye holy; for I am holy" (1 Pet. 1:16, quoting Lev. 20:7). Fred Moritz rightly titled his study of separation *"Be Ye Holy": The Call to Christian Separation*, observing, "The purpose of separation is the ongoing effort by the local church or the believer to imitate the holiness of God."[15] Love, as nonseparatists practice it, is a violation of holiness and is therefore unbiblical.

Holiness and love are not opposites like the pairs discussed earlier. That some people view them as opposites does not mean that they are. Once we understand the terms *holiness* and *love*, we will see that many nonseparatists are reacting to a misconception of holiness, while some separatists are reacting to a misconception of love, both misconceptions arising from unbiblical practices carried out under the guise of holiness or love. If separatists misunderstand holiness, they will practice separation in unbiblical ways, and the same holds true for the nonseparatist's misunderstanding of love.[16]

THE MEANING OF HOLINESS

Holiness is essentially uniqueness or "differentness." It does not follow, of course, that uniqueness is necessarily praiseworthy. A lunatic is different from other people, but the difference is not praiseworthy. Biblical holiness is different in that it represents good rather than evil, moral light rather than darkness, God rather than Satan. Our fallen world is characterized by evil, darkness, and the domination of Satan. To be holy in the biblical sense is to manifest a character displaying goodness, light, and the rule of God.

The Bible expresses this uniqueness as moral purity and separation from that which is unclean. As Ernest Pickering and Myron Houghton write, "God is a separatist. He is separated from all that is evil. Holiness is a principle of His nature. It is consistent, therefore, to expect that bodies which He would establish upon this earth to represent Him would be required to be holy (separated) as well. They would be expected to mirror His character."[17]

As we noted in Chapter 1, through justification God regards the believer as being as righteous and holy as Jesus is. The goal of progressive sanctification is to grow toward greater holiness and purity of life. Critics of fundamentalism do not deride holiness or purity, but they imply there is something false or artificial about the fundamentalist stress on holiness, characterizing it as a "prideful quest for purity."[18] Fundamentalism's emphasis is often caricatured as an overemphasis on externals.

But one implication of the biblical teaching of holiness—perhaps the most important one—is that holiness is not primarily an external attribute. Satan's external appearance, the Bible says, can be indistinguishable from that of God's angels (2 Cor. 11:14). The fact that he looks good does not mean that he is good. The same is true of people. Jesus describes the scribes and Pharisees as whitewashed tombs—outwardly beautiful but utterly corrupt within (Matt. 23:27–28). Holiness is first and foremost a matter of the heart. God gave Israel the physical rite of circumcision as a sign of this nation's "differentness" from its neighbors, but He really desired the circumcision of hearts. The subject is mentioned seven times in the Old Testament (Lev. 26:41; Deut. 10:16; 30:6; Jer. 4:4; 9:25–26; Ezek. 44:7, 9), and Paul drives it home: "Circumcision is that of the heart, in the spirit, and not in the letter; whose praise is not of men, but of God" (Rom. 2:29).

If the character of the world were morally neutral, believers could be like the world without compromising the holiness of their hearts. Remember, the point of difference with which true holiness concerns itself is the difference between right and wrong. Where right and wrong are not at stake, holiness demands no difference. Whether to wear a red or a blue shirt is not an issue of holiness unless it becomes a question of right and wrong when, for example, a parent instructs a child to wear one or the other. But the character of the world is not morally neutral. The world's entertainment, for example, reflects the ungodliness of a worldly heart. A Christian whose consumption of entertainment is indistinguishable from that of people of the world has no right to claim that his or her heart is truly holy toward God. Wherever there is a choice to be made between what reflects the character of God and what reflects the character of Satan, the heart that chooses for God is the holy heart, and the heart that sides with Satan is unholy. Since true holiness is a matter of the heart, it follows that those who conform to the world's pattern on moral issues are unholy. Jesus' teaching supports this claim because He says that immorality proceeds from within, out of the heart (Mark 7:14–23).

A truly holy life, then, is one that is different from the world in a way that identifies it with God. Holiness begins in the heart; without holiness of heart there can be no holiness of life. But holiness never ends in the heart. The disposition of the heart manifests itself outwardly, and, to an increasing degree, as a believer matures in Christ.

So what are the differences of life that identify a holy person with God? Consider an illustration from the life of Frederick Douglass (1818–95), a slave who escaped bondage and became a leading opponent of slavery and a defender of the rights of black Americans. As a boy, while still a slave, Douglass heard the gospel with interest. He was happy at the age of fifteen when his master, Thomas Auld, professed conversion during a Methodist revival meeting. Auld testified proudly of his conversion, and he often invited ministers to visit him. Yet Frederick saw no difference in Auld's treatment of his slaves. When Douglass began attending a black Sunday school led by a free black, a mob from the Methodist church, led by Auld himself, violently broke up the meeting. Douglass was later sent to another master, Edward Covey, who also claimed to be a devout Methodist, but Covey was a "slave breaker" whose job it was to break the wills of stubborn slaves. He beat Douglass often, on one occasion until he was bloody. Douglass observed these men, saw even Methodist preachers using the whip on slaves, and finally concluded that "of all slave holders . . . religious ones are the worst. I have found them, almost invariably, the vilest, meanest, and basest of their class."[19] Disgusted with such men, Douglass turned his back on evangelical Christianity.

Consider another illustration. J. Frank Norris (1877–1952) was a fiery fundamentalist known as "the Texas tornado." He denounced liberalism in the Southern Baptist Convention so pointedly that the convention expelled him. His newspaper, with more than eighty thousand subscribers, printed scathing attacks against evolution,

communism, and especially religious liberalism. Norris was unquestionably a powerful preacher. He built large churches in Fort Worth,
Texas, and Detroit, Michigan, and pastored both of them at the same
time. His radio broadcasts covered most of the nation. He became
perhaps the best-known fundamentalist in the South.

At the same time, Norris was notoriously difficult to get along with.
Evangelist John R. Rice broke a nine-year association with Norris
because he felt Norris was trying to control him. Norris called Rice
a heretic and warned him that he would never get anywhere without
Norris's support. Rice even briefly stopped calling himself a *fundamentalist* because the term was so associated with Norris.[20] When G.
B. Vick and a number of other men broke from Norris to form the
Baptist Bible Fellowship in 1950, Norris savaged them in print. He
called them "gangsters" and accused them and their family members
of adultery, sodomy, and other moral offenses. Norris's own son left
his father's church and founded another church in Fort Worth. The
angry father offered to pay for the younger Norris to change his last
name.[21] In 1926, in the middle of a prolonged controversy with the
Catholic mayor of Fort Worth, Norris shot and killed a supporter of
the mayor in the pastor's study. Norris said that he thought his life was
being threatened, and a jury acquitted him of murder, but the incident
forever branded him as a "gun-totin' parson."

Of course, the hypocrisy of professing Christians does not excuse
Frederick Douglass before God, and God was able to use even a man
as flawed as J. Frank Norris to defend His truth. But holiness does
not consist in professing conversion and attending church or even
defending the Christian faith. These are, at most, the outward signs
of a holy heart. The differences that identify a person with God are
supernatural character traits such as selflessness toward others, joy in
the midst of suffering, a genuine love of the Scriptures, and a prayer-
ful recognition of and confidence in God's hand at work where others
see only fate and random chance. A minister may certainly defend
the faith and be characterized by holiness, but such a man will conduct his ministry as the outgrowth of a genuinely holy heart. Holiness
softens a Christian's manners and seasons his speech.

Someone who claims to live by biblical standards of holiness can
be exactly like the Pharisees, whose circumcision affected their flesh
but not their hearts. To live like a Pharisee is, at least in part, to lack
love for God and for one's neighbor. Onlookers who observe such

pharisaical lives are correct to point out the obvious lack of love. It does not follow, however, that holiness is less important than love. The onlooker is reacting against a false holiness rather than against true holiness. He or she is reacting to a hypocritical stress on externals, not a difference in lifestyle that reflects the character of God in contrast to that of the world.

True holiness is not always understood and appreciated. Because the world has always hated God, it will always hate those who are like Him. But it is one thing to be hated for manifesting the character of God that rebukes sinners and quite another to be disdained as a hypocrite who pretends to be holy while living the same sort of sinful life as the non-Christian.

THE MEANING OF LOVE

Just as holiness is often misperceived as a fastidious preoccupation with external details to the neglect of inner character, love is often misperceived as a feeling of goodwill and an unconditionally affirmative attitude toward all people as they are. The loving thing to do in any situation, according to this misunderstanding, is whatever makes people feel accepted and increases their self-esteem.

The Bible leaves no doubt, though, about the nature of genuine love. Because God is the source of love (1 John 4:16, 19), we must form our conception of love on the basis of how the Bible describes God's love. Perhaps the best place to begin is the most familiar verse in the Bible: "For God so loved the world, that he gave his only begotten Son, that whosoever believeth in him should not perish, but have everlasting life" (John 3:16). God's love prompted Him to sacrifice Himself for the benefit of those He loves. We know love is not just a feeling of attachment because elsewhere the Bible teaches that sinners are revolting to God and that He is full of wrath toward them. Paul emphasizes this self-sacrificial character of God's love: "But God commendeth his love toward us, in that, while we were yet sinners, Christ died for us" (Rom. 5:8).

So let us lay down a provisional definition of love along these lines: love is a disposition to act in the highest interests of the loved one, regardless of the cost to the one who loves. Such a disposition may or may not involve an emotional attachment to the loved object. Emotion is a negotiable component; self-sacrificial commitment is not. A love that lacks this commitment is not the love that God exercises and commands us to exercise.

Now the question arises whether God really commands us to have this kind of love, or whether this is a love that only He can have, a love far above human capacity. In the first place, the New Testament's commands to love invariably use the same word for love that normally describes God's love even though several synonyms were available to the writers. This is not a conclusive argument, though. The same word is also used for lesser kinds of love (e.g., Matt. 23:6; John 12:43), and the Bible sometimes uses the synonyms to describe God's love (John 5:20; 16:27).

The passage in which Jesus commands us to love our enemies comes very close to requiring a self-sacrificial love like God's (Matt. 5:43–48), and in John's Gospel the requirement to love as God loves is clear. "As the Father hath loved me, so have I loved you: continue ye in my love," Jesus says (John 15:9). But does this mean to continue loving as Christ loves or to continue being an object of Christ's love? The passage goes on: "If ye keep my commandments, ye shall abide in my love; even as I have kept my Father's commandments, and abide in his love" (15:10). So it does not sound as though Jesus is commanding the disciples to exercise love but is rather commanding them to live so that they may continue to be objects of His love. But the passage is not finished. What commandment(s) must they keep? "This is my commandment, That ye love one another, *as I have loved you*" (15:12; emphasis added). Still, Jesus has not explicitly demanded self-sacrifice. Perhaps He means that it should be true that we love one another just as it is true that He loved us, not necessarily that we should love one another just as much as He loved us. But, again, we must read on: "Greater love hath no man than this, that a man lay down his life for his friends" (15:13). There is no avoiding the fact that the Bible requires us as believers to love others with the same kind of love He has for us.

John learned Jesus' teaching about love. Decades later he described love as one of the preeminent qualities of the Christian life (1 John 3:10–23). He wrote, "My little children, let us not love in word, neither in tongue; but in deed and in truth" (3:18). John stressed that believers must love one another with a divine kind of self-sacrificial love. The presence or absence of this sort of love is directly related to our assurance of salvation (3:19), and John gave love an importance equal to that of faith in Christ (3:23).

The Bible clearly demands that believers love as God loves. Although it is impossible for us to love to the *full extent* that God loves, it is nevertheless possible, through the work of the indwelling Holy Spirit, to love with the *same kind* of love God has, a self-sacrificing commitment to serve the highest interests of those we love. We see this in the example of Paul, who wrote to the Corinthians (his most troublesome church, by the way), "I will very gladly spend and be spent for you; though the more abundantly I love you, the less I be loved" (2 Cor. 12:15). Paul follows the pattern of divine love. So should every Christian.

THE RELATIONSHIP BETWEEN HOLINESS AND LOVE

Remember we are exploring whether holiness and love are opposites that must be balanced against one another. We have defined our terms: holiness is a difference from the world that identifies us with God in opposition to Satan, and love is a self-sacrificing commitment to act in the highest interest of those we love. Once we understand these terms, we see that there is no reason to limit either of them. Is there a degree of godlike holiness beyond which it is harmful to go? Can we be too much like God and too little like the world? Regarding love, can we be so willing to sacrifice for the sake of others that we displease God or harm someone? Obviously, there is no limitation to be placed on these virtues of holiness and love, and we will spend our Christian lives continually growing in our exercise of them. In fact, we can equate perfect love and holiness with sinlessness. To the extent that we are like God, we do not sin. To the extent that we strive unselfishly to press forward the work of God in people's lives, we do not sin. If holiness and love, properly understood, equate with sinlessness, then we must place no limit on either.

> **THOSE WHO TRULY LOVE WILL ZEALOUSLY PURSUE TRUE HOLINESS BECAUSE THEIR BECOMING LIKE CHRIST IS BOTH GOD'S DESIRE AND THEIR OWN HIGHEST GOAL.**

Nonseparatists who complain, "You fundamentalists would do better to quit worrying about holiness and be more concerned about love" set up a false tension between these two virtues. Fundamentalists would make a mistake if they responded by reversing the terms: "You compromisers should quit worrying so much about love and be more concerned about holiness." That response accepts the premise that the two virtues are in tension. Worse for fundamentalists, nonseparatists have the Bible on their side when they rank love before holiness since Jesus Himself singles out love rather than holiness as the first and greatest commandment.

We must hasten to add, however, that it does not follow that holiness is unimportant. In rebuking the Pharisees, Jesus put these virtues in order like this: "But woe unto you, Pharisees! for ye tithe mint and rue and all manner of herbs, and pass over [i.e., overlook] judgment [i.e., justice] and the love of God: these ought ye to have done, and not to leave the other undone" (Luke 11:42). The error of the Pharisees is that they attempted to be holy without having laid a foundation of love for God on which to build that holiness. A holiness not based on genuine love for God will always be a false holiness. The command to imitate God's holiness presupposes a love for God. Without that love there is no motive for obeying that command. If contemporary fundamentalists try to be holy without a genuine love for God and man, they become modern-day Pharisees deserving the rebuke of those who see through their hypocrisy.

But there is a better way. Once the foundation of true love for God and neighbor is laid in the heart, a Christian's reason for living is to serve God and others rather than himself or herself. This order is crucial. Jesus ranks love for God as the first commandment because a love for others that does not keep God's interests as the highest priority will always go astray and content itself with serving the baser human interests. Notice these words: "By this we know that we love the children of God, when we love God, and keep his commandments" (1 John 5:2). Love for God must come first, and love for others inevitably follows, just as love in general must come first, and holiness follows.[22]

Those who truly love will zealously pursue true holiness because their becoming like Christ is both God's desire and their own highest goal. The proper response of fundamentalists who are charged with a lack of love is twofold. First, fundamentalists must examine themselves to consider the validity of the charges, repenting of any failure that may validate them. Second, having reaffirmed the conviction that they are acting in obedience to Scripture, for the sake of God and others rather than self, they should point out any evident misunderstanding by nonseparatists of the true meaning of love and holiness.

CONCLUSION

The theological context of separation demands two things of us. First, we must balance Scripture's requirement of separation against its requirements of unity and association and its warnings against schism. As they practice separation, fundamentalists must take God's desires concerning Christian unity seriously. They must guard against the sin of schism, which separation can easily become if not practiced scripturally.

> **WE MUST GUARD AGAINST THE SIN OF SCHISM, WHICH SEPARATION CAN EASILY BECOME IF NOT PRACTICED SCRIPTURALLY.**

They must also realize the necessity of association with sinners for evangelism and witness. Otherwise biblical separation becomes unscriptural isolation.

Second, the theological context demands that we recognize that a scripturally balanced separation is an expression both of holiness and of love. We must simultaneously maximize these two virtues in our daily living, not balance one against the other. We will fail in the areas of both holiness and love if we become excessive either in separatism or inclusivism. Of course, *excessive* must be understood in terms of what the Bible teaches, not in light of what makes us comfortable. To develop and apply that scriptural definition will be the task of the remainder of this book.

CHAPTER THREE
SEPARATION FROM THE WORLD

In the first two chapters, we have argued that biblical separation is a practice rooted in the teaching of Scripture. It is now time to examine specific scriptural evidence for this doctrine. Since the Bible alone is our authority for doctrine and practice (2 Tim. 3:16–17), it does not merely inform us of God's will but also guides us in how we should live and act (Ps. 119:105; Prov. 6:23). Only by giving attention to Scripture under the guidance of the Holy Spirit will we be able to maintain a balanced view of separation, avoiding the extremes of ignoring the principle entirely or of separating unnecessarily over customs or minor points of interpretation.

We will discuss separation under three divisions: separation from the world (this chapter), separation from false teachers (Chapter 4), and separation from disobedient fellow believers (Chapter 5). Our goal is to demonstrate that separation is not optional but absolutely necessary when circumstances demand it because it is a matter of obeying Scripture and thereby reaping the benefits of fellowship with God.

Separation is not an obscure teaching dragged out of some forgotten corner. It runs through the whole of God's Word. Because the Bible contains many Old Testament examples as well as New Testament warnings and commands about separation, we will also cite Old Testament parallels to the New Testament teaching.

Nevertheless, three chapters in a slender book cannot cover all biblical teaching about separation. You will need to meditate on this concept as you read God's Word and hear it preached. Also, it is important to keep in mind that categories such as personal and ecclesiastical separation often overlap. False teaching occurs in the world as well as in the church. Sinful practices of the unsaved sometimes enter the church. Classifications are only guides to help us understand God's Word. Scripture does not always fit neatly into manmade categories. It is impossible to lay down absolute rules that prescribe the proper course of action in every situation that might arise in the life and ministry of a Christian. Mature Christians must take the responsibility for making sure their own decisions follow biblical principles. With these thoughts in mind, let us look more closely at the first of our topics: separation from the world.

> **ONLY BY GIVING ATTENTION TO SCRIPTURE UNDER THE GUIDANCE OF THE HOLY SPIRIT WILL WE BE ABLE TO MAINTAIN A BALANCED VIEW OF SEPARATION**

DEFINITIONS

In this chapter and the two that follow, we will introduce the discussion with definitions of basic terms. These definitions will help you follow the arguments of a particular passage by showing you how these terms are used in the whole of Scripture.

World system: The ways the unregenerate people of this earth think and behave as organized and dominated by Satan, "the god of this world" (literally, *this age*; 2 Cor. 4:4). This system opposes Christ and His goals for the earth (John 15:18–19). Sometimes we call the world system simply "the world," but it is very important that we do not confuse the physical world with the spiritually corrupt realm of Satan. The physical world was created by God and is sustained by Him (Gen. 1:1; Col. 1:16–17). Although it suffers from the effects of sin (Rom. 8:19–22), it is still the possession of God. The world system, on the other hand, as the realm of Satan is characterized by rebellion against God.[1]

Worldliness: An attitude of friendship toward, a desire for, and a wish to be recognized by the world system. Although it is something we often talk about in terms of certain actions (e.g., smoking, drinking, etc.), at its root worldliness is the opposite of a friendship with, a desire for, and a seeking after the approval of God. As a result of this inner attitude, people indulge in worldly behavior. Worldly behavior is not merely the things that worldly people do but, as one writer points out, those actions "that display [the world's] vanity, ignorance, darkness, and alienation from God" (based on Eph. 4:17–18).[2] Any act that arises from a worldly motive will identify you with the world system and thus hinder your love for God, your spiritual growth, and your Christian testimony.

BIBLICAL PRINCIPLES

In Chapters 3–5 we will look at key passages concerning each facet of separation and establish guidelines for how separation should be practiced. Although separation is not just an idea contained in a handful of isolated spots in the New Testament, the Bible is God's Word and does not have to state a command repeatedly in order for us to be obligated to obey. One command given by God is enough. Still, separatists are sometimes charged with "proof-texting," that is, citing a few verses (often out of context) to prop up a weak position. We will examine the context and teaching of each passage to demonstrate that our approach is in harmony with the overall teaching of God's Word. Cross-references to other passages, as well as to Old Testament parallels, reveal that separation is a theme that runs throughout the Word of God.

KEY NEW TESTAMENT TEXTS

1 John 2:15–17

> Love not the world, neither the things that are in the world. If any man love the world, the love of the Father is not in him. For all that is in the world, the lust of the flesh, and the lust of the eyes, and the pride of life, is not of the Father, but is of the world. And the world passeth away, and the lust thereof: but he that doeth the will of God abideth for ever.

In these verses, the apostle John gives all believers a categorical command to avoid loving the world. Any person who makes the things of the world system the center of his or her interest and desire has exalted the world to a place of idolatrous worship. An idol is not just a piece of wood or stone that someone kneels in front of. It is anything we regard as the supreme interest of our lives. A person who loves the world, John says, excludes the proper love for the Father from his or her life. Although God has made the material things of the world, we can pervert them into idols by regarding them as our supreme interest. Thus even the beauties of nature, art, music, or literature can become idols if they displace God.

"The things that are in the world" can be the source of temptations in three general areas. "The lust of the flesh" is the desire that the flesh produces. This desire might be for an object that is good in itself, such as food (Matt. 4:3), but when food becomes more important than the will of God, it becomes an idol. "The lust of the eyes" is the desire for anything beautiful or attractive that can be exalted in place of God. It may be an object as good as a tree (Gen. 3:6). "The pride of life" is the selfish display of even good things that may replace the desire for God.[3] One writer, noting the difficulty of interpreting "pride of life," characterizes it as "arrogance" and says, "Arrogance and lust summarize the attitude of those who subscribe to the world's system."[4]

John tells us that the world system and all its appeals are passing away, but the believer who has made God the object of his or her existence—the supreme interest—will continue forever. God will make such a believer the heir of all things in Christ (Rev. 21:7).

2 Corinthians 6:14–7:1

> Be ye not unequally yoked together with unbelievers: for what fellowship hath righteousness with unrighteousness? and what communion hath light with darkness? and what concord hath Christ with Belial? or what part hath he that believeth with an infidel? and what agreement hath the temple of God with idols? for ye are the temple of the living God; as God hath said, I will dwell in them, and walk in them; and I will be their God, and they shall be my people. Wherefore come out from among them, and be ye separate, saith the Lord, and touch not the unclean thing: and I will receive you, and will be a Father unto you, and ye shall be my sons and daughters, saith the Lord Almighty. Having therefore these promises, dearly beloved, let us cleanse ourselves from all filthiness of the flesh and spirit, perfecting holiness in the fear of God.

In this passage the apostle Paul first states the principle that believers are not to be "unequally yoked together with unbelievers" (6:14). He is probably alluding here to Deuteronomy 22:10, where

God forbids plowing with an ox and a donkey yoked together. Such a mismatched pair cannot pull or plow effectively. Paul supports this principle with a series of contrasts that should be self-evident to Christians. Righteousness and unrighteousness as well as light and darkness have nothing in common (2 Cor. 6:14). Christ has no agreement with Belial, a name for Satan that comes from a Hebrew word meaning "worthless." A believer can have no "part" with an unbeliever (6:15). Finally, Paul contrasts the temple of God with idols (6:16), explaining that believers are the temple of God.

Paul warns of idolatry throughout the Corinthian letters (e.g., 1 Cor. 5:10–11; 8:1–10; 10:14, 19–28). As "the temple of God," believers enjoy a special relationship with God in which He dwells among them. The idea of setting up idols in the temple of God is abominable. Against this background Paul gives the command of the Lord: "Wherefore come out from among

SEPARATION IS NOT AN OBSCURE TEACHING DRAGGED OUT OF SOME FORGOTTEN CORNER. IT RUNS THROUGH THE WHOLE OF GOD'S WORD.

them, and be ye separate, saith the Lord" (2 Cor. 6:17). The result, he says, is that God will receive believers, and they will be sons and daughters to Him. Paul defines what it means to "be . . . separate" and to "touch not the unclean thing" by urging believers to obey this command in cleansing themselves "from all filthiness of the flesh and spirit" and in "perfecting holiness in the fear of God" (7:1).

Thus we see that the practice of separation is grounded in the character of God. Paul provides example after example of how the kingdom of God is completely opposed to the world system with no basis of agreement between them. In light of Paul's five contrasts, "when the nature of the believer is contrasted with that of the unbeliever, it is incongruous," says Moritz, for them to have any genuine fellowship.[5] Because Christians are children of God and citizens of His kingdom, they must be separated *to* God and *from* sin and worldliness.

This passage, rightly called "the keystone passage in the New Testament which deals with separation,"[6] is one of the most cited as well as the most disputed. Often it is used in the context of ecclesiastical separation, in part because it is addressed to a church and in part because the clear command "Come out from among them, and be ye separate" applies so satisfactorily when urging believers and churches to leave apostate denominations. Also, Paul uses the temple as an image of the church (1 Cor. 3:16–17; Eph. 2:21) as well as of the individual Christian (1 Cor. 6:19). Critics of the separatist position protest that this passage does not apply to separation from professing Christians.[7] For instance, Eenigenburg states that "nowhere in the New Testament are some Christians given the privilege of declaring other professing Christians 'unbelievers'" so that they may separate from them.[8] Runia is subtler but questions the application: "How [this passage] is to be applied in the case of an unfaithful church must be decided by the teaching of the whole New Testament. A straightforward appeal to verse seventeen . . . in defense of separatism is an oversimplification of the issue."[9]

These critics generally recognize that separation from the world system is appropriate, even necessary. They also rightly note that the immediate application concerns separation from unbelievers. What they ignore is the possibility that a church can become so identified with the world system that it has effectively become part of that realm of unrighteousness, darkness, Belial, infidelity, and idolatry that God condemns.[10] God, for example, condemns "Babylon," the apostate religious system of the end times, and commands, "Come out of her, my people, that ye be not partakers of her sins, and that ye receive not of her plagues" (Rev. 18:4). Fundamentalist Chester Tulga seems almost bewildered by Christians who argue that 2 Corinthians 6:14 "forbids fellowship with idolaters but does not forbid fellowship with those who deny the fundamentals of the Christian faith."[11] Paul elsewhere warns Timothy about the "doctrines of devils" getting into the church (1 Tim. 4:1).

In fact, 2 Corinthians 6:14–7:1 does deal primarily with the Christian's separation from the world system, but as we will see in the next chapter, it also applies to separation from false teachers. For now, keep in mind the main teaching of this passage, namely that God's kingdom is holy and therefore separate from Satan's realm. Christians, as citizens of His kingdom, are to imitate that holiness by clinging to God and spurning the world. The practice of separation rests on "the basic fact of incompatibility between the like and the unlike."[12]

Ephesians 5:11

> Have no fellowship with the unfruitful works of darkness, but
> rather reprove them.

Perhaps the best place to start in understanding Paul's message
in Ephesians 5:11 is to define our terms. The "unfruitful works of
darkness" are defined earlier in 5:3–4 as sexual immorality, impurity,
greed, obscenity, and foolish talking or coarse joking. This is not an
exhaustive list, of course, but more of a representative sampling. It is
worth noting in light of 1 John 2:15–17 that Paul calls a person who
practices these things an idolater (Eph. 5:5). These works of darkness
are the supreme interest of his or her life.

Paul instructs the Ephesians not to "fellowship" with these works
but to "reprove" them. The picture of "fellowshipping" with "works"
might seem strange at first, but the idea is that we must not share or
participate in such acts. By *reproof*, Paul means to expose these "works."
Charles Hodge points out that this same word is used in John 16:8 for
the ministry of the Holy Spirit: "When the Spirit is said to reprove people of sin," he writes, "it means that he sheds such
light on their sins that it reveals their true character and produces
the consequent consciousness of guilt and pollution."[13] In contrasting
fellowship with reproof, the apostle highlights the chasm that exists
between those devoted to the "unfruitful works of darkness" and
those devoted to the fruitful works of light. Believers not only refuse
to share in such sinful acts but also actively oppose them.

Nevertheless, though Paul forbids sharing in the works, he does
not forbid interacting with the people who practice them. Christ
pointed out the sin of the woman at the well of Samaria, but He nonetheless spoke with her about her need to drink from the "well of water

> **GOD'S KINGDOM IS HOLY AND THEREFORE SEPARATE FROM SATAN'S REALM. CHRISTIANS, AS CITIZENS OF HIS KINGDOM, ARE TO IMITATE THAT HOLINESS BY CLINGING TO GOD AND SPURNING THE WORLD.**

springing up into everlasting life" (John 4:14). We should befriend the lost even though we refuse to share in their works.

1 Thessalonians 1:9

> They themselves shew of us what manner of entering in we had unto you, and how ye turned to God from idols to serve the living and true God.

According to 1:7–8, the people mentioned in the opening of 1:9 were believers in Macedonia (the region where Thessalonica was) and Achaia (where Paul was when he wrote 1 Thessalonians). He had heard reports from these other believers about the activities of the Thessalonian Christians in demonstrating the results of the ministry of Paul and the other missionaries ("what manner of entering in we had unto you"). Specifically, the Thessalonians had "turned to God from idols to serve the living and true God."

The construction of this verse markedly contrasts serving idols with serving God. Hiebert points out that *turned* is a translation of the usual New Testament word for conversion.[14] To serve God is to move in a direction completely opposite from that of serving idols. Furthermore, the verse also artfully describes the nature of idols. Because God is "living and true," then idols must be dead and false. Although the Thessalonians likely turned from literal idols, anything that a person substitutes for God is equally dead and false.

James 4:4

> Ye adulterers and adulteresses, know ye not that the friendship of the world is enmity with God? whosoever therefore will be a friend of the world is the enemy of God.

James intends his words to be shockingly blunt: Adultery is sexual unfaithfulness in marriage. James accuses his readers of spiritual adultery, of unfaithfulness in their relationship to God. He has warned them against lusts in the previous verses (4:1–3). This use of *lust* reinforces the imagery of adultery. Just as lust leads a partner in a marriage into unfaithfulness, so the lusts of the flesh can make Christians unfaithful to their God. Those who allow the world to turn their hearts away from God commit spiritual adultery. James describes two allegiances that no one can reconcile. The world system is God's enemy; friendship with the world system is "enmity," literally "hatred," toward

God. People are either friends of the world and enemies of God, or friends of God and enemies of the world. There is no middle ground.

OLD TESTAMENT PARALLEL

Worldliness was a constant problem for the people of Israel. When they rejected Samuel's sons as judges and asked for a king, their reason was so that they could "be like all the nations" (1 Sam. 8:20).[15] God taught His people to be separate from other peoples. This was not an arbitrary command because holiness is expressed by separateness: "Ye shall be holy unto me: for I the Lord am holy, and have severed you from other people, that ye should be mine" (Lev. 20:26). When they made alliances with pagans, God sent prophets to condemn them for their evil associations (Isa. 30:1–17). Because of His grace and mercy, God called Israel to be His "peculiar treasure" and His "holy nation" (Exod. 19:5–6). Therefore, the Israelites were to reflect that holy calling in their lives by separating from the false gods of the heathen and refusing to intermarry with those who worshiped them. Yet their holy calling also involved experiencing the love, mercy, and faithfulness of their God (Deut. 7:1–11) and testifying to other nations that He is the one true God (4:4; Isa. 43:30).

God judged Israelites who apostatized from the Word of God and worshiped the gods of the heathen so that they became like the heathen, followed their practices, and intermarried with them. The book of Judges records a recurring cycle of unbelief and judgment because of such worldliness (Judg. 3:5–8). God says that the Northern Kingdom of Israel fell because it followed the ways of ungodly nations (2 Kings 17:6–8).

Proverbs has much to say about avoiding evil people (e.g., 4:14–19). God also promises blessing to those who do not associate with the wicked and their pagan lifestyle. Psalms is filled with such promises. Psalm 1 contrasts these two ways: "Blessed is the man that walketh not in the counsel of the ungodly, nor standeth in the way of sinners, nor sitteth in the seat of the scornful. But his delight is in the law of the Lord; and in his law doth he meditate day and night. And he shall be like a tree planted by the rivers of water, that bringeth forth his fruit in his season; his leaf also shall not wither; and whatsoever he doeth shall prosper" (Ps. 1:1–3).

EXPLANATION AND APPLICATION

Note in the passages we have discussed in this chapter how God constantly reminds us about the gulf between His kingdom and the world system. Christ describes the normal relationship of the Christian to the world: "If the world hate you, ye know that it hated me before it hated you. If ye were of the world, the world would love his own: but because ye are not of the world, but I have chosen you out of the world, therefore the world hateth you" (John 15:18–19). The apostle John told first-century Christians, "Marvel not, my brethren, if the world hate you" (1 John 3:13). If this deep hatred between the world system and the Christian ceases, it is because the Christian, not the world, has changed.

Separation from the world begins with recognizing the completely evil character of the world system. The Christian should not desire or expect approval—or even fair treatment—from the world. In addition, separation from the world means avoiding all actions that might fall into the category of worldliness as we have defined it. Sources of contamination from the world today include ungodly media, music, movies, and fashions. The Bible often specifically warns against being influenced by the worldly thinking of those we associate with (1 Cor. 15:33). Subtler sources of contamination can include worldly philosophies and ideologies less evident to the eye (1 Cor. 3:18–20; Col. 2:8). Christians belong to God and should turn their backs on the sins of the world. A Christian should overthrow the world's idols and reject all its unbiblical ambitions and schemes. Further, because actions arise from the heart, only the person whose heart belongs to God and is inclined toward holiness can truly understand what it means to forsake worldly behavior. Christians are not holy because they reject worldliness. They reject worldliness because they have been set apart by God in salvation and are being transformed by the Holy Spirit.

> **CHRISTIANS ARE NOT HOLY BECAUSE THEY REJECT WORLDLINESS. THEY REJECT WORLDLINESS BECAUSE THEY HAVE BEEN SET APART BY GOD IN SALVATION AND ARE BEING TRANSFORMED BY THE HOLY SPIRIT.**

Yet as we said in the previous chapter, God's command to separate from the world does not mean that Christians should isolate themselves from society. Christians are to be the "salt of the earth" (Matt. 5:13). They are responsible for evangelizing the world (Acts 1:8). Therefore, separation from the world should by no means discourage earnest efforts to win the world to Christ, something that God certainly desires (John 3:16; 2 Pet. 3:9). Jesus Himself spent so much time with "publicans and sinners" that He was criticized for being their friend (Matt. 11:19). In fact, when Jesus and His disciples went to a party Matthew threw for his fellow tax collectors, the legalists were quick to complain about their associating with sinners (Luke 5:29–30).

Furthermore, separation from the world does not prohibit associating with worldly people in the course of daily life. Paul tells the Corinthians that he does not expect them to leave the world in order to avoid contamination from sinners (1 Cor. 5:9–13). As already noted, our Lord prayed that believers would be kept from the evil of the world, not removed from it (John 17:15). "As we have therefore opportunity," says the apostle Paul, "let us do good unto all men, especially unto them who are of the household of faith" (Gal. 6:10). The Christian may cooperate with unsaved people in beneficial community projects, such as electing worthy leaders or helping to relieve the poor, the ill, and the underprivileged, though the Christian should be careful not to imply that unsaved people are Christians. Nor should these joint efforts promote organizations that use social or political efforts to further unbiblical causes. Joseph, Daniel, and Nehemiah were men who worked in pagan sociocultural environments while remaining true to God.

Finally, we should note that the charge of legalism is often made against those who stress separation from the world. Defined biblically, legalism is a serious heresy. Basically, it is trying to earn merit with God by performing good works. Paul dealt with this problem in Galatians. False teachers in Galatia were saying that people could be justified (Gal. 2:16) or sanctified (3:1–5) by performing good works, in this case by following the Mosaic law. Paul would have no part of such teaching. We do not become holy by doing certain things; actions express what is in our hearts.

Those who charge separatist Christians with *legalism* probably are not using the term in this technical sense. Rather they are usually referring to requiring standards of behavior that have no biblical basis.[16] Certainly, there is a danger in requiring people to dress a certain way or in forbidding some action when there is no biblical command. For example, around 1900 the Church of God (Anderson, Indiana) underwent a major conflict over worldliness. The cause of this bitter struggle? Wearing neckties. Eventually, part of the anti-necktie faction founded its own church.[17]

Our reply to the charge of legalism is similar to the one we made in the previous chapter about the charge of schism. While we should be careful about establishing human standards, God does impose certain standards on His people (e.g., Eph. 4:22–32; Col. 3:8–17; 1 Tim. 3:2–13.) Obeying God's Word can never be the sin of legalism.

PURPOSES

Christians, therefore, separate from the world and from worldliness for the following reasons:

- To avoid the ever-present danger of contamination by the world (1 Cor. 11:32; 15:33; 2 Cor. 11:3; 1 Thess. 4:5; 1 Pet. 2:12)

- To maintain close fellowship with God (John 15:15; James 4:4)

- To base their lives on that which is enduring (John 15:16)

- To make clear to Christians and non-Christians alike by their actions that they belong to God, not to the world (Isa. 43:21; 1 Thess. 5:22; 1 Pet. 2:9)

- To avoid sin (James 4:17)

These purposes contribute to the overall goal of Christlikeness for the believer. Jesus Christ was sinless; there was certainly no hint of worldliness about Him. He lived to reveal His Father to the world, and He maintained a close fellowship with the Father. Christ's focus was the eternal will of God, not temporal, temporary advantage or comfort. Jesus overcame "the lust of the flesh, and the lust of the eyes, and the pride of life" in His temptation by Satan (Matt. 4:1–11; Luke 4:1–13). This is the pattern we desire to follow.

CONCLUSION

Christians who practice personal separation demonstrate in conduct and attitude a strict obedience to God and His Word. In addition, they testify to the world of their inner love for God and their desire to be like Him.

Separation has what may be seen as a negative side: believers refuse to imitate the world because they have no desire for the world. From conception, all were subjects of Satan's world system. The Christian's salvation from sin is separation from Satan's world, even though the pull of the flesh constantly wars against separation in the Christian's life by inducing him to sin.

PROPERLY PRACTICED, SEPARATION IS AN ACT OF WORSHIP.

The Christian therefore has to oppose the flesh to exercise separation.

But there is a positive side of separation too—the believer is to become more like Christ. Separation is not a sacrifice you make for God. Rather it is a submission to God's wisdom, a testimony to your faith that He knows what is best for you. Certainly, you should not view separation as a way to earn God's favor. "Salvation does not begin with giving up something but with receiving Someone."[18] God has already showed Christians His favor by saving them. The Almighty has entered into a personal relationship with mere humans. Separation should be a response to God for His goodness toward us. Properly practiced, separation is an act of worship.

CHAPTER FOUR
SEPARATION FROM FALSE TEACHERS

As mentioned in Chapter 1, many discussions of separation divide the topic into personal and ecclesiastical separation. Those who follow this approach view the topic of the previous chapter—separation from the world—as personal separation. This chapter about separating from false teachers focuses on ecclesiastical separation. Positively, ecclesiastical separation involves identification with groups faithful to the truth and the practice of God's Word. Negatively, it is the refusal to be identified with any teacher, church, denomination, or other religious organization that does not hold to and defend the fundamentals of the faith concerning the Bible, Christ, and salvation.

Yet we should not draw hard and fast lines between different types of separation. Sin does not always fall into neat categories. Although we often speak of worldliness and the world system in connection with personal separation, the concepts are also important in discussing ecclesiastical separation. Douglas McLachlan defines ecclesiastical separation as "radical non-conformity to Babel," that is, a refusal to conform to the "satanic" religious pattern of the world system.[1] Paul's well-known call for separation, "Wherefore come out from among them, and be ye separate, saith the Lord" (2 Cor. 6:17), is an allusion to Isaiah 52:11, where God calls

> **WE SHOULD NOT DRAW HARD AND FAST LINES BETWEEN DIFFERENT TYPES OF SEPARATION. SIN DOES NOT ALWAYS FALL INTO NEAT CATEGORIES.**

His people out of literal Babylon and specifically charges the priests (those "that bear the vessels of the Lord") not to be spiritually defiled.

Regardless of whether we can pigeonhole sins into certain classifications, we need to understand the danger of false teaching—the world system's religious belief, which is inspired by Satan and is a threat to the souls of humanity. That some false teachers are sincere or well-meaning does not change the nature of their teaching. Christians must guard themselves against false doctrine, and they must warn others. "Thus saith the Lord of hosts, Hearken not unto the words of the prophets that prophesy unto you: they make you vain: they speak a vision of their own heart, and not out of the mouth of the Lord" (Jer. 23:16).

DEFINITIONS

False teacher: Someone who professes to be a Christian but who attempts to deceive the church by false doctrine. Scripture describes false teachers as wolves in sheep's clothing, who are to be judged on the basis of their works (doctrinal teaching and its effects) and not merely by their profession (Matt. 7:15–20; Titus 1:16). Although such deceivers give the appearance of being angels of light and ministers of righteousness, the Bible calls them false apostles, deceitful workers (2 Cor. 11:13–15), servants of corruption (2 Pet. 2:19), ungodly men (Jude 1:4), filthy dreamers (1:8), and mockers (1:18). We normally assume that false teachers are unregenerate even though we cannot always know for sure. Regardless of their personal standing with God, false teachers are unquestionably promoting doctrine that threatens the eternal well-being of human souls.

Fundamental doctrine: A clear scriptural teaching that the Bible itself indicates is an important truth of Christianity, a teaching so essential that it cannot be denied without destroying the faith. Such fundamentals of the faith do not include points of doctrine that are matters of particular interpretation. Genuine Christians have differed with each other on many points of doctrine, but they agree on the fundamentals. There can be no room for difference of opinion concerning the full inspiration, inerrancy, and authority of the Bible; the virgin birth of Christ; His essential deity and proper humanity; His absolute sinlessness; His power to save the sinner through His substitutionary death on the cross; His bodily resurrection; His personal return; and the reality of heaven and hell.

Of course, to distinguish between what is essential and what is a matter of interpretation requires spiritual discernment. True teachers of the Word have disagreed with one another about such things as church ordinances or the details of Christ's return. Rolland McCune lists several teachings that he sees as "doctrinal non-issues" in fundamentalism, including preference for certain families of biblical manuscripts, Calvinism and Arminianism, questions of church polity, and differing systems of prophetic interpretation.[2] This is not to say that such issues are unimportant, just that they are not fundamental to the Christian faith.

BIBLICAL PRINCIPLES

KEY NEW TESTAMENT TEXTS

Galatians 1:8–9

> But though we, or an angel from heaven, preach any other gospel unto you than that which we have preached unto you, let him be accursed. As we said before, so say I now again, If any man preach any other gospel unto you than that ye have received, let him be accursed.

Satan seeks to corrupt Christ's church through false ministers who preach a false message. Having warned against "another gospel: which is not another" (1:6–7), Paul adamantly teaches that no change can be introduced into the apostolic gospel and states this teaching in unmistakably strong terms.

But what does Paul mean by "another gospel"? According to passages such as Luke 24:44–47 and 1 Corinthians 15:1–4, the gospel includes teachings such as Christ's death for our sins, His resurrection, and the forgiveness of sin only through Him. These truths are certainly central to the gospel. In Galatians, however, Paul specifically accuses believers of turning away from the grace of Christ (Gal. 1:6) by adopting the heresy of legalism (as mentioned in Chapter 3). False teachers were saying that believers had to follow the Mosaic law to be saved (Gal. 2:16; 3:1–5). Such legalism is "another gospel."

In 1:6–7 Paul uses two different words meaning "another" in the phrase "another gospel, which is not another." The first means "something entirely different," and the second means "something of the same kind." These false teachers presented a "gospel" that had nothing in common with the true gospel. Their teaching is "so different from Paul's message that it constitutes . . . 'a different gospel'—and therefore, in fact, no gospel at all, since there can be no 'other gospel.'"[3]

If any human being, or even an angel from heaven, preaches another gospel (another of a different kind), Paul prays that that person would be accursed. J. Gresham Machen points out that Paul is not just saying that false teachers have no right to change the gospel. *No one* has the right to change it.[4] Martin Luther said, "Whatever does not teach Christ is not yet apostolic, even though St. Peter or St. Paul does the teaching. Again, whatever preaches Christ would be apostolic, even if Judas, Annas, Pilate, and Herod were doing it."[5] Machen also notes that Paul was willing to endure those who preached the true gospel for wrong motives (Phil. 1:15–18), but he was unwilling to put up with anyone who preached a "bad gospel," even with good intentions.[6]

The word translated "accursed" is *anathema*, which originally had the meaning of "offering." The idea is something being handed over to God—in this case, handed over for judgment. Paul almost certainly meant that such teachers should be excluded from the church, but more than that they are to be given over to a severe judgment at God's hands. Boice says that the literal sense is "Let them be damned" and that anybody, even Paul himself, is included.[7] This emphatic language demonstrates Paul's fervor in denouncing any who would modify the gospel he preached.

2 John 1:9–11

> Whosoever transgresseth, and abideth not in the doctrine of Christ, hath not God. He that abideth in the doctrine of Christ, he hath both the Father and the Son. If there come any unto you, and bring not this doctrine, receive him not into your house, neither bid him God speed: for he that biddeth him God speed is partaker of his evil deeds.

The apostle John gives one of the Bible's sternest warnings about false teachers in 2 John 1:9–11. He has just said (1:7) that "many deceivers are entered into the world, who confess not that Jesus Christ is come in the flesh." Such a person "is a deceiver and an antichrist." The word *antichrist* here does not refer to the Beast of the end times (Rev. 13:1–10) but to anyone who sets himself against Christ and attempts to take His place. An antichrist, then, reflects the character of Satan.

John describes the consequences of such false teachings. Anyone who goes beyond and will not continue abiding in the biblical doctrine of Christ has abandoned God. The word translated "transgresseth" could perhaps be translated "progresses," which would indicate that these teachers claimed to have "progressed" to a higher level in their teaching of Christ. "Such progress beyond the revelation in Christ, however, was not spiritual advancement but a fatal plunge into spiritual darkness."[8]

What is the "doctrine of Christ" that they deny? The most obvious idea, based on the phrase "confess not that Jesus Christ is come in the flesh" in 2 John 1:7, is that they deny the incarnation of Jesus as truly human. An early heresy called Docetism denied that Jesus had a real body and viewed Him as a sort of ghost who only appeared to be human. Other teachings about Christ that John stressed in his writings against false teachers are that Jesus is the Messiah ("the Christ"; 1 John 2:22) and that Jesus is the Son of God (2:23). The tense of the verb translated "is come" in 2 John 1:7 might even imply that these teachers deny the Second Coming of Christ.[9] All of these are essential teachings concerning Christ.

We need not extract particular doctrinal teachings from the passage. John says that believers must continue abiding in the doctrine of Christ to have fellowship with the Father and the Son. The "doctrine of Christ" is the Bible's whole teaching concerning who Jesus is and what He has done. The true teacher is not just someone who believes certain truths about Jesus. He accepts the entire person and work of Christ. One writer comments, "We are taught that any Christian teacher who does not truly believe in Christ as the incarnate Saviour, is devoid of any personal relationship with God." He argues that this is not simply a matter of whether a teacher believes in the incarnation but whether such a teacher is genuinely converted.[10]

Because denying the doctrine of Christ is so seriously wrong, believers are to have nothing to do with anyone who claims authority as a teacher but who denies the Bible's teaching about Christ. Christians should not give such a person religious recognition of any kind or do anything that could be construed as accepting the false teaching or aiding the teacher in spreading his or her falsehood. To do so would mean that believers would share in the wrongdoing. To pray for God's blessing on such a false teacher would be asking God to bless apostasy and heresy. Those who wish false teachers well or help them on their way are aiding in the destruction of souls by false teaching. Critics often accuse fundamentalists of being unloving for refusing to work with liberals, but in reality fundamentalists are properly loving the souls of others by refusing to promote destructive heresy.

Romans 16:17–18

> Now I beseech you, brethren, mark them which cause divisions and offences contrary to the doctrine which ye have learned; and avoid them. For they that are such serve not our Lord Jesus Christ, but their own belly; and by good words and fair speeches deceive the hearts of the simple.

At the conclusion of his epistle to the Romans, Paul urges his readers to deal wisely with false teachers. He says, "Mark them [that is, to watch out or be on the lookout for them, because they] cause divisions and offences contrary to the doctrine which ye have learned." It is not just that the divisions themselves are contrary to "the doctrine" (although that is true). The false teachings *cause* the divisions. The Roman Christians' standard for judging these false teachings was the doctrine that they had learned. Paul is not referring to some teaching he had given them. As one commentator points out, Paul had not yet been to Rome and this was his first contact with this church.[11] The doctrine learned is the Christian faith that Roman Christians had embraced. They were to "avoid" such teachers, to stay away from them altogether. Christians achieve true unity only by eliminating the errors that cause divisions, not by overlooking the errors.

Paul does not identify the group he is warning against, but 16:18 makes clear that they are false teachers. They serve their "belly" (their own selfish appetites) instead of Christ. They speak "good words" and give "fair speeches" but they deceive "the simple," the naive and uninformed. False teachers are slickly eloquent, but their teaching is poisonous.

1 Timothy 6:20–21

> O Timothy, keep that which is committed to thy trust, avoiding
> profane and vain babblings, and oppositions of science falsely so
> called: which some professing have erred concerning the faith.
> Grace be with thee. Amen.

In the conclusion of this letter, Paul offers the last of a series of warnings concerning false teaching (1:3–7, 18–20; 4:1–3; 6:3–5). Positively, he tells Timothy, "Keep that which is committed to thy trust." Timothy is to guard what has been deposited with him, like someone guarding a treasure. (Paul uses similar language in 2 Tim. 1:14.) The context of 1 Timothy makes evident that what has been entrusted to Timothy is "sound doctrine" (1 Tim. 1:10; 4:6, 16; 6:3).

Negatively, Timothy is to guard this treasure by "avoiding profane and vain babblings, and oppositions of science falsely so called." In other places as well Paul describes the teaching of false teachers as pointless chattering that leads only to ungodliness (1 Tim. 1:6; 4:7; 2 Tim. 2:16). The word translated "science" is normally translated *knowledge* in the New Testament. The false teachers claim that they have true knowledge, but Paul declares that they do not. He tells Timothy that what these teachers say opposes the truth that Timothy guards. Furthermore, Timothy is to turn from such teaching in order to protect the truth entrusted to him.

Paul highlights the danger of false teachings by stating that those who profess them have "erred concerning"—that is, turned aside or wandered from—the faith. This is not a simple difference of opinion but a distinction between truth and error with the fate of souls hanging in the balance.

Revelation 2:2, 6, 14–16

> I know thy works, and thy labour, and thy patience, and how
> thou canst not bear them which are evil: and thou hast tried
> them which say they are apostles, and are not, and hast found
> them liars. . . . But this thou hast, that thou hatest the deeds of
> the Nicolaitanes, which I also hate. . . . But I have a few things
> against thee, because thou hast there them that hold the doc-
> trine of Balaam, who taught Balac to cast a stumbling block be-
> fore the children of Israel, to eat things sacrificed unto idols,
> and to commit fornication. So hast thou also them that hold the
> doctrine of the Nicolaitanes, which thing I hate. Repent; or else

> I will come unto thee quickly, and will fight against them with
> the sword of my mouth.

Revelation 2–3 contains seven letters that Jesus directs to seven churches in Asia Minor. Christ first addresses the churches at Ephesus (2:1–7) and Pergamum (2:12–17), praising the church at Ephesus for resisting false teaching and condemning the church at Pergamum for tolerating it. The Ephesians had tested false teaching and rejected it. The believers at Pergamum, although not denying the faith (2:13), had permitted false teaching to exist in their assembly and therefore needed to repent.

The teaching Christ condemns in these churches is that of the Nicolaitans. We have no certain knowledge about this group. The earliest references in the writings of the church fathers say that this group taught that Christians could "lead lives of unrestrained indulgence."[12] Christ describes their teaching as "the doctrine of Balaam." (Revelation 2:15 translates more literally, "Thus you are likewise having those who hold the teaching of the Nicolaitanes." The Nicolaitans held to the same teaching described in 2:14, not a different one, as we might think from a casual reading of the KJV.)

Balaam, the greedy prophet of Numbers 22–24, is best known for blessing the children of Israel almost against his will. However, the incident to which Christ refers to took place soon afterwards. Numbers 25 describes how the Israelites joined the pagan worship of the Midianites and intermarried with them. Numbers 31:16 tells us that it was Balaam who advised King Balak of the Midianites to try this policy of "If you can't beat them, get them to join you." Like Balaam, these false teachers of Revelation 2 urged compromise with idolatry by eating meat sacrificed to idols. (See Paul's warnings about this practice in 1 Cor. 8:1–13; 10:14–33.) Furthermore, they "commit fornication." This may be a reference to spiritual unfaithfulness (see James 4:4), but some people in the church at Pergamum may actually have taught that Christians could indulge in sexual immorality, perhaps in pagan temples. Jude warns of false teachers who change "the grace of our God into lasciviousness" (Jude 1:4).

Note the clarity of the statement about Christ's attitude toward false teaching. He says that He hates both the deeds (Rev. 2:6) and the doctrines (2:15) of the Nicolaitans. The only solution for the church at

Pergamum is to repent for buying in to this false teaching. Otherwise Christ Himself will fight against those who hold it.

OLD TESTAMENT PARALLEL

The presence of false prophets among the people of God in the Old Testament was a common problem (2 Pet. 2:1), and the condemnation of such teachers was a constant theme. God taught His people to totally reject a false prophet. If what some prophets predicted did not happen, the people would know that those prophets were false (Deut. 18:20–22). Even if they correctly predicted the future and verified it with miracles, the people would know that the prophets were false if they tried to lead the people away from the true God (Deut. 13:1–5). The people were supposed to judge teachers by their actions as well as by the content of their teaching (Isa. 8:20).

Both Jeremiah and Ezekiel faced false prophets (Jer. 23; Ezek. 13) who discouraged backslidden people from repenting by telling them that peace was on the way. As a result of their lies, many perished. Of course, Jeremiah and Ezekiel preached against these deceivers. Other Old Testament prophets also used strong language to condemn false prophets (1 Kings 22:19–23; Isa. 28:7; Hos. 4:5; Mic. 2:6–8, 11; Zeph. 3:4). All God's prophets strongly denounced false worship, condemning any tendency by the Israelites to combine their religious practices with those of the surrounding nations.

EXPLANATION AND APPLICATION

We saw in the previous chapter that there is an absolute distinction between the kingdom of God and the world system. The passages discussed in this chapter demonstrate the same divergence between true doctrine and false teaching. The two have nothing in common. Just as Paul warned the Ephesian elders that they would have problems with false teachers (Acts 20:29–31), so believers today can expect to face similar problems. How should Christians deal with false teachers?

First, Christians must judge all doctrinal teaching in the light of Scripture. If a preacher or a teacher of God's people denies scriptural teaching and practice, true believers should recognize that person as a false teacher.

Second, it is necessary to rebuke the false teachers in order to deliver those who have been influenced by their teaching. This rebuke should be as strong as those given by Christ (Matt. 23:13–36) and His apostles (Gal. 1:9; 5:12).

Third, all conduct toward false teachers should be based on the truth that an apostate gets progressively worse in his or her false doctrine (2 Tim. 3:13) and that there is no scriptural evidence that an apostate ever returns to Christ (Heb. 6:4–6). An apostate has deliberately rejected revealed truth.

> **OBEYING GOD IS OFTEN DIFFICULT, AND SEPARATION FROM FALSE TEACHERS REQUIRES EFFORT.**

Such false teachers must be expelled from the church and from any positions of influence involving a religious institution, publication, or missionary society.

Finally, when expelling false teachers becomes impossible because a majority of the members of a church or group support them, then it is necessary for believers to withdraw from that group. Undoubtedly, this point of separation is the most controversial. Few conservative Christians question the legitimacy of separating from outright apostasy. Eenigenburg, writing against separatism, comes close to denying separation from apostasy, but even he is willing to admit the possibility.[13] Instead, critics offer qualifications and limitations to the idea of separation. Runia is typical in saying that believers should not tolerate heresy in the church, but they should expel it, not withdraw from the church.[14] Nash criticizes conservatives for leaving denominations when they became a minority and were unable to expel false teachers. They should have hung on, he says, to maintain their influence and perhaps win the struggle later on.[15]

Some argue that there is no clear New Testament example of a faction withdrawing from a church for scriptural reasons, but Runia allows that in the first century "the New Testament church separates itself from the Jewish church."[16] But nothing in the New Testament parallels a situation in which a God-honoring minority faction faced an unyielding majority unwilling to expel false teaching. Opponents of separation seem to say that if expulsion fails, then the believers who lose a battle must simply tolerate serious error until they can expel it. This argument, however, flies in the face of the passages we have examined in this chapter. Christians are to avoid false teaching (Rom. 16:17) and refuse to have fellowship with it (2 John 1:9–11). Expelling the error is the first course of action, but if the majority fails to do so, then the minority must obey the scriptural principle of refusing to fellowship with error by withdrawing.

A common argument against such separation is an appeal to the parable of the wheat and the tares (Matt. 13:24–30, 36–43).[17] The basic argument is that the church is a mixed multitude, containing both wheat (true Christians) and tares (unregenerate people posing as Christians). Jesus says that the two should remain mixed until the final judgment, when He will reveal which believers are true and which are spurious. Therefore, Christians should not try to separate the wheat from the tares themselves but should endure this mixed condition. There is a legitimate application of this idea (as we will see in a moment), but there are major problems with this manner of presenting it. The biggest difficulty is that Jesus says in 13:38 that the field is the *world*, not the church. This world is a mixture of the saved and the unsaved, and Christians cannot use force to uproot or coerce unbelievers. In addition, the interpretation of this parable cannot be used to invalidate God's commands elsewhere to put away false teaching.[18] As we have mentioned before, Scripture cannot contradict Scripture.

There are three cautions about separation from false teaching. First, separation from false teachers does not involve separation from ordinary hypocrites—church members who secretly do not believe what they profess to believe. God has not called us to judge the motives of others. If people believe false doctrine but give no outward sign of their attitude and do not teach anything false to other members of the church, they may remain in the church until they reveal that they are "tares." Judas, one of the twelve chosen by Christ, remained part of the group until he betrayed Christ. He never revealed himself to the disciples as a false teacher or even as an unconverted man. Christians cannot know someone's heart and cannot act until someone gives open evidence that he or she is a false teacher.

FOR THE PROTECTION OF THE CHURCH, WE MUST EXPEL FALSE TEACHERS.

Second, we must remember that only God knows the heart of a false teacher. Possibly some who proclaim apostate teaching are themselves deceived.[19] A true apostate is without hope, but we cannot always know who is a true apostate. After warning Timothy against false teachers, Paul urges him to "be gentle unto all men, apt to teach, patient, in meekness instructing those that oppose themselves; if God peradventure will give them repentance to the acknowledging of the truth" (2 Tim. 2:24–25). Even so, we must treat anyone who holds to apostate teaching as though he or she were an apostate. Immediately after warning Timothy to be gentle, Paul goes on to describe false teachers in pointed terms and tells the younger man, "From such turn away" (3:5).[20] For the protection of the church, we must expel false teachers. If such a teacher is merely deceived, expulsion may be a means of confronting him or her with the truth.

Third, separation from false teachers does not mean rejecting a new believer who may express some views contrary to fundamental doctrine. If the novice submits to correction and chooses to obey the teaching of Scripture, he or she should not be regarded as a false teacher.

PURPOSES

The Christian separates from false teachers and their teaching for the following reasons:

- To maintain the doctrinal integrity of the church (1 Tim. 3:15; Jude 1:12)

- To protect the sheep from error that not only inhibits spiritual growth but that can also destroy faith (Matt. 7:15; Acts 20:28; 2 Tim. 2:16–18; Titus 1:11; 2 Pet. 2:1–2)

We may again see a pattern of Christlikeness here. It is Christ's purpose to save and to sanctify the church "that he might present it to himself a glorious church, not having spot, or wrinkle, or any such thing; but that it should be holy and without blemish" (Eph. 5:27). Furthermore, Christ is the Good Shepherd (John 10). He knows His sheep and they know Him, and He protects them, lays down His life for them, and gives them abundant life; He protects His flock from the wolves. Peter tells the leaders of the church to "feed [literally, *shepherd*] the flock of God" as their duty to "the chief Shepherd," Jesus Christ (1 Pet. 5:1–4).

CONCLUSION

Obeying God is often difficult, and separation from false teachers requires effort. Believers must be alert to the danger of false teaching and be discerning about what they hear and accept. Christians must be courageous enough to denounce error and either to expel the error or (what can often be harder) leave a group if the false teacher cannot be expelled. A church that teaches error or permits error to be taught within its ranks cannot fulfill its scriptural mandate to serve as "the pillar and ground of the truth" (1 Tim. 3:15). The reward for obedience is great. After commanding, "Wherefore come out from among them, and be ye separate," the Lord promises, "I will receive you, and will be a Father unto you, and ye shall be my sons and daughters" (2 Cor. 6:17–18).

CHAPTER FIVE
SEPARATION FROM DISOBEDIENT CHRISTIANS

"As long as biblical separation is discussed on a theoretical level, many Christians do not question its importance," writes Fred Moritz. "When separation is applied in practice to people and institutions they know, however, some believers bristle."[1] With no aspect of separation is this observation truer than in separation from disobedient fellow believers. Most Christians will acknowledge at least the concept of separation from worldliness or apostasy, but many argue vehemently against separation from other Christians. For example, E. J. Carnell writes, "Christian fellowship repudiates *any* separation of brother from brother in the community of faith."[2] Our purpose in this chapter is to show that, to the contrary, the Bible does at times command such separation.

First some cautions. We are using the term *disobedient* to mean the willful, unrepentant practice of disobedience. No believer is perfect, and all Christians disobey God at some point. We all need God's grace to triumph over the power of sin in our lives, and we need love and discernment to deal with and help other Christians in their weakness. Separation should never exclude Christian sympathy.

> SEPARATION SHOULD NEVER EXCLUDE CHRISTIAN SYMPATHY. . . . THE GOAL OF SEPARATION IS NOT ONLY TO PRESERVE THE PURITY OF THE CHURCH BUT ALSO TO RESTORE THE DISOBEDIENT ONE.

In this chapter we will deal with situations in which professing Christians consistently violate important biblical commands and, having been confronted about those violations, refuse to repent. Even then, the goal of separation is not only to preserve the purity of the church but also to restore the disobedient one. Through separation we endeavor to bring a fellow Christian back into the full fellowship with other believers in Jesus Christ.

Separation from disobedient Christians can involve personal separation (separation from a Christian who refuses to forsake some form of worldliness) or ecclesiastical separation (separation from someone who refuses to forsake some form of false teaching or unscriptural practice). But since it is usually practiced as an exercise of church discipline, we normally think of it as a form of ecclesiastical separation.

DEFINITIONS

Disobedient believer: A professing Christian who deliberately refuses to change some aspect of his conduct to conform to the clear teaching of Scripture. The significant considerations to keep in mind are the seriousness of the sin and the persistence with which it is practiced. Our approach toward such a person will differ from the approach we would take toward a false teacher because we assume the disobedient believer has faith in Christ's saving work.

Church discipline: Action taken by a body of believers to correct the disobedience of one of its members. Anyone who loves fellow Christians desires for them to do right (1 Cor. 13:6). Proper church discipline results in the building up of the church, not in its destruction (2 Cor. 13:10). The goal of such discipline is to reclaim the disobedient Christian (Matt. 18:15).[3]

BIBLICAL PRINCIPLES

KEY NEW TESTAMENT TEXTS

Matthew 18:15–17

> Moreover if thy brother shall trespass against thee, go and tell him his fault between thee and him alone: if he shall hear thee, thou hast gained thy brother. But if he will not hear thee, then take with thee one or two more, that in the mouth of two or

three witnesses every word may be established. And if he shall neglect to hear them, tell it unto the church: but if he neglect to hear the church, let him be unto thee as an heathen man and a publican.

Only twice do the Gospels record teachings by Jesus concerning the church. In Matthew 16:18–19, He speaks of the foundation and building of His church. In Matthew 18:15–17, He speaks of discipline within it.

Jesus outlines the procedure that believers should follow in church discipline. Christ says that if your brother sins against you in some way, you must first go to him. Perhaps such a meeting will settle matters immediately and you will have "gained thy brother." If this visit does not settle the matter, you are then to return with one or two witnesses, presumably to report on this encounter to the church and ensure that the actions and attitudes of the brother are accurately reported (Deut. 19:15). Separation should never be based on rumor or hearsay. If this meeting fails, then the question should come before the whole church (that is, the local assembly of believers). If the offender refuses to heed the church, the other members must exclude him and treat him as they would a pagan or a tax collector. Because Jews would have nothing to do with Gentiles or with tax collectors (even those who were themselves Jews), Christ's teaching is that the church is to break fellowship with the offender and treat him as no longer part of the church.

Immediately after Christ gives this teaching, Peter asks how often he should forgive someone who sins against him. Christ replies "seventy times seven" and tells the parable of the unforgiving servant (Matt. 18:21–35). When Christians consider to what extent they should forgive an offending brother, they should remember how much God has forgiven them. If a brother refuses to repent, he should be treated as an unregenerate man, but if he asks forgiveness, then believers are to welcome him back.

1 Corinthians 5:1–13

It is reported commonly that there is fornication among you, and such fornication as is not so much as named among the Gentiles, that one should have his father's wife. And ye are puffed up, and have not rather mourned, that he that hath done this deed might be taken away from among you. For I verily, as absent in body, but present in spirit, have judged already, as though I were present, concerning him that hath so done this deed, in the name of our Lord Jesus Christ, when ye are gathered together, and my spirit, with the power of our Lord Jesus Christ, to deliver such an one unto Satan for the destruction of the flesh, that the spirit may be saved in the day of the Lord Jesus.

Your glorying is not good. Know ye not that a little leaven leaveneth the whole lump? Purge out therefore the old leaven, that ye may be a new lump, as ye are unleavened. For even Christ our passover is sacrificed for us: therefore let us keep the feast, not with old leaven, neither with the leaven of malice and wickedness; but with the unleavened bread of sincerity and truth.

I wrote unto you in an epistle not to company with fornicators: yet not altogether with the fornicators of this world, or with the covetous, or extortioners, or with idolaters; for then must ye needs go out of the world. But now I have written unto you not to keep company, if any man that is called a brother be a fornicator, or covetous, or an idolater, or a railer, or a drunkard, or an extortioner; with such an one no not to eat. For what have I to do to judge them also that are without? do not ye judge them that are within? But them that are without God judgeth. Therefore put away from among yourselves that wicked person.

As Matthew 18 represents the concept of church discipline, 1 Corinthians 5 reflects its practice. The apostle Paul rebukes the Corinthians for failing to discipline one of their number who has committed incest, probably with his stepmother. Paul writes sternly to them, commanding that the guilty person "be taken away from among [them]" (5:2). He is to be delivered "unto Satan for the destruction of the flesh, that the spirit may be saved in the day of the Lord Jesus" (5:5). Paul uses the same language in 1 Timothy 1:20 concerning Hymenaeus and Alexander. Although there is debate about what being delivered to Satan means,[4] its connection with "be taken away from among you" indicates that it refers at least partly to excluding such a person from the church with the goal of eventual restoration.

Paul explains the danger of this situation to the church at Corinth. He uses the imagery of yeast (leaven) in baking (1 Cor. 5:6–8). A little yeast spreads through an entire lump of dough, affecting the whole batch and causing it all to rise. Paul says the effect of sin will be similar. If the church tolerates the practice of sin by one member, that sin will affect the whole body. Having been cleansed from the penalty and power of sin by Christ, our desire should then be to live free from sin. The goal of church discipline is purity—for the church to cleanse itself from sin.

Paul does not encourage believers to abandon their relationships with immoral non-Christians (1 Cor. 5:10), but he warns that believers must not associate with professed believers whose doctrine or practice contradicts scriptural standards (5:11). The offenses Paul lists (5:10–11) are mostly moral offenses, such as sexual immorality, covetousness, and drunkenness. However, he also includes idolatry, which involves, as one writer notes, "separation from a disobedient brother . . . on doctrinal as well as moral grounds."[5] The chapter concludes with the command, "Put away from among yourselves that wicked person" (5:13). The church should not stand by and watch the disobedient member continue his downward course without warning. Rather the Corinthian assembly is to warn him in an attempt to turn him from his destructive course, and, until he repents, believers are to have no fellowship with him.

> IF THE CHURCH TOLERATES THE PRACTICE OF SIN BY ONE MEMBER, THAT SIN WILL AFFECT THE WHOLE BODY.

There is a footnote to this passage. In 2 Corinthians 2:5–11, Paul discusses an individual who had sinned, had been disciplined by the church, and had repented. We have no way of knowing whether this is the same person that Paul condemns in 1 Corinthians 5, but the passage nonetheless teaches that a Christian who repents after church discipline is to be welcomed back without hesitation.

2 Thessalonians 3:6, 14–15

> Now we command you, brethren, in the name of our Lord Jesus Christ, that ye withdraw yourselves from every brother that walketh disorderly, and not after the tradition which he received of us. . . . And if any man obey not our word by this epistle,

note that man, and have no company with him, that he may be ashamed. Yet count him not as an enemy, but admonish him as a brother.

Here the apostle commands believers to "withdraw . . . from every brother" who "walketh disorderly, and not after the tradition" received from the apostles. Central questions in understanding this passage concern the meanings of *withdraw, disorderly,* and *tradition.*

Withdraw means simply "to separate from or to withhold fellowship from." One commentator argues that in the context of 6:15 "this does not mean 'abstain from all intercourse,' but it stands for the withholding of intimate fellowship. . . . They had to be made to see that complete fellowship is possible only when there is complete harmony."[6]

The word translated "disorderly" originally had the meaning of being out of line, like a soldier who breaks rank from a march. By Paul's time it had acquired a meaning of idleness.[7] Paul had warned about this matter in his earlier epistle (1 Thess. 5:14) when he confronted Christians who had apparently claimed that the Lord's return was so imminent that they could stop working and had become meddlers as a result (2 Thess. 3:7–12). Paul says "that if any would not work, neither should he eat" (3:10), and he tells the Thessalonians to withdraw from those Christians who refuse to obey.

Paul does not leave the reader to wonder what tradition is. He refers to instruction he has already given them. In this instance, Paul was instructing them as he had in 1 Thessalonians 4:11 that they should work to support themselves. But *tradition* means more than that. In 2 Thessalonians 2:15 the apostle declares the traditions to be his own teaching, whether by word or epistle. In that verse Paul is contrasting the Christian message with the false teaching prevalent in the last days (2:2–12). When he tells them to "hold the traditions" in 2:15, he is referring to the great truths of salvation, election, sanctification, and the gospel that he has just mentioned in 2:13–14. If any brother's

> **IF ANY BROTHER'S PRACTICE OR TEACHING ON ANY POINT DOES NOT AGREE WITH THE TEACHING OF SCRIPTURE, BELIEVERS ARE TO WITHDRAW FROM HIM.**

practice or teaching on any point does not agree with the teaching of Scripture, believers are to withdraw from him.

Lest any believer fail to recognize the importance of this discipline, the apostle repeats the command at the end of the next chapter. If any man does not obey the teaching in Paul's epistles, Christians should "note that man, and have no company with him, that he may be ashamed" (2 Thess. 3:14). To allow him to continue in his error without trying to get him to repent would be both wrong and unkind to the man himself. Other Christians are not to treat him as an enemy but to "admonish," or warn, him as a brother (3:15).

As we said at the beginning of this chapter, many Christians deny the appropriateness of separating from other Christians, but both here and in 1 Corinthians 5, Paul teaches that such separation is appropriate. Another approach to limiting such commands is to narrow their focus. For instance, some argue that the passage applies only to the refusal to work and laziness, not to other forms of disobedience.[8] They are right to note Paul's focus on the problem of idlers, but this idleness is only one example of willful disobedience. The broader definition of *traditions* in 2 Thessalonians 2:15 invalidates attempts to limit the application to one particular practice. Anyone who refuses to abide by apostolic teaching (3:14) is subject to church discipline.

OLD TESTAMENT PARALLEL

Under the Mosaic law, God required an Israelite to rebuke someone who had fallen into sin. "Thou shalt not hate thy brother in thine heart: thou shalt in any wise rebuke thy neighbour, and not suffer sin upon him" (Lev. 19:17). The Israelites who entered the Promised Land understood the principle that if some of God's people became disobedient, their fellow Israelites should be the first to reprove them and then take appropriate action against them (Josh. 22:11–20). The story of the sin of Achan (Josh. 7) illustrates this principle in action as well as God's judgment on the congregation for the presence of sin. The book of Proverbs also has a great deal to say about the principle of rebuke (e.g., 25:12; 27:5).[9]

This principle is also illustrated by the situation that followed the return of the Israelites from the Babylonian captivity. Some of the Jewish returnees had followed the religious practices of the pagans and intermarried with them, and both Ezra and Nehemiah confronted this issue. Ezra realized the seriousness of his fellow Hebrews' sin and the need for action (Ezra 9:3–10:17). He mourned and prayed. Then he led the people in public penitence before God and in the putting away of the foreign wives. Several years later Nehemiah likewise recognized the importance of cleansing and disciplinary action (Neh. 13:1–29). He excluded foreigners from God's assembly, cleansed the temple, commanded the resumption of the tithe, restored the celebration of the Sabbath, and demanded the end of mixed marriages.

EXPLANATION AND APPLICATION

Although many Christians see the necessity of separation from the world system and from teachers of false doctrine, they find it more difficult to accept the need for separation from another Christian. Ideally there should be a spiritual unity in the church, a oneness that pervades the entire body of Christ. If all believers acted as they should, there would be unity in the church. The church, however, does not always live up to this ideal. It has not yet been presented without spot or wrinkle, and believers are not yet all that they should be or will be. In the present everyday life of the church, it is sometimes necessary to break fellowship with a fellow believer. "It is often said that the divided condition of Christendom is an evil, and so it is," writes J. Gresham Machen. "But the evil consists in the existence of the errors which cause the divisions and not at all in the recognition of those errors when once they exist."[10]

Separation from a disobedient brother is only a part of corrective discipline in the church. Anytime a member disobeys a clear command of God's Word, it becomes necessary first to rebuke him (Matt. 18:15–17; 2 Tim. 2:25). Matthew 18 teaches that if the offender fails to respond to the initial rebuke, then we must make various other efforts to correct his errant lifestyle, beliefs, or practice. Only as a last resort is it necessary to separate from this brother, and this action must not be done in a spirit of self-righteousness. Christians have to break fellowship with regret while maintaining the hope that repentance will result. Furthermore, the act of separating from a fellow Christian may vary in extent and nature from one case to another according to the severity and persistence of his disobedience.

Because Christians sometimes ignore this kind of separation or press it beyond the guidelines set down in Scripture, it is helpful to consider examples of situations likely to arise. First, when a Christian chooses to live like the world in open sin or when he adopts a worldly lifestyle, he becomes a danger to other Christians. The church is obligated by Scripture to deal with him. Depending on the extent of his backsliding, he may be counseled, excluded from positions of leadership, forbidden to take part in the public programs of the church, or even excluded from membership.

Second, if a brother becomes enamored with some teacher of false doctrine, lends support to him, and gives him Christian recognition, then he is becomes a "partaker of his evil deeds" (2 John 1:11). He may thereby deceive other Christians and lead them astray. The church must deal with him in much the same manner as described above.

Third, a Christian leader who refuses to take action against those who have been disobedient but instead encourages them is himself disobedient to the commands of the Bible. It is the responsibility of other Christian leaders to rebuke him and eventually to separate from him if he does not repent.

Fourth, a member who causes divisions in the church must also be disciplined. In New Testament times the word *heresy* meant a division, and the Bible condemns such schisms. The local assembly must, therefore, deal with any Christian who by his conduct or teaching disrupts the unity of the church. Ironically, some extreme separatists themselves cause unnecessary divisions by separating over minor issues of interpretation or personal differences.

Separation should not result from merely personal conflicts or differences of opinion on minor matters of interpretation. Denominational differences on matters of church government or the mode of baptism should not preclude fellowship and cooperation with spiritual Christians of other denominations (1 Cor. 1–3). Furthermore, biblical separation is not total rejection that allows no place for repentance. We should make every effort to restore the other, making full allowance for possible ignorance, errors of judgment, and momentary weakness. We should allow time for those young in the faith to achieve a degree of spiritual maturity that enables them to understand these truths. The member who has realized his responsibility and is in the process of moving away from compromise may be treated differently from one who is abandoning a separated position and beginning to compromise the Christian faith. For example, if someone remains a member of an apostate denomination but has begun to see the problems of such an association, we should work with him, encouraging him to make a complete break.

We cannot stress too strongly that separation from another Christian is not the same as separation from an apostate teacher. In both cases, purity is a goal. However, in separation from a Christian, restoration is also a goal. Although we might hope that separation from a false teacher would be a means of reaching him with the truth (2 Tim. 2:24–25), we are commanded to remember that erring Christians are our brothers and need to be restored to a harmonious family relationship. "If we lump our [disobedient] brothers together with apostates under the general heading of 'ecclesiastical separation,' it isn't long before we are speaking of and treating our brothers as though they were apostates."[11]

Exactly how do we practice separation in everyday life? The Amish practice what is known as "shunning." When the Amish exclude someone from their church, they forbid all communication with him. Even a wife whose husband is shunned cannot eat with him or she too will be excluded. Shunning, however, is far more extreme than the separation taught in the Bible. We should remember that separation deals with religious and spiritual associations, particularly church-related relationships. The question sometimes arises about the nature of a Christian's relationship to a family member involved in sin. Sin hampers Christian fellowship, but it does not destroy a family relationship. Christians should still love and help parents or siblings ensnared in sin. What separation from a disobedient Christian involves is refusing religious recognition that gives approval to wrongdoing.

A Christian whose sin is not publicly known and who is not leading others astray by his example should be rebuked privately by a fellow Christian who is stronger in the faith. The latter should attempt to restore the weaker one in a spirit of meekness, remembering that he may also be tempted. However, public sin committed by a public figure must be publicly rebuked for the sake of those who are being deceived. For example, a person who advocates fellowship with apostasy and who cooperates with false teachers and unbelievers is guilty of public defiance of God's command. For the sake of those he is leading astray or may lead astray if they are not properly warned from Scripture, a faithful minister of Christ must warn people about that person even though he claims to, and perhaps to an extent does, preach the gospel. At best, this is a situation in which a disobedient Christian is behaving like a false teacher. The difficulty is that people are associated with positions. It would be easier if we could concentrate on the *principle* of scriptural disobedience or compromise, but when a *person* is a prime instigator, promoter, and advocate of an unbiblical position, we must expose that person as well as the sin he is promoting.

The question may arise of what a believer should do about the disobedience of a fellow Christian who is not part of the same church or denomination. The procedure described in Matthew 18 does not readily apply to such situations. It might be that in such a case a Christian should contact the leadership of the disobedient Christian's church, depending on the circumstances. More often in such cases, however, the wrongdoing has become public (or otherwise a believer would not even be aware of it). Even if another church refuses to discipline one of its members for disobedience, a believer is responsible to God for his own obedience and the proper conduct of the church he belongs to. In such cases, Christians must still reject the wrongdoing and refuse to extend recognition and fellowship to those who are in obvious disobedience to God's Word.

Some Christians who object to separating from disobedient Christians argue that such separation from other Christians must be based only on moral grounds. Donald Grey Barnhouse insisted, "There must be separation where there is *moral* lapse, but *there is never a hint of separation because of doctrinal differences.*"[12] Barnhouse even offered a hundred dollars to anyone who could cite a single verse in the Bible justifying separation from a fellow Christian on doctrinal grounds.[13] Walter Martin joined him in contending that separation can be based only on moral grounds unless the doctrinal error is causing divisions in the church.[14] We mentioned earlier that the reference to idolatry in 1 Corinthians 5:11 weighs against this view because idolatry is certainly a doctrinal error.[15] Furthermore, this argument misses the central point of separation. We do not simply itemize all the sins specifically mentioned in Scripture and say, "These are the only grounds for separation." Rather, we affirm the principle that the willful, unrepentant practice of any sin is grounds for separation because all such sin is an affront to the holiness of God.

As we mentioned in Chapter 1, some Christians speak of first-degree and second-degree (or primary and secondary) separation. By first-degree separation they mean separation from those who teach false doctrine, and by second-degree separation they mean separation from believers who do not practice first-degree separation. Some Christians ridicule the position

> **WE AFFIRM THE PRINCIPLE THAT THE WILLFUL, UNREPENTANT PRACTICE OF ANY SIN IS GROUNDS FOR SEPARATION BECAUSE ALL SUCH SIN IS AN AFFRONT TO THE HOLINESS OF GOD.**

of second-degree separation as unscriptural, saying that it may lead to extremes.[16] One writer asks, "What about what has been called second-degree separation or third-, fourth-, or even fifth-degree separation? Are God's people to separate from others of God's people who do not separate? How far removed from the original offender should one carry the matter of separation? Specific answers to these questions are not given in the Bible."[17]

We should not let terminology distract us from the truth that faithfulness to biblical principles sometimes makes separation from other believers necessary. Some staunch separatists have even used the term "second-degree" separation to distinguish the difference between separation from fellow Christians and separation from false teachers.

We should likewise not lose sight of the fact that we are trying to practice of *biblical* separation; *first-degree* and *second-degree* are merely manmade descriptive terms. The question is not how some behavior fits into artificial categories. Rather, how does the character of any behavior appear in light of the Bible? As another writer argues, "There is no such thing as first-degree separation, second-degree separation, and so forth. There is only Scriptural separation."[18] Paul illustrates this point in the warnings to the Thessalonians to "have no company with" disobedient fellow believers. Had the Thessalonians refused, they would not have been guilty simply of associating with someone who was disobedient (i.e., a "degree" of separation); they would have been guilty themselves of disobedience for refusing to heed Paul's command.

In addition to underestimating the seriousness of disobedience, those condemning "secondary" separation miss the Bible's warnings about the contaminating effects of associating with disobedience. Citing 1 Corinthians 15:33, Rolland McCune observes, "While some may debate whether or not there is a legitimate 'condemnation by association,' there is certainly a genuine 'corruption by association' that takes place in wrong alliances."[19] It is not a question of separating from those who do not separate; it is a matter of separating from sin, from a willful disobedience to what God commands.

PURPOSES

Concerned Christians separate from disobedient Christians, therefore, for the following reasons:

- To preserve the testimony of God's people in the eyes of the world (1 Pet. 2:12)

- To prevent a disobedient brother from influencing others to do wrong (1 Cor. 5:6–7; Gal. 5:9)

- To set an example which will encourage others to be obedient (1 Tim. 5:20)

- To bring about repentance in the one who has been disobedient (2 Tim. 2:25; Rev. 3:19)

We may at first be perplexed when we try to think of separation from disobedient Christians in terms of Christlikeness. We know that Jesus invites sinners to Himself and says, "Come unto me, all ye that labour and are heavy laden, and I will give you rest" (Matt. 11:28). But we have already mentioned that Christ's purpose is to save and cleanse His church as a bride for Himself (Eph. 5:25–27). Christ Himself gave the first teaching concerning church discipline (Matt. 18:15–18). Those He loves, Christ says, He rebukes and chastens so that they may repent (Rev. 3:19). We can also repeat as a caution that any church discipline or form of separation undertaken without a concern for love and holiness is not a Christlike practice.

CONCLUSION

As we look back on Chapters 3–5, we should recall some general conclusions about the practice of biblical separation. First, in separation, as in other aspects of Christian living, believers must act according to the principle of love. But Christian love is not weak sentimentality: "Biblical love is to be informed, discerning, and discriminating (Phil. 1:9–10)."[20] True biblical separation is manifested in love—a love for God that rejects the world system, a love for the church that will not tolerate false teachers who desire to lead the sheep astray and to devour them, and a love for fellow Christians that is willing to endure even a break in fellowship in order to provoke them to do right. In the practice of separation, Christians should not become frustrated or vindictive. They should not be hasty to condemn others on the basis of unproven rumors. Instead they should demonstrate a godly patience because they know that God will eventually judge all ungodliness (Jude 1:14–15), whether the ungodliness of the world, a false teacher, or disobedient believers.

Second, many who argue against scriptural separation as presented here do not oppose separation as a principle but argue that separation endangers imperatives such as Christian unity and compassion. We need a balanced view that encompasses all the teachings of Scripture. The seriousness of the sin makes separation absolutely necessary. The believer who immerses himself in the Word of God and seeks to mature spiritually must learn to view sin the way God does.

> **IN SEPARATION, AS IN OTHER ASPECTS OF CHRISTIAN LIVING, BELIEVERS MUST ACT ACCORDING TO THE PRINCIPLE OF LOVE . . . NOT WEAK SENTIMENTALITY.**

Third, there is always the danger of extremism in separation. Some elevate personal interpretations to points of division and separate almost for separation's sake rather than for sound biblical reasons. "Separation is God's answer to apostasy. Separation is God's answer to the problem of disobedient brethren who will not separate from apostasy. But, separation is not the answer to every disagreement between brethren."[21]

This third consideration highlights an aspect of separation that Christians also need to appreciate, the matter of prudence in associations. Scripture, particularly the book of Proverbs, highlights the virtue of prudence (e.g., Prov. 13:16; 14:8, 15). Christians should separate from a person or institution only about a matter that clearly violates God's Word. But Christians may choose not to associate publicly with a person or group because of disagreement in methodology, a concern for raising questions among other believers, or even just a lack of full knowledge of a situation. Not every choice against cooperation is necessarily a stand for separation from sin. The story of Paul and Barnabas in Acts 15:36–41 might serve as an example. The Bible reveals no ethical principle involved in this separation. Rather it appears to have been a prudent move because of disagreement, and it resulted in two teams doing evangelistic work, instead of just one.[22]

In summary, believers practicing biblical separation should avoid individuals who are evil in conduct, false in teaching, and unspiritual in lifestyle. They should do so to the glory of God and to be conformed to the image of Jesus Christ.

CHAPTER SIX
FUNDAMENTALISM

Biblical separation is closely identified with fundamentalism—
indeed, so closely identified that we have spent five chapters laying
out the biblical basis of separation to correct the misconception that
separation is nothing more than a practice of some contemporary
"ism." Since the 1970s a steady stream of books and articles have
discussed American fundamentalism.[1] Although we can only survey
the history and beliefs of fundamentalism here, the endnotes provide
a guide for additional reading. In this chapter we will define *fundamentalism*, briefly survey its history, and discuss general considerations necessary to understand its nature. We will emphasize how
fundamentalism has taught and practiced separation in a way that
illustrates how the principles examined in previous chapters have actually been applied, and we will also demonstrate that contemporary
fundamentalism represents the fullest, though not the only, expression of the principles of biblical separation.

DEFINING FUNDAMENTALISM

In popular usage, the word *fundamentalist* has been frequently
applied to various religious extremists that sensible people would
likely despise. Journalists have labeled snake handlers, Mormon
polygamists, and people who let their children die rather than take
them to doctors as "fundamentalists." Even academics have used the
term to describe non-Christian religious groups, especially violent
ones. For instance, Islamic terrorists may be called "Muslim fundamentalists" while Hindus attacking Muslims may be called "Hindu

fundamentalists." What makes these groups "fundamentalist" in secular eyes is their intolerance towards other religions (including secularism), not any substantive views they hold in common. Thus Christians who insist on the truth of the Trinity as essential to their faith are placed in the same category with Muslims and Jews who think the doctrine of the Trinity is heresy.[2]

A basic definition of fundamentalism is the belief that (1) there are certain truths so essential to Christianity that they cannot be denied without destroying Christianity and (2) these essentials are the basis of Christian fellowship. The first point distinguishes fundamentalism from liberalism, neo-orthodoxy, and Roman Catholicism (discussed in Chapters 7, 8, and 11). The second point distinguishes fundamentalism from broader evangelicalism and the charismatic movement (discussed in Chapters 9 and 10). In terms of our theme of separation, the first point concerns biblical teaching about separation from false teachers and the second point separation from disobedient Christians.

There are also characteristics of the movement not covered by this basic definition: theological development, cultural factors, and historical continuity. First, fundamentalism has reaped the benefit of centuries of development in Christian theology. The truth of God is eternal and unchanging. Truth does not develop, and we do not invent it. But the Bible is not a book of systematic theology. Throughout history the church has grappled with important questions for which Christians have searched the Scripture for answers. The doctrine of the Trinity is a good example. Until Arius denied Christ's deity in the fourth century, Christians had not examined the Bible's teaching concerning that doctrine in a systematic way. The challenge of Arius led the Councils of Nicea (AD 325) and Constantinople (AD 381) to issue a creed that summarized biblical teaching about Christ.[3]

Likewise, fundamentalism incorporated theological development. Dispensationalism, which developed in the nineteenth century, was important to the development of fundamentalism. Likewise, the inerrancy of Scripture, though not a new doctrine, took on new importance in response to liberal attacks on the Bible. Although some writers argue that fundamentalism either "invented" inerrancy or put more stress on the doctrine than the church did in previous centuries, inerrancy has been a historic teaching of the Christian faith.[4] Yet like many teachings of Scripture in history, inerrancy was emphasized by fundamentalists when it came under attack by liberals.[5]

Cultural factors also shaped fundamentalism. Some Christians find it difficult to distinguish scriptural mandates from ideas that arise from their cultural heritage. Hudson Taylor believed he must overcome such cultural factors, and he shocked his fellow missionaries in the 1800s by abandoning Western cultural norms to live and dress like the Chinese people he wanted to reach with the gospel. Sometimes we can be blind to such factors. Early fundamentalists often viewed American culture as the height of Christian civilization. For instance, William Jennings Bryan opposed evolution partly because he saw it as an enemy of America's Christian civilization.[6] Although the United States has a rich Christian heritage, the nation has never been a model of perfection, as is easily demonstrated by such ugly episodes of its history as slavery, racial prejudice, and the mistreatment of native Americans. The model for Christianity is found in the Bible, not in the history of any nation.

Some writers have tried to define fundamentalism entirely by its cultural features. Historians of a feminist bent, for instance, have defined fundamentalism as primarily a reaction to changing gender roles in America. Some of their observations are valid, but their conclusions are not. It is true that fundamentalists reflect their culture because everyone does. It is quite another thing to say that the root of fundamentalism is found in the culture. To argue that culture is the determining factor is to ignore much evidence to the contrary.[7]

It is important to balance theological development and cultural factors by noting historical continuity. Orthodox Christians of the past did not share all the beliefs or practices of fundamentalism, but fundamentalism shares the orthodox theology of historic Christianity. The liberal New Testament scholar Kirsopp Lake of Harvard made a prescient observation about fundamentalism in 1925:

> But it is a mistake, often made by educated persons who happen to have but little knowledge of historical theology, to suppose that Fundamentalism is a new and strange form of thought. It is nothing of the kind: it is the partial and uneducated survival of a theology which was once universally held by all Christians. How many were there, for instance, in Christian churches in the eighteenth century who doubted the infallible inspiration of all

Scripture? A few, perhaps, but very few. No, the Fundamentalist may be wrong; I think that he is. But it is we who have departed from the tradition, not he, and I am sorry for the fate of anyone who tries to argue with a Fundamentalist on the basis of authority. The Bible and the *corpus theologicum* [doctrinal body] of the Church [are] on the Fundamentalist side.[8]

Christians of past ages were not fundamentalists, but if it were somehow possible for earlier Christians to consider the points on which fundamentalists and liberals differ today, it is hard to imagine them not preferring the fundamentalist side. Even the various movements that gave rise to fundamentalism did not agree with each other on all points of interpretation even though they shared a common commitment to historic Christian orthodoxy.

> ORTHODOX CHRISTIANS OF THE PAST DID NOT SHARE ALL THE BELIEFS OR PRACTICES OF FUNDAMENTALISM, BUT FUNDAMENTALISM SHARES THE ORTHODOX THEOLOGY OF HISTORIC CHRISTIANITY.

Although fundamentalism is a contemporary movement with contemporary features, it expresses the historic Christian faith. Fundamentalists affirm the teachings of the creeds of the early church councils regarding the Trinity, Christ's deity, His divine and human natures, and other biblical doctrines. They claim the doctrines held in common by the great Reformation confessions concerning the nature of salvation, the sufficiency of Scripture, and other teachings the reformers proclaimed in opposition to Catholic error. Whatever its other features, at the heart of fundamentalism lies "the faith which was once delivered unto the saints" (Jude 1:3).

A BRIEF HISTORY OF FUNDAMENTALISM

Although historical movements do not break into neat periods, we will divide fundamentalism into five periods, each of which represents a development in its practice of separation.

FORMING THE FUNDAMENTALIST COALITION (1865 TO 1919)

Fundamentalism has no true founding date. A number of movements—each with its own origins and influenced by a number of
different factors—came together in response to liberalism to form
what we now know as fundamentalism. The term *fundamentalist* was
not even coined until after 1919. Also some Christians involved in
the movements that contributed to the rise of fundamentalism later
distanced themselves from fundamentalism.

Until after the American Civil War, evangelical Protestantism
dominated American culture. Although the United States had no
established state church under the First Amendment, Protestantism
was virtually—if unofficially—the established religion. For example,
almost all non-state colleges were church-related and had clergy-
men as their presidents. Catholics considered the public schools so
Protestant that they often established their own parochial schools to
protect their children from Protestant influence.

This interdenominational Protestantism expressed its dominance
through cooperative efforts in establishing Bible societies, mission
agencies, and movements for social reform (e.g., the abolition of
slavery and the prohibition of the sale of alcohol). One facet of evangelical Protestantism that fundamentalists treasured was the nation's
heritage of revivals and evangelism. The Prayer Meeting Revival of
1857–59 contributed directly to the movements that gave rise to
fundamentalism, such as Bible conferences. After the Civil War came
the citywide campaigns of evangelists such as D. L. Moody. Later Billy
Sunday and other prominent evangelists became major figures in
fundamentalism.[9]

Protestant dominance of American culture began to break down
in the late 1800s. Immigration of non-Protestants increased, reduc-
ing Protestantism's numerical advantage. Intellectual movements
challenged the Christian faith. Charles Darwin's *Origin of Species*
promoted the theory of biological evolution and in so doing challenged the authority of Scripture. Reason and particularly science
were widely assumed to be the roads to truth. Critics implied that
if Christianity clashed with science, then so much the worse for
Christianity.

The invasion of naturalism and rationalism into the church
sparked the formation of fundamentalism. Liberalism, referred to as

modernism in the late 1800s and early 1900s, represented this spirit of naturalism and rationalism. (We will look more fully at the development of liberalism in the next chapter.) Early modernists were less extreme than secular rationalists. The modernists agreed that Protestantism should dominate American culture, but they wanted to maintain that dominance by changing Christianity to suit the temper of the times. They would modernize the faith to appeal to modern humans. Regrettably, "modernizing" the faith meant abandoning the inerrancy and authority of Scripture and questioning Christ's deity, His miracles, and His physical resurrection.[10]

The challenge of modernism united a coalition of conservatives within existing movements who began to resist it. For example, one rising force in nineteenth-century American Christianity was premillennialism. There had been premillennialists throughout history, but premillennialists became influential in American religious history only after the Civil War. Most American Christians until that time were postmillennialists who believed that the Holy Spirit would work through the church until the gospel spread throughout the world. When the world had come to Christ, then Jesus Himself would return for the final judgment.

> **THE INVASION OF NATURALISM AND RATIONALISM INTO THE CHURCH SPARKED THE FORMATION OF FUNDAMENTALISM.**

Premillennialists, on the other hand, believed that there would be a great outpouring of God's wrath on the earth followed by Christ's return to establish a millennial (thousand-year) kingdom. Premillennialists were especially opposed to the modernist perversion of postmillennialism. Modernists argued that mankind would build a better world through teaching and practicing Christian principles and did not believe, as the conservative postmillennialists did, in the person and work of the Holy Spirit or the literal return of Christ.[11]

Books, tracts, and religious newspapers popularized premillennial teaching. Two new vehicles for promoting premillennialism were Bible conferences and Bible training schools. At Bible conferences, Christians gathered at vacation spots to hear concentrated Bible teaching from leading ministers and teachers. The audiences at such conferences absorbed orthodox Bible teaching and returned home to spread it further. One of the most important of these conferences in the late 1800s was the Niagara Bible Conference led by James H. Brookes. This conference, a center of premillennial teaching, also became a rallying point for those who affirmed the essential doctrines of Christianity that modernism had denied. The creed of this conference, adopted in 1878, is often considered the first creed of the fundamentalist movement.[12]

Some Christians also began to form Bible training schools. As their name suggests, these schools concentrated mostly on Bible teaching as well as practical topics such as personal evangelism and Sunday school work. Their goal was to train lay workers or sometimes ministers and missionaries for Christian work. These schools based their curriculum on theologically conservative study of the English Bible, usually with a heavy stress on premillennialism. Many of the early Bible schools were Bible institutes. That is, they did not offer a full college curriculum but a Bible-study program with perhaps a few courses in English or speech. The most famous Bible institute, founded by D. L. Moody in Chicago, was after his death renamed Moody Bible Institute. Later, many Bible institutes adopted full collegiate programs and became Bible colleges, Christian liberal arts colleges, and seminaries.[13]

These Bible conferences, schools, and publications taught different varieties of premillennialism. One important variety was dispensationalism, a theological system named for the different ages, or *dispensations*, it sees in history. In each dispensation, God tests mankind in some way, and each age ends with man's failure and God's judgment. Central to dispensationalism is a distinction between Israel and the church. Certain parts of the Bible, including a great deal of prophecy, apply only to the Jews, and other parts apply only to Christians. Dispensationalists also stressed teachings that later characterized fundamentalism in general—the inerrancy of Scripture, the falling away of most of Christendom from the truth before the return of Christ, and the Rapture (the coming of Christ for His church just before God's wrath is poured out on earth). J. N. Darby of the Plymouth Brethren in Britain is usually considered the founder of dispensationalism, but the system was popularized in America by Congregationalist minister C. I. Scofield through his *Scofield Reference Bible* (first edition 1909).[14]

Another influence on fundamentalism was Keswick Holiness teaching. (Methodist Holiness teaching exercised less influence on fundamentalism than the Keswick variety.) Named for a conference site in England, the Keswick approach stressed the need for personal holiness through the power of the Holy Spirit. Although they did not necessarily accept all Keswick teachings, many fundamentalists embraced some of its ideas such as the "victorious" or "abundant life" and the existence of two distinct natures in the believer (a corrupt old nature and a regenerate new nature). Particularly popular was the idea of a special experience following conversion, often called "surrender," in which a Christian moves to a higher level of spiritual development and maturity.[15]

Modernism was initially a movement of scholars, and therefore among its most gifted opponents were orthodox academics who disputed the liberal teachings. A major center of orthodox scholarship was Princeton Theological Seminary, which stood firmly against liberalism and upheld the inerrancy of the Bible. Princeton's Benjamin B. Warfield was probably the leading scholarly defender of inerrancy at the turn of the twentieth century. The Princeton men were not concerned only about inerrancy. They realized that modernism was cutting out the heart of Christianity as a redemptive religion, and they opposed the movement's errors on a range of issues. Warfield died in 1921, but J. Gresham Machen continued to defend the Princeton theology during the Fundamentalist-Modernist Controversy.[16]

A blending of premillennialism, Keswick Holiness, and conservative scholarship occurred in a series of twelve pamphlets titled *The Fundamentals* (1910–15).[17] Sponsored by two Christian businessmen, these pamphlets contained articles written by prominent orthodox writers, such as Warfield and Scofield, in which they defended the authority and inspiration of the Bible, attacked evolution, and set forth biblical teaching about Christ. The sponsors mailed thousands of free copies of these pamphlets to pastors, missionaries, and laymen. As the subtitle said, the booklets were "a testimony to the truth." Within a few years the pamphlets and their purpose to defend Christian truth probably contributed to the coining of the term *fundamentalism*.

In this early period, expulsion of false teaching rather than withdrawal was the usual pattern of separation. An exception was the pastor of the Wealthy Street Baptist Church in Grand Rapids, Oliver Van Osdel, who led his church out of the Northern Baptist Convention in 1909. Since conservatives for the most part controlled the major denominations, they took steps to eliminate heresy within them. In 1910, the Presbyterian Church in the USA (PCUSA) began requiring candidates for the ministry to affirm their belief in five essential doctrines: the inerrancy of the Bible, the virgin birth of Christ, His vicarious atonement, His bodily resurrection, and the genuineness of biblical miracles. Furthermore, Presbyterians conducted heresy trials of liberal theologians and ministers in an attempt to expel them from the church.[18]

FUNDAMENTALIST-MODERNIST CONTROVERSY (1919 TO 1936)

Most people who know at least a little about fundamentalism often associate it with what is known as the Fundamentalist-Modernist Controversy of the 1920s. During that period modernists and fundamentalists clashed over which faction would control the major denominations and their agencies (schools, mission boards, publishing houses).[19]

A prelude to the controversy was the founding of the World's Christian Fundamentals Association (WCFA) in 1919 under the presidency of Minnesota Baptist W. B. Riley. The WCFA represented the first major attempt to unite conservatives and coordinate their efforts against modernism.[20] The following year Baptist editor Curtis Lee Laws coined the name for this movement when he wrote, "We suggest that those who still cling to the great fundamentals and who mean to do battle royal for the fundamentals shall be called 'Fundamentalists.'"[21]

Major battles took place in the PCUSA and the Northern Baptist Convention (NBC). The fundamentalists tried to exclude modernism from their denominations; modernists attempted to allow denominations to include all shades of theological belief. The fundamentalist slogan was "Truth," and the modernist slogan was "Tolerance."

Fundamentalists in the NBC began organizing in 1920, founding the Fundamentalist Fellowship to lobby for orthodoxy. The climax was an effort in 1922 to adopt a creed and thereby force the modernists out. The modernists offered a counterproposal affirming "that the New Testament is the all-sufficient ground of our faith and practice, and we need no other statement."[22] The New Testament proposal won the vote hands down. Although skirmishing continued for several years, the NBC rejected the fundamentalist position and committed itself to tolerating theological diversity.[23]

Another effort organized by conservative Baptists was the Baptist Bible Union (BBU), founded in 1923. This organization attempted to rally all Baptists for the fundamentalist cause in their respective denominations. W. B. Riley in the North, J. Frank Norris of Texas in the South, and T. T. Shields in Canada were the main leaders. The BBU foundered, however, especially after two public-relations disasters. Norris shot a man in his office in 1926. Although he was acquitted of murder, Norris's reputation was seriously damaged. (See Chapter 2.) In 1927, Shields led a BBU attempt to transform an NBC school, Des Moines University, into a fundamentalist institution. The student body rioted and forced the closing of the school in 1929. These disasters wrecked the BBU almost beyond repair.[24]

In the Presbyterian Church the major fundamentalist leader was J. Gresham Machen of Princeton Seminary. He wrote the most important fundamentalist apologetic, *Christianity and Liberalism* (1923), arguing that modernism was not even Christian. However, an alliance of liberals and tolerant conservatives in the PCUSA attacked the denomination's five-point doctrinal test for ministers. When that test was finally overturned in 1927, the denomination then reorganized Princeton Seminary to remove it from conservative control. Machen and several others left Princeton to found Westminster Theological Seminary. When Machen protested liberalism among the denomination's missionaries by founding an independent mission board in 1933, the Presbyterians tried him for violating church discipline and suspended him. Machen then organized a new denomination in 1936 that eventually became known as the Orthodox Presbyterian Church (OPC). In essence, the fundamentalists lost almost all their denominational battles.[25]

IN ESSENCE, THE FUNDAMENTALISTS LOST ALMOST ALL THEIR DENOMINATIONAL BATTLES.

Another aspect of the Fundamentalist-Modernist Controversy was the crusade against evolution in the South. Christians sought legislation to forbid the teaching of evolution in public schools, which climaxed with the Scopes Trial in Dayton, Tennessee, in 1925. A local schoolteacher, John Scopes, was tried for violating Tennessee's anti-evolution law. Agnostic attorney Clarence Darrow defended Scopes, supported by the American Civil Liberties Union. Statesman and Presbyterian fundamentalist William Jennings Bryan led the prosecution, supported by the WCFA. The devout Bryan opposed evolution in part because it conflicted with the Bible's account of Creation, but, as mentioned earlier, he also attacked evolution because he thought it was a cruel philosophy that would destroy Christian civilization in the United States. Scopes was convicted, but the press made fundamentalism look ridiculous. Liberals as well as the general public viewed the Scopes Trial as yet another defeat for fundamentalism.[26]

INDEPENDENT FUNDAMENTALISM (1925 TO 1957)

When the attempt to expel liberals from the major denominations proved unsuccessful, fundamentalists began to emphasize separation and organize their own independent fundamentalist network of institutions, including schools, publishing houses, mission boards, and eventually denominations. If they could not clean up the denominational institutions, then they would found their own.[27]

We have already mentioned how Machen founded the OPC. The remnant of the BBU reorganized itself into the General Association of Regular Baptist Churches (GARBC) in 1932. Other fundamentalists left the NBC in 1947 and formed the Conservative Baptist Association (CBA). Fundamentalists also relied on Bible schools founded before the controversy, such as Moody Bible Institute, Biola, and Wheaton College as well as newer schools including institutions such as Dallas Theological Seminary, a center of dispensationalist teaching (founded in 1924), and Bob Jones College (1927), later Bob Jones University. Fundamentalist mission boards quickly surpassed the boards of the major denominations in sending missionaries to the field. Bible conferences also continued to function as centers for spreading orthodox theology and to provide opportunities for fellowship.

Fundamentalists further made use of mass media. They published periodicals and religious newspapers, such as the *Sunday*

School Times and the *Sword of the Lord* (founded in 1934). Radio also became a popular vehicle for promoting the fundamentalist cause. One of the most successful broadcasters was Charles Fuller. His *Old-Fashioned Revival Hour* became one of the most popular religious radio programs in America during the 1930s and 1940s, surpassing even the most popular secular shows. Fuller's listening audience was estimated at twenty million.[28]

When fundamentalists and modernists battled to control the major denominations, an assumption had been that whoever won would then superintend Protestantism's historic dominance in American culture. Although the modernists won, the historic denominations began in the 1960s to suffer a precipitous decline in membership. Meanwhile, fundamentalists flourished. Their churches and larger organizations grew and thrived so that by the 1950s and 1960s some religious observers began to refer to fundamentalism/evangelicalism as a "third force" in American religion alongside Catholicism and mainline Protestantism.[29]

The word *independent* describes fundamentalism in this period. Fundamentalism remained opposed to liberalism and was separatist in refusing to cooperate with liberalism, hence its many independent agencies. But fundamentalists did not always agree among themselves about breaking all official ties to liberalism. Ernest Pickering and Myron Houghton have rightly pointed out how the GARBC and the CBA represented differing philosophies. The GARBC from its founding refused to allow its churches to hold membership in organizations such as the NBC, which also included modernists. The CBA allowed its members to hold dual membership.[30] Nevertheless, both the GARBC and the CBA were initially considered fundamentalist organizations.

Fundamentalists agreed that they should not support liberalism, but the question was what was meant by the term *support*. Was the kind of association practiced by the CBA a form of support? In the 1950s this question of the Christian's precise relations to liberalism became the focus of a new controversy.

SEPARATIST FUNDAMENTALISM (1957 TO 1976)
The use of the word *separatist* for this period does not mean that fundamentalism had not previously been separatist. Separatism had

earlier been expressed not only as withdrawal but also through expulsion of liberals and building independent organizations. Nevertheless, events of this period brought the question of separatism to the forefront.

In the 1940s and 1950s, a number of evangelical scholars and spokesmen, taking the name *new evangelicals* (discussed in Chapter 9), began to call for the reform of fundamentalism. They wished to see greater evangelical involvement in scholarship, especially discussion of theological issues with liberals. They also repudiated the idea of separation and called for the infiltration of evangelicals back into the major denominations in an attempt to recapture them.

The man who became the symbol of this movement and whose actions marked this division was not a scholar but the evangelist Billy Graham, probably the best-known evangelical preacher in America. The break between the new evangelicals and fundamentalists was highlighted in 1957 when Graham announced, "I would like to make myself quite clear. I intend to go anywhere, sponsored by anybody, to preach the Gospel of Christ, if there are no strings attached to my message."[31] In his New York campaign of that year, he accepted liberal sponsors on his committee, and he sent converts from his campaign to liberal churches.

Many fundamentalists denounced this action as a betrayal of what they had been fighting for since the 1920s. In 1958, more than 150 fundamentalist leaders met in Chicago to respond to Graham. Led by John R. Rice of *The Sword of the Lord* and by Bob Jones Sr. of Bob Jones University, the attendees signed a pledge to have no fellowship or other religious connection with liberalism. Among the signers were important leaders of fundamentalist associations, such as Robert Ketcham of the GARBC, G. B. Vick of the Baptist Bible Fellowship, and Ernest Pickering of the Independent Fundamental Churches of America.[32] Graham's action, the pledge implied, was not some vague question of associations. It was a conscious embrace of liberals.

The result of Graham's action was to make separatism a major issue among conservative Christians. Graham's alliances with liberals caused fundamentalists to look closely at the dangers of even casual religious ties to liberals. Fundamentalists would no longer be vague about what constituted "support" of liberalism. They insisted on breaking all connections so that there would be no question of association.

Conservative Protestants soon divided into two camps. Some who did not consider themselves "new" evangelicals still supported Graham because of his extensive, apparently successful evangelistic work. Those who opposed Graham's methodology and the new evangelical philosophy it represented kept the name *fundamentalist*. As we will discuss more fully in Chapter 9, the initial disagreement between these two factions was not on an essential point of doctrine (as it had been with the liberals) but on the matter of biblical separation itself.

Some groups, such as the GARBC, came down solidly on the fundamentalist side, but many others split. The CBA, as we mentioned, had allowed its members to maintain some ties to organizations that tolerated liberalism. The majority of the CBA sided with the new evangelical policy, but a sizable minority left the CBA to pursue a fundamentalist separatism.[33]

FUNDAMENTALISM IN TENSION (1976 TO THE PRESENT)

In 1976, the World Congress of Fundamentalists met in Edinburgh, Scotland. Some two thousand delegates gathered for a week of meetings. They heard papers read, listened to sermons, and joined in prayer sessions. They also heard resolutions affirmed, including a seven-point definition of what a fundamentalist is.[34] Noticing the preparations for this meeting, leading evangelical theologian Carl Henry reported in *Christianity Today* that "the evangelical far-right is regathering for a massive initiative all its own."[35] The congress seemed to mark a high point of unity and testimony for the separatist cause.

Yet separatist fundamentalism experienced increasing tension in the coming decades. From the outside, events such as the founding of an Islamic republic in Iran increasingly identified the term *fundamentalism* with political and religious extremism. Other contemporary cultural and theological movements challenged fundamentalism and its separatist practices from outside.[36] There was dissent, even at the time of the World Congress of Fundamentalists. Opposing what he saw as an unreasonable application of separation, John R. Rice and his newspaper *The Sword of the Lord* remained aloof from the congress. At the other end of the spectrum, the militant Carl McIntire rejected the congress as an ill-conceived "New Fundamentalism," which he believed was insufficiently separatist and designed to undercut his own organization, the International Council of Christian Churches.[37] Rice and McIntire highlight a challenge to contemporary fundamentalism, the tendencies to be either looser or stricter in separation.

Two major controversies have troubled separatist fundamentalists since the 1970s. Curiously, these controversies parallel contemporary conflicts within broader evangelicalism. As evangelicals battled over the inerrancy of Scripture (described in Chapter 9), fundamentalists struggled over the role of the King James Version. While evangelicals debated the concept of "cobelligerence" with Roman Catholics (discussed in Chapter 11), fundamentalists faced an internal conflict over political action as a threat to separation.

The roots of the so-called King James Only position lay in the nineteenth century.[38] Drawing on a new methodology and using Greek manuscripts discovered since the publication of the KJV, scholars compiled a new edition of the Greek Scriptures, often known as the eclectic text. A minority of scholars, led by Anglican scholar John Burgon (1813–88), argued for the superiority of the traditional Greek text, variously called the Majority Text or Received Text (*Textus Receptus*), which underlay the translations of the Reformation era. (Although these labels are sometimes used interchangeably, the two are not identical. The Majority Text is a group of actual manuscripts that represent the majority of surviving Greek manuscripts. The Received Text is the published edition of the Greek text from the Reformation era, based on Majority Text manuscripts.)

Among twentieth-century fundamentalists, this clash over Greek manuscripts turned into a battle over translations. Defense of the Greek text used during the Reformation slipped into a defense of the King James Version. Because the KJV was the last translation to come out of the English Reformation, supporters of the Majority Text saw the KJV as the best, most faithful rendering of God's Word in English. Particularly as modern translations began to proliferate (e.g., the Revised Standard Version in the 1950s and the New International Version in the 1970s), some fundamentalists insisted on retaining the KJV as the safeguard against doctrinal error and theological drift.

A problem arose when defenders of the KJV made their position a test of fellowship and even a test of true fundamentalism. To complicate matters, KJV defenders fell along a continuum. Some fundamentalists held strongly to the KJV and its underlying text but did not insist on their position as a basis of fellowship. Others believed the Majority Text/KJV position was a serious point of disagreement among believers. Some fundamentalists believed not only in the superior textual basis of the KJV but also thought that providential activity in its translation made the KJV uniquely the Word of God for the English-speaking world. And finally, most extreme were a few who held the KJV to be superior to any Greek or Hebrew text.

SOME FUNDAMENTALISTS INSISTED ON RETAINING THE KJV AS THE SAFEGUARD AGAINST DOCTRINAL ERROR AND THEOLOGICAL DRIFT.

Some fundamentalist institutions, while expressing appreciation for the King James Version, declared that views on Bible translations were a matter of personal conviction. Others adopted declarations and statements of faith directly affirming the KJV as God's specially preserved Word. The divisions showed few signs of diminishing even in the twenty-first century.[39] The stronger, more adamant defenders of the KJV had drawn a new line of separation.

A second post-1970s controversy arose over what Earle Cairns referred to as "Open Fundamentalism," in contrast to the "Closed Fundamentalism" of militant separatists.[40] The militants devised the label *pseudo-fundamentalism* for the opposing group.[41] However, *neo-fundamentalism* probably comes closest to a neutral term.[42]

Neo-fundamentalism took reforming fundamentalism as its goal, much as the new evangelicalism had sought to do thirty years before. (See Chapter 9.) Like the new evangelicals, the neo-fundamentalists argued that fundamentalism had become too narrow and was insufficiently vocal about social issues. Neo-fundamentalism, however, demonstrated no interest in interacting with liberalism, and by social action, neo-fundamentalists intended greater involvement in behalf of conservative political causes.[43]

A forerunner of this position was John R. Rice. As mentioned earlier, he questioned what he called the unnecessary practice of secondary separation from other Christians. Rice also lent warm support to two formative figures in the movement: Jack Van Impe and Jerry Falwell. Van Impe was a well-known fundamentalist evangelist and television preacher. He had held numerous successful citywide campaigns and had addressed the first World Congress of

Fundamentalists. In the late 1970s, however, he began to denounce what he called a hate movement among fundamentalists, claiming that they were majoring on (and separating over) minor issues. In 1984, he published *Heart Disease in Christ's Body*, in which he outlined these charges and finalized his own break with separatist fundamentalism.

Far more important to the neo-fundamentalist movement was Baptist pastor Jerry Falwell of Lynchburg, Virginia. A member of the Baptist Bible Fellowship (one of the largest independent Baptist groups), Falwell began to attract attention in the 1960s. The remarkable growth of his congregation, Thomas Road Baptist Church, made its Sunday school one of the ten largest in America by 1969.

Falwell achieved national renown after he founded the political action group known as the Moral Majority in 1979. This organization was one of many conservative religious groups credited with helping elect Republican Ronald Reagan to the presidency in 1980. Political liberals accused Falwell of trying to force his religious beliefs on the nation while fundamentalists charged him with compromising the faith. Despite opposition, Falwell maintained an extensive national outreach through his television program, *The Old Time Gospel Hour*, and his school, eventually named Liberty University.

Neo-fundamentalists initially criticized new evangelical tolerance and Billy Graham's cooperation with liberals.[44] The movement, however, based its practice of separation on the distinction between first-degree and second-degree separation (discussed in Chapters 1 and 5). As a result, neo-fundamentalists rejected false teaching but were much less likely to separate from other Christians.[45] Neo-fundamentalists insisted strenuously on the cardinal doctrines of the faith, especially the inerrancy of Scripture. But the movement used this doctrinal stance as a basis for suggesting closer alliances between themselves and conservative evangelicals who had become disillusioned by trends in broader evangelicalism.[46] Neo-fundamentalists maintained that they represented an earlier, purer form of fundamentalism that the militants had obscured.

Fundamentalists became concerned that Falwell was actually promoting an ecumenical movement more inclusive than anything proposed by Billy Graham and the new evangelicals in the 1950s. In the Moral Majority, Falwell claimed he had founded a nonreligious political organization that would lobby for morality through legislation and politics. Therefore, he did not hesitate to invite Roman Catholics, Jews, Mormons, and other religious groups to work with him. Militant fundamentalists pointed to the near-impossibility of holding a "nonreligious" crusade for morality, especially when its leaders were all clergy. Inclusion of these groups in the Moral Majority, critics argued, would lead Bible-believers to accept the validity of their positions.[47] One critic described Falwell's approach to political action as "the ultimate ecumenism."[48]

Falwell and Van Impe had genuine grievances. Some militant fundamentalists were harsh or extreme in their criticism, and some separatists certainly majored on minors. However, although the neo-fundamentalists claimed to be reformers calling fundamentalism back to its original position, they regularly shifted their own theological alliances. For instance, Falwell moved from opposition to the charismatic movement to cooperation with it. Liberty University began to accept charismatic students after Falwell had earlier said it would not do so.[49] Van Impe moved even farther to an embrace of Roman Catholicism as a partner not just in moral reform, but also in evangelism and discipleship.[50]

One historian observes that neo-fundamentalists "tended to blur the distinction between fundamentalist and evangelical."[51] Neo-fundamentalism's position on ecclesiastical separation—the crucial difference between fundamentalist and non-fundamentalist evangelicalism—is virtually indistinguishable from the position of most

> **ALTHOUGH WE CAN DRAW MODELS FROM HISTORY, THE FUNDAMENTALIST PAST SHOULD NOT DETERMINE ONE'S ATTITUDE TOWARD SEPARATION.**

evangelicals. Falwell began calling himself a fundamentalist less and less and more often used the term *evangelical*. He openly affirmed his cooperation with non-fundamentalist evangelicals, charismatics, and Catholics. By the time Falwell invited Billy Graham to speak at the commencement of Liberty University in 1997 (when Graham's grandson was in the graduating class), there appeared to be little distinction between his position and that of mainstream American evangelicalism.

Fundamentalism entered the twenty-first century a little uncertainly. Although perhaps four million Americans still identified themselves as fundamentalists,[52] it was unclear how these people defined the term.

CAUTIONS ABOUT USING HISTORY

Scripture, not history, sets the pattern of how we should believe and live. Although we can draw models from history, the fundamentalist past should not determine one's attitude toward separation. Some evangelicals have argued that *The Fundamentals* (published 1910–15), in their adherence to the fundamentals of the faith, scholarly defense of the truth, and alleged openness on questions such as inerrancy and evolution, were actually closer to new evangelicalism than to mid-twentieth-century fundamentalism.[53] Likewise, Robert L. Sumner accused David Beale of "changing the rules in the middle of the game" by arguing that after 1930 fundamentalists began to practice separation in a different manner in the light of a different situation.[54] We should always remember that the Bible is our only guide for faith and practice. Scripture alone should control our conduct.

UNDERSTANDING FUNDAMENTALISM

Some additional characteristics of the fundamentalist movement and questions concerning it should be considered if we are to answer the charge that fundamentalism reduces theology to a "lowest common denominator." We also need to consider what is meant by fundamentalist "militancy" and to acknowledge the testimony of other separatists who do not consider themselves fundamentalists.

FUNDAMENTALISM'S "REDUCTION" OF THEOLOGY

Some critics charge that fundamentalists reduce Christianity to just a few doctrines. Harold O. J. Brown, for example, says that Protestant orthodoxy "is doctrinally comprehensive, while fundamentalism is highly selective." Orthodoxy, he says, "presents a broad range of doctrines it considers vital, and integrates them into a dogmatic system" whereas fundamentalism "selects a small number of doctrines as fundamental and fights for them."[55]

SET APART

This common charge misunderstands the nature of fundamentalism. Broadly speaking, the movement holds to the beliefs of orthodox
Protestantism. Specifically, the movement insists that there are essentials of Christian belief apart from which Christianity cannot exist.
Fundamentalism does not argue that these essentials are the whole
of Christian doctrine. In fact, fundamentalist essentials are generally
those that have been challenged by liberalism. Were fundamentalism
confronting Roman Catholicism, then doctrines such as justification
by faith alone and the sole mediation of Christ would become prominent. Fundamentalism aims to unite believers in defense of the faith
despite their differences. Christians may hold competing systems of
theology (dispensationalism, Calvinism, Arminianism) and yet be
united in testimony to the truths of Christianity. No one need deny
his theological heritage or system of theology in order to be a fundamentalist. Indeed, we must ask Brown, which system of Protestant
orthodoxy should all Christians adopt?

FUNDAMENTALIST MILITANCY

Another common misunderstanding is the idea of "militancy" or
"militant fundamentalism." Common synonyms for *militant* include
combative, *belligerent*, *contentious*, *extreme*, *pugnacious*, and *disputa-
tious*. Ronald Nash castigates fundamentalism on this basis: "One of
the prime 'virtues' of the twentieth-century separatist is theological
pugnaciousness. One can hear them speak proudly and boastfully of
their 'militant fundamentalism,' 'uncompromising fundamentalism,'
'fighting fundamentalism,' and so on, *ad nauseam*."[56] Furthermore,
those who speak of "Muslim fundamentalism" or "Jewish fundamentalism" base their argument on the claim that being "militant"
about your faith (whatever that faith may be) is what makes you a
fundamentalist.

A standard theological definition of the word *militant* explains the
meaning of the phrase "militant fundamentalism." Christians have
historically used the phrases "the church militant" and "the church
triumphant." The church triumphant consists of the redeemed in
heaven who enjoy the presence of God. The church militant is the
church on earth engaged in warfare against sin. It is in this sense—
warfare against sin—that the fundamentalist is militant. Paul uses
this imagery, telling the Ephesians to put on a spiritual soldier's

equipment, "the whole armour of God" (Eph. 6:10–17). He urges Timothy to "endure hardness, as a good soldier of Jesus Christ" and warns that "no man that warreth entangleth himself with the affairs of this life; that he may please him who hath chosen him to be a soldier" (2 Tim. 2:3–4; see also 1 Tim. 6:12; 2 Tim. 4:7).

Because they truly believe in the Christian faith, fundamentalists defend that faith. The idea of basing Christian fellowship on the fundamentals assumes militancy and commitment to essentials as the basis of all alliances. Fundamentalism starts with theological belief, and "militancy" results. Yet militancy is no excuse for sin. As Moritz notes, fundamentalists must be militant, but they must also manifest the fruit of the Spirit.[57] A "good soldier of Jesus Christ" is not a plundering soldier of fortune but a servant who obeys his or her commander in all things.

> **FUNDAMENTALISTS MUST BE MILITANT, BUT THEY MUST ALSO MANIFEST THE FRUIT OF THE SPIRIT.**

OTHER SEPARATISTS

Finally, we must acknowledge other separatists who are not fundamentalists. Sometimes fundamentalists lose heart as Elijah did in the wilderness. In the midst of despair, the prophet told God, "The children of Israel have forsaken thy covenant, thrown down thine altars, and slain thy prophets with the sword; and I, even I only, am left" (1 Kings 19:14). But God replied to Elijah, "I have left me seven thousand in Israel, all the knees which have not bowed unto Baal, and every mouth which hath not kissed him" (19:18).

We will discuss in Chapter 12 the testimonies of Charles Spurgeon (1834–92) and D. Martyn Lloyd-Jones (1899–1981). Before fundamentalism ever arose in America, Spurgeon condemned the rise of liberalism in Britain's Baptist Union. When that group determined to tolerate unbelief, Spurgeon withdrew from it in 1887. Lloyd-Jones, a British evangelical, never referred to himself as a fundamentalist, but like fundamentalists he criticized not only liberal theology but also alliances with liberals. In 1966, he issued a vain call to British evangelicals to consider leaving their compromised denominations.

Plainly, there were and are separatists seeking to follow the biblical pattern who do not use the label *fundamentalist.*

Some Christians practice ecclesiastical separation from false teachings such as liberalism because they adhere to their theological or denominational distinctives in addition to the fundamentals of the faith. In this group are staunchly conservative Calvinists, Lutherans, Baptists, and others. They also treat liberalism as a non-Christian religion and refuse to have anything to do with it. Usually, though, Christians in these groups differ with fundamentalists. Sometimes that disagreement arises over a matter of personal separation. For instance, some Reformed (Calvinistic) Christians reject prohibitions on tobacco or alcohol, maintaining that such questions are matters of Christian liberty to be decided by the individual Christian.[58]

Sometimes these other separatist Christians think fundamentalists require *too few* "fundamentals." They believe the boundaries of Christian fellowship should be narrower. The Protestant Reformed Churches of America, for example, is a small Calvinistic body that is strictly separatist. A writer in this denomination criticizes fundamentalism for not carrying its essentials far enough. He says, "We would add to the list of fundamental truths many more truths, such as the truth of sovereign predestination, the truths of the five points of Calvinism, and the truth of the covenant."[59] In explaining why the Lutheran Church-Missouri Synod did not work with fundamentalism, Milton Rudnick says that fundamentalists stress points of agreement and "agree to disagree" about other points so that they may work or even worship together. "Missouri Synod Lutherans considered this controlling principle of fundamentalism completely unacceptable and even sinful," Rudnick writes. Christians must observe all that Christ commands, he argues, such as the Lutheran views of the sacraments.[60] Baptist David E. Gonnella says that fundamentalists err in excluding baptism by immersion and other Baptist distinctives from their list of fundamentals. "I further submit," he says, "that fundamentalism is nothing more than a ploy of Satan . . . to dilute New Testament doctrine and practice."[61] For these Christians, fundamentalists are either not Calvinistic enough, not Lutheran enough, or not Baptist enough. Yet these believers unquestionably practice separation from unbelief.

CONCLUSION

At least two themes mark the history of fundamentalism: the idea of doctrinal "fundamentals" and the practice of separation. We discussed in Chapter 4 the difference between a fundamental doctrine and a matter of interpretation. In the course of this chapter we have mentioned some of the doctrines defended by fundamentalists: the inerrancy and authority of the Bible, Christ's deity and virgin birth, His vicarious atonement and resurrection, and the biblical teaching about creation. Adherence to these and other fundamental doctrines has unquestionably characterized fundamentalism.

Fundamentalism is also a movement characterized by its practice of separation. More than that, it has attempted to practice separation in a balanced manner. Groups such as the Protestant Reformed Churches and the Lutheran Church-Missouri Synod also practice a form of separation, but unlike fundamentalists, they add denominational and interpretational distinctives as tests of fellowship. Fundamentalism, ideally, insists that fundamental doctrines—not matters of interpretation—are the only beliefs that may be required of a Christian brother. Fundamentalism does not, however, surrender fundamental doctrines to accommodate anyone.

Fundamentalism is certainly imperfect. Critics will always be able to cite its shortcomings. The question, however, should be the central beliefs of the movement. Are there truths so essential to Christianity that they cannot be denied without destroying Christianity? Should these essentials be the basis of Christian fellowship? If the answer to both these questions is yes, then fundamentalists have a strong case to offer in defense of their practices.

CHAPTER SEVEN
LIBERALISM

Why do people believe what they believe? One basic reason is the authority they appeal to. In medieval Europe, the authority was the institutional church and the Bible as interpreted by the church. The church was assumed to have the answer to every problem, not only in religion but also in philosophy, politics, and the arts as well.

During the Reformation of the 1500s, leaders such as Martin Luther and John Calvin demonstrated that what the Roman Church declared was opposed to what God had said. They argued that the Bible, God's Word, was an authority sufficient in itself to reveal God's message. "Scripture alone" was a central theme of the Reformation. At his famous appearance at the Diet of Worms, Luther told Emperor Charles V and his court, "Unless therefore I am convinced by the testimony of Scripture, or by the clearest reasoning—unless I am persuaded by means of the passages I have quoted, and unless they thus render my conscience bound by the Word of God, *I cannot and I will not retract,* for it is unsafe for a Christian to speak against his conscience. *Here I stand; I can do no other; may God help me. Amen.*"[1]

The Reformation's stress on the Bible, however, did not end the debate about religious authority. During the Age of Reason in the 1600s and 1700s, human reason began to displace the Bible as an authority, and it is in this post-Reformation era with its stress on reason that we find the roots of the many movements that are part of what is called liberalism.

PHILOSOPHICAL BACKGROUND OF LIBERALISM

Sometimes the Age of Reason is referred to as the Enlightenment, a reexamination of all knowledge in the light of human reason. "We ought never let ourselves to be convinced," philosopher René Descartes (1596–1650) wrote, "except on the evidence of our reason."[2] During the Enlightenment people looked to reason, not the church or the Bible. Leaders of the Enlightenment especially viewed science as providing the surest way of discovering truth. Some thinkers of this period claimed to be Christians looking for what God had to say, but they maintained that they would find God's Word not through revelation (the Bible) but through reason.

But how exactly does reason work? More particularly, where does knowledge come from—through mental processes or through our senses and experiences? Philosophers debated these questions. Descartes said that pure reason alone was enough. He believed, for example, that he could prove his own existence by the very fact that he thought. "I think, therefore I am" was his famous declaration. Scotsman David Hume (1711–76), on the other hand, said that only experiences received through the senses could provide knowledge.

The German philosopher Immanuel Kant (1724–1804) suggested an answer to this dilemma. He agreed with Hume that sensory experience was necessary for scientific knowledge—knowledge about things in time and space. But Kant also said that reason played a role in knowledge. The human mind combines sensory experiences with *a priori* understandings (facts perceived as true before and apart from experience) to formulate valid scientific knowledge. The mind plays a role in shaping sensory experiences into knowledge. Furthermore, Kant said there is another realm beyond time and space, a realm of ideas, or "things in themselves." Here reason cannot operate, for there is no "data" for reason to examine. Faith is the only way to understand these "things in themselves," and one cannot demonstrate the truth of faith through scientific or mathematical proof. Instead, Kant said, the realm of things in themselves is validated by what he called "the categorical imperative," roughly the conscience, a universal sense of right and wrong.

We have greatly simplified Kant's ideas here, but his views sparked a revolution in philosophical thought. Important to our discussion is how Kant's ideas spurred the growth of religious liberalism. Kant says that the things of God (e.g., His existence and attributes) are not perceptible to the senses. They lie in the realm of things in themselves, a realm of faith where reason cannot operate. Faith, in other words, cannot be based on rational proof.

Kant's views had two important consequences for religious studies. First, he made whatever exists within the realm of the senses fair game for applying reason. We cannot know anything about God from reason, but we can apply rational methods to the study of the Bible as one of the phenomena available to our senses. In fact, according to Kant's scheme, we can thoroughly criticize the Scripture without damaging faith. Second, the appeal to the categorical imperative based religious truth on something *within* humans and their experience. Religious truth was not something revealed to humans from above but from inside humans themselves. Also, because religion is inward, it is ultimately about morality. Kant said that "true religion is to consist not in the knowing or considering of what God does or has done for our salvation but in what we must do to become worthy of it,"[3] a position exactly opposite to the Bible's teaching about grace.

Other ideas were combined with Kant's philosophy to shape modern religious liberalism. We mentioned in the previous chapter how Charles Darwin's theory of biological evolution shook the intellectual world after *Origin of Species* was published in 1859. Also, German philosopher Georg Hegel (1770–1831) popularized a scheme in which history was viewed as moving civilization along a path of inevitable progress (a view Karl Marx revamped as the basis for his theory of communism). The ideas of Darwin and Hegel led scholars to assume mankind's inevitable progress as virtually a law of science. These concepts of Kant, Darwin, and Hegel—religious truth being internal to man, evolution, and the inevitability of progress—contributed significantly to the rise of liberalism.

RATIONALISM AND HIGHER CRITICISM

At first, cautiously in the 1700s, rationalistic Bible scholars began to scrutinize Scripture with the professed goal of discovering through historical research a solid foundation for religious belief and practice. Not surprisingly, the result was not certainty but a confusing and contradictory range of human opinions.

Scholarly study of the Bible is often called criticism.[4] Lower criticism, also called textual criticism, is the study of the surviving manuscripts of the Bible. Textual critics endeavor to determine the exact wording of Scripture by a careful study of all available manuscripts. Higher criticism is the study of the content of the Bible and deals with questions of authorship, date, and literary structure. Despite its name, biblical criticism is not necessarily critical in the sense of being disparaging. A Bible-believing scholar who studies the manuscripts of the Bible or carefully studies the content and structure of a book of the Bible also engages in biblical criticism in the sense of being analytical about the text. A believing scholar, for example, might conduct an intensive study of the epistle to the Hebrews to argue that the apostle Paul was or was not its author. Nevertheless, liberal higher critics approach the Bible with human assumptions that undermine its authority. On this point R. A. Torrey wrote, "It is often said that we should study the Bible just as we study any other book. That principle contains a truth, but it also contains a great error. The Bible it is true is a book as other books are books; the same laws of grammatical and literary construction and interpretation hold here as hold in other books. But the Bible is an entirely unique book. It is what no other book is—the Word of God."[5]

Nineteenth-century higher criticism took different forms. For instance, borrowing ideas from Hegel, Ferdinand Christian Baur suggested that Christianity had an evolutionary development. Baur said that originally Christianity was a kind of reformed Judaism, represented by Peter. This system clashed with Greek philosophy, represented by the teachings of Paul. The resulting synthesis became early Christianity. Another popular investigation was the "search for the historical Jesus." Critics assumed that the New Testament accounts of Christ were encrusted with legends. Therefore, they sought to rediscover the "true" Jesus of history. "Unreasonable" teachings about Christ's miracles, virgin birth, and deity were eliminated until critics had created a first-century philosopher/teacher who had little similarity to the Christ of the Gospels.

The Old Testament received similar treatment. Critics particularly sought to uncover the various sources allegedly used in compiling the books of the Old Testament. The most famous example is the critical treatment of the Pentateuch. Building on the work of earlier scholars, Julius Wellhausen (1844–1918) theorized that the books credited to

Moses (even by Jesus Himself) were actually written over a period of centuries by combining different sources. The two oldest sources, although still not going back to the time of Moses, each used a different name for God: *Jehovah* and *Elohim*. These sources were called "J" and "E." A later source from the era of King Josiah added the legal requirements, such as those found in Deuteronomy, so it was called "D." Finally, after the Babylonian captivity, a team of priestly editors brought all these sources together into the five books we know today. This priestly work represented the "P" document. Underlying all of this study—Old Testament and New—was an evolutionary view of history. Critics argued that Judaism and later Christianity had developed from simple, crude systems of belief into more complex forms. They did not believe God gave a complete revelation to His people.

Nineteenth-century liberalism put a strong emphasis on morality and good works. For example, Albrecht Ritschl (1822–89), following Kant, said we cannot really know or prove the "facts" (or doctrines) of Christianity. All we can know are the value judgments we make about those facts. For example, we cannot know that Jesus Christ made an atonement for our sin to the Father. All we can know is that Jesus' death moves us to love as He loved and to serve others. Ritschl therefore also represented the liberal tendency to stress building the kingdom of God on earth.

The climax of nineteenth-century liberalism came in Adolf von Harnack (1851–1930). Harnack believed that Christianity had a kernel of truth covered by a husk of legend, and he saw his task as removing the husk. Harnack reduced Christ's teaching to three main principles: the need to proclaim and establish the kingdom of God, the fatherhood of God and the brotherhood of all men, and an ethic of loving God and loving your neighbor as yourself.[6]

Even this brief survey of liberalism reveals many ways it deviated from the Christian faith. The authority of the Bible was first discarded and then everything else that was "unreasonable"—the miracles recorded in Scripture, for example. Liberals assaulted the biblical presentation of the person and work of Christ. Jesus was no longer God incarnate but simply a man who was "divine" in the sense that He had a superior conception of God and God's will. His death was not a payment for sin but an example of sacrificial love. Liberals believed that God dwelt in all His creation in some fashion. Therefore, in every person there existed a "spark of divinity." To become a child of God only required fanning that spark into a flame.[7]

LIBERALISM IN AMERICA

Religious liberalism was far advanced in Europe before it came to America. Before the Civil War, the only important form of liberalism in the United States was Unitarianism. The Unitarians denied the deity of Christ, His atonement, and other essential doctrines, but their views were largely confined to their own denomination. After the Civil War, liberalism began to invade the major evangelical Protestant denominations.[8]

Liberalism in America appeared first in the schools of higher education. Baptist William Newton Clarke (1841–1912) is often said to have written the first liberal systematic theology in America, *An Outline of Christian Theology* (1898). Even more influential was William Rainey Harper (1856–1906). As president of the University of Chicago, he made that university and its divinity school a major center of liberalism in the United States. Even before the Fundamentalist-Modernist Controversy, conservatives criticized the liberalism of the University of Chicago and founded conservative seminaries to counteract its effects.[9]

> **LIBERALISM IS NOT TRUE CHRISTIANITY, AND WE SHOULD TREAT IT AS WE WOULD ANY FALSE TEACHING.**

From the schools, liberalism went into the pulpits. Some early liberals began accommodating evolution in their sermons. Henry Ward Beecher (1813–87) was one of the first to try to cross evolution with Christianity. The great pulpit representative of liberalism, however, was Harry Emerson Fosdick (1878–1969), an eloquent and learned defender of liberal theology. His *Guide to Understanding the Bible* was a leading—and readable—introduction to liberal views, and his popular radio program carried liberalism into homes across America. Although a Baptist, Fosdick was serving at the First Presbyterian Church in New York City in 1922, where he preached the sermon "Shall the Fundamentalists Win?" and thereby touched off the

Fundamentalist-Modernist Controversy within the Presbyterian Church. Fosdick eventually became the founding pastor of Riverside Church in New York, a bastion of liberalism in America.

Another expression of liberalism was the social gospel. The Father of the Social Gospel, Walter Rauschenbusch (1861–1918), taught that the gospel needed to be applied to social institutions. Accepting the teachings of liberal higher criticism, Rauschenbusch redefined the gospel. He denied the importance of the Fall of Adam and Eve (thus ignoring the root of all human sin) and made little of man's need for grace. He acknowledged the need for individual redemption from sin, but he did not refer to the biblical conception of salvation. Instead, he saw sin more as an offense against other people than an offense against God and defined salvation as a process characterized by a life of love and service. Therefore, Rauschenbusch could speak of the "salvation" of social institutions. By this, he meant bringing all social organizations under the law of Christ. The goal of the social gospel was to build the kingdom of God on earth by human effort. Unsurprisingly, the phrase "social gospel" ultimately came to mean a system of social reform that had little or nothing to do with the redemption of souls through the atonement of Jesus Christ.[10]

THE GOAL OF THE SOCIAL GOSPEL WAS TO BUILD THE KINGDOM OF GOD ON EARTH BY HUMAN EFFORT.

The result of the growth of liberalism in the United States was the distortion of biblical Christianity. Neo-orthodox writer H. Richard Niebuhr satirized this liberal message as teaching that "a God without wrath brought men without sin into a kingdom without judgment through the ministrations of a Christ without a cross."[11]

EVOLVING LIBERALISM

Considering its evolutionary foundation, it is not surprising that liberalism continued to develop. The first major revision in American liberalism came in the 1930s after the Fundamentalist-Modernist Controversy. Neo-liberalism, as it was called, reacted to changing circumstances. Worsening world conditions—such as worldwide war, the rise of dictatorships, and the Great Depression—undercut the rosy optimism of the liberals. Further discoveries in archeology and biblical manuscripts likewise undermined some of the "assured results" of nineteenth-century higher criticism. Fosdick symbolized this transition to neo-liberalism in 1935 when he preached a sermon titled "The Church Must Go Beyond Modernism." Neo-liberalism was more realistic, not naively optimistic, and addressed the concerns of the common man but not that common man's need of salvation.

One of the most important expressions of liberalism since World War II has been the ecumenical movement. *Ecumenical* means "universal" or "worldwide." The ecumenical movement attempted to unite all churches on a liberal basis through organizations such as the World Council of Churches and (in the United States) the National Council of Churches. Ecumenists (those who support the movement) downplay doctrine and call for tolerance of many viewpoints. One organization promoting the movement, for example, took as its motto "Doctrine divides, but service unites." In recent years, liberal ecumenical organizations such as the World Council of Churches have even welcomed non-Christian religions.

Each new variety of liberalism seemed more radical than the last. Terms such as "theology of hope," "process theology," and "secular theology" were bantered about in scholarly circles. The depths or radicalism seemed to be reached in the 1960s with the short-lived "death of God" theology, an extreme form of secular theology that argued that the concept of God has no relevance for modern man and should be abandoned.[12]

In the 1960s, liberal theologians mixed religious and political radicalism in attempts to make their theology more relevant. Liberation theology is an example of such a political theology. Borrowing heavily from Marxism, liberation theologians argued that God was on the side of the poor and oppressed. Therefore, Christians must devote themselves to relieving oppression, even to the point of supporting violent revolutions. Liberation theology had great appeal among Roman Catholic theologians in Latin America and black theologians in the United States. Feminist theology combined liberation theology with a growing interest in gender-related views of history. Feminist theologians argued that history was the story of female oppression and that theology was a tool for ending that oppression. Feminist theologians rejected traditional Christianity as being the product of a biased, male-dominated, patriarchal society.

In the latter half of the twentieth century, liberalism faced a challenge from postmodernism that denied the liberal ideological basis altogether. Postmodernism rejected the rationalist basis of the Enlightenment that has characterized much of Western thought since the 1700s. Contending that human reason does not lead to a unified view of reality and that scientific study is not a sure means to truth, postmodernism took Kant's ideas about how the individual perceives reality and made "truth" a matter for the individual: "There are no facts, only interpretations." Postmodernism therefore denied the validity of liberalism's supporting structure but proved no friend to orthodox Christianity either. Liberalism looked to the collective knowledge of humanity as an authority whereas postmodernism preferred the interpretations of the individual as the authority. Many spin-offs of classic liberal theology, such as feminist theology and black theology, relied on postmodernist ideas.[13]

POSTMODERNISM DENIED THE VALIDITY OF LIBERALISM'S SUPPORTING STRUCTURE BUT PROVED NO FRIEND TO ORTHODOX CHRISTIANITY EITHER.

EVALUATION OF LIBERALISM

Liberalism is certainly more diverse than fundamentalism, but all forms of liberalism place human authority above biblical authority. Even postmodernist systems that reject the Enlightenment's belief in science and reason still base authority on the individual's reason and perceptions.

The question is, "What is our starting point—divine authority or human reason?" As Christians, we believe that the revelation of God is superior to human reason. Is the Bible the revelation of God? If you argue this point by reason (as some conservative theologians have tried to do) to show the reasonableness or authoritativeness of Scripture, you are claiming that human reason must prove that the Bible is God's revelation.

Roman Catholics appeal to the authority of the church to establish the Bible's authority, but Bible-believing Protestants look to the self-authenticating Scripture itself. The mind and the ways of God are beyond human comprehension (Rom. 11:33–34). On this point Immanuel Kant was right. The basis on which a person accepts God's Word as true is the internal witness of the Holy Spirit. Paul explained this matter when he wrote, "The natural man receiveth not the things of the Spirit of God: for they are foolishness unto him: neither can he know them, because they are spiritually discerned" (1 Cor. 2:14). For the Christian, reason must presuppose faith. In the words of Anselm of Canterbury (1033–1109), "For I do not seek to understand that I may believe, but I believe in order to understand. For this also I know—that unless I believed, I should not understand."[14]

The denial of biblical authority is at the root of liberal errors. Liberals saw their rational conclusions about religion as authoritative, or they looked to the Bible as it inspired religious experiences, which were then authoritative. Either way, the authority lay within man and not in God's revealed Word. Liberalism therefore discarded teachings that did not accord with reason or were not validated by the liberals' own religious experiences. As a result, they discarded the cardinal doctrines of the faith.[15]

Jesus said of false teachers, "Ye shall know them by their fruits" (Matt. 7:16). The moral bankruptcy of liberalism is an example of such fruit. The early liberals were often very moral. Some modernists supported prohibition in America with as much fervor as the fundamentalists. But liberalism has grown more immoral through the years. Acceptance of sexual relations outside of marriage, the ordination of homosexuals to the ministry—these and other fruits reveal the true nature of liberalism. Jude aptly summarized the moral character of such false teachers: "Clouds they are without water, carried about of winds; trees whose fruit withereth, without fruit, twice dead, plucked up by the roots; raging waves of the sea, foaming out their own shame; wandering stars, to whom is reserved the blackness of darkness for ever" (Jude 1:12–13). As Jude says, they "walk after their own ungodly lusts" (1:18).

Liberalism is, in short, "another gospel." When Machen wrote his great defense of orthodoxy, he did not title it *Fundamentalism and Liberalism* but *Christianity and Liberalism*. When Clarence Macartney preached a sermon in response to Fosdick's "Shall the

Fundamentalists Win?" in 1922, he did not title his message "Shall the Modernists Win?" but "Shall Unbelief Win?"[16] Liberalism is not true Christianity, and we should treat it as we would any false teaching.

Though it may seem presumptuous to judge the eternal destiny of professing Christians, the seriousness of such false teaching should not be underestimated. If, as the Bible says, doctrines such as the incarnation of Christ (2 John 1:7–9) and His resurrection (1 Cor. 15:12–19) are essential to the Christian faith, then individual liberals are, to say the least, in a precarious position. As Machen wrote, "We are not presuming to say whether such and such an individual man is a Christian or not. God only can decide such questions; no man can say with assurance whether the attitude of certain individual 'liberals' toward Christ is saving faith or not. But one thing is perfectly plain— whether or not liberals are Christians, it is at any rate perfectly clear that liberalism is not Christianity."[17]

CHAPTER EIGHT
NEO-ORTHODOXY

As fundamentalists and modernists battled for control of the major denominations in the 1920s, another system of theology was beginning to criticize liberalism. Neo-orthodoxy ("new orthodoxy") claimed to reconcile orthodox Christianity with the revolution in thought brought about by the Enlightenment. "The fundamentalist has something to say to his world," said one neo-orthodox writer, "but he has lost the ability to say it. The modernist knows how to speak to his age, but he has nothing to say."[1] Although neo-orthodoxy was not orthodox, it did have a significant effect on American religion, including conservative Christianity.

BACKGROUND OF NEO-ORTHODOXY

Neo-orthodoxy described itself as "orthodoxy rethought and reinterpreted for our times."[2] The neo-orthodox did not question scientific theories such as evolution, and they accepted the results of rationalistic higher criticism. Nevertheless, they argued that liberalism had abandoned the essential truths of Christianity, such as a notion of sin, the transcendence of God, and the need for redemption. Neo-orthodoxy revived the language of orthodoxy, but its critics charged that it changed its meaning in the process.[3]

The forerunner of neo-orthodoxy was Danish philosopher and theologian Søren Kierkegaard (1813–55). Called the Father of Christian Existentialism, Kierkegaard, like Kant, had a belief system that is complex and difficult to summarize. In brief, according to existentialism, existence is the basic truth of life. We find meaning in life not from external authority but from within ourselves, from our own decisions and actions. Because life has no purpose or meaning, we create our own meaning by our actions. At its most extreme, existentialism holds that truth is completely subjective. There is no such thing as absolute truth; each individual develops his or her own truth.

The desire to find meaning in life apart from reason gave rise to Kierkegaard's so-called Christian existentialism. Kierkegaard agreed with Kant that reason cannot lead people to God. He believed that an individual must make a blind leap of faith and commit himself or herself to God without—or even in spite of—reason. Then and only then can a person live an authentic Christian life. Because this leap of faith is often the consequence of a major internal crisis, some refer to neo-orthodoxy as the theology of crisis.

KARL BARTH

The thinking of Karl Barth (1896–1968) was important in formulating neo-orthodox theology, and he was probably the most conservative of the major neo-orthodox leaders. If Barth cannot bear up under scriptural scrutiny, then it is unlikely that any other major leader of neo-orthodoxy can.[4]

Born in Switzerland, Barth attended seminary in Germany, where he embraced liberalism. While serving as pastor of a church in Switzerland, however, he found idealistic liberalism inadequate to meet the needs of his people during the troubled era of World War I. During a great inner struggle, Barth wrote a commentary on the book of Romans (1919) that became the first major document of neo-orthodoxy. Later, as a university lecturer and prolific writer, Barth remained the leader of the movement.

AT ITS MOST EXTREME, EXISTENTIALISM HOLDS THAT TRUTH IS COMPLETELY SUBJECTIVE.

Barth rejected many ideas of liberalism. He denied natural theology, for example, saying that God cannot be known through nature by human reason. Instead, he argued that God is "wholly other," completely transcendent and set apart from His creation. Only as God reveals Himself can anyone know Him. Rather than having a spark of divinity in our hearts, as liberals claimed, humans are sinful and separated from God. Only as God chooses to reveal Himself to an individual can he or she be saved from sin.

These concepts sound orthodox, but there was also a "new" side to Barth's teachings as well. The main problem is that neo-orthodoxy had an inadequate view of Scripture. The Bible was not an inerrant revelation of God. Instead, it was simply a witness to revelation, a means God could use to communicate His revelation to humans. Only as God meets with the individual as he or she reads the Bible does it become God's Word to that person. Barth's view of Scripture is revealed in a 1934 conversation he had with American evangelical Donald Grey Barnhouse:

> "You say that the Bible is the only source of revelation, but do you believe that all of the Bible is God's revelation?"
>
> Dr. Barth had a book in his hand. He divided a page with a gesture of his hand and said, "If this part of the Bible speaks to me, it is God's Word to me." And then indicating the other part of the page, "If this part does not speak to me, it is not God's Word to me."
>
> That is enough to make some people's hair stand on end, but I was convinced that there was something more than appeared upon the surface of his speech, so I said, "But Doctor, suppose the part that hasn't spoken to you really speaks to me. Is it then God's Word?"
>
> "Certainly," he replied. "It is then God's Word for you."
>
> "And do you believe that the part which is God's Word to me may someday become God's Word to you?"
>
> "Of course. Anything in the Bible may become God's Word to me."[5]

Because he viewed the Bible as an errant, human book that only testified to God's Word, Barth accepted the idea of historical criticism of the Bible. In fact, he claimed God's power was revealed in His ability to use such an error-filled book of human origin to convey His revelation to man.

Barth and the neo-orthodox also seemed to teach two kinds of "history." For Barth, biblical events such as Christ's resurrection took place in the realm of "super history" but not necessarily in the world of everyday events. In other words, Barth could say Christ truly rose from the grave without meaning that the resurrection occurred in the same historical sense that Napoleon's invasion of Russia in 1812 did.

When Barth visited the United States in 1962, evangelical theologian Carl Henry attended a question-and-answer session with Barth in Washington, DC. Henry introduced himself as editor of *Christianity Today* and asked about Barth's belief in the resurrection of Jesus. Noting the many reporters present, Henry asked whether there would have been anything to report had they been present at the resurrection. Henry asked, "Was it news in the sense that the man in the street understands news?"

Rather than reply to the question, Barth replied angrily, "Did you say Christianity *Today* or Christianity *Yesterday*?" Barth then asked sarcastically if photographers could have taken pictures of the virgin birth. The risen Christ, Barth said, appeared to believers only and not to others.[6]

Evangelical Bernard Ramm staunchly defends Barth against the charge of believing in two kinds of history and cites examples from Barth's writings,[7] but Reformed theologian Cornelius Van Til argues just as strongly that Barth did make such a distinction, quoting extensively from Barth.[8] Barth's writings are so complex that it is difficult to determine what sort of history he believed in. Reading Barth is like looking at a piece of abstract art with each viewer seeing something different in the picture. However, even if Barth did not believe in two "kinds" of history, no one denies that he was still willing to view parts of Scripture as "myth" or "saga." For example, he did not believe that Genesis 1–3 was historical. Consequently, the Fall of man was not the result of a real individual named Adam eating from a real tree in a real place called Eden. Humanity was naturally sinful because human beings are separated from God and have always been separated from God.

There are additional problems with Barth's theology. His view of the Trinity, for example, sounds a great deal like the ancient modalistic heresy, which said that the persons of the Godhead are simply three manifestations of the same being. Likewise, some of Barth's comments sound as though he believed that everyone will ultimately be saved (universalism). Here we have focused on Barth's views about which there is little debate even from his defenders. His view of

Scripture and his denial of the historicity of Adam and the Fall indicate in themselves that his "neo-orthodoxy" is unorthodox.

OTHER NEO-ORTHODOX LEADERS

Other notable neo-orthodox theologians include Swiss theologian Emil Brunner (1889–1966), who emerged in the public eye about the same time Barth did. In fact, he was initially better known in America than Barth and introduced neo-orthodoxy to the United States.[9] Brunner disagreed with Barth about the role of natural theology. Whereas Barth said that God revealed Himself only through the Bible, Brunner claimed that God could reveal Himself through other means, such as nature or history. Brunner also helped popularize the major neo-orthodox concept of revelation as "personal" rather than "propositional." In other words, God reveals Himself personally to an individual. He never reveals Himself through propositions, that is, statements of fact about Himself. Hordern illustrated Brunner's view this way: To say that Jesus is the Christ, the Messiah, is not revelation. It is only a proposition that points to revelation because it points to Christ.[10] Concepts such as God's holiness and almighty power do not reveal God but only point to Him.

Two other influential representatives of neo-orthodoxy in the United States were the brothers Reinhold Niebuhr (1892–1970) and H. Richard Niebuhr (1894–1962).[11] Their version of neo-orthodoxy is sometimes called realistic theology because it takes a more realistic view of human nature than traditional liberalism does. Ryrie suggests that Reinhold Niebuhr represented the neo-orthodox preservation of the social gospel because he was so concerned with social ethics.[12] Niebuhr's writings deeply influenced both Martin Luther King Jr. and President Jimmy Carter. Although willing to acknowledge the truth of man's sinfulness, Niebuhr denied the biblical basis for human sin, criticizing the "absurd notion" that "man's sinfulness is determined by the Biblical account of the fall of Adam." Niebuhr argued instead that the reality of sinfulness "is supported by overwhelming evidence taken both from a sober observation of human behavior and from introspective analysis."[13] In a manner typical of neo-orthodoxy, Niebuhr redefined biblical terms, such as saying that original sin "is not so much an inherited corruption as an inevitable taint upon the spirituality of a finite creature."[14]

Another notable theologian sometimes associated with neo-orthodoxy is Dietrich Bonhoeffer (1906–45). A German theologian who was a student of Barth, Bonhoeffer was caught up in resistance against the Nazis and was executed for his part in a plot to assassinate Hitler. Because he died before his ideas were fully developed, it is difficult to know how to classify him theologically. In the 1960s, however, the "death of God" theologians claimed his writings as their inspiration.[15]

EVALUATION OF NEO-ORTHODOXY

Neo-orthodoxy has serious shortcomings. As is the case with liberalism, neo-orthodoxy has an inadequate view of the authority of Scripture. The truly orthodox Christian can never accept the relativistic view of revelation reflected in statements such as Hordern's: "God's Word never consists of black marks on the pages of a book called the Bible; God's Word is the living Word which he speaks through the Bible and to which man must respond by saying yes or no."[16] The authority for religion, according to neo-orthodoxy, lies within the individual as God speaks to him or her.

> **THE AUTHORITY FOR RELIGION, ACCORDING TO NEO-ORTHODOXY, LIES WITHIN THE INDIVIDUAL AS GOD SPEAKS TO HIM OR HER.**

Neo-orthodoxy finds "truth" in the Bible without allowing Scripture itself to be true. For instance, the neo-orthodox may agree that the story of Noah reflects the truth that God hates sin but they do so without believing that the ark, the animals, and the worldwide Flood were actually true. Such word games lead Charles Ryrie to conclude, "Neo-orthodoxy is a theological hoax. It attempts to preserve the message of the Bible while denying the facts of the Bible."[17]

Nevertheless, neo-orthodoxy often sounds good. Consider, for example, H. Richard Niebuhr's blunt and accurate critique of liberalism, quoted in the previous chapter. Many evangelicals likewise quote Bonhoeffer's indictment of "cheap grace": "Cheap grace is the preaching of forgiveness without requiring repentance, baptism without church discipline, communion without confession, absolution without personal confession. Cheap grace is grace without discipleship, grace without the cross, grace without Jesus Christ, living and incarnate."[18] Can this perhaps be a pointed way of stating the principle that Paul enunciated: "What then? shall we sin, because we are not under the law, but under grace?" (Rom. 6:15).

But as Cornelius Van Til notes, "Final alliances and final hostilities depend upon the content rather than the sound of words."[19] Revelation is not simply personal but is also propositional. Propositions do not save, but they describe the Person who does. One writer observes that

> orthodox theology has always recognized the necessity of a personal encounter with God in and through the Lord Jesus Christ. Mere knowledge about God cannot save the soul. A saving revelation of God must be such a personal revelation of Him and by Him to the heart as will impart new life and yield faith in Christ. But this personal revelation must have an objective and verifiable basis.[20]

Neo-orthodoxy is subjective. It does not provide believers anything outside of themselves on which to base their faith. To the neo-orthodox it is thoughts, feelings, and convictions that provide the source of faith, but this reliance on internal emotions is unscriptural. Peter says that although he and the other apostles had seen and heard Jesus Christ, they and other believers "have also a more sure word of prophecy" (2 Pet. 1:19). Scripture, which "came not in old time by the will of man" but was the result when "holy men of God spake as they were moved by the Holy Ghost" (1:21), is more certain than any experience, even that of an eyewitness.

Likewise Luke, in the opening of his Gospel, mentions that many had attempted to write an account "of those things which are most surely believed among us" (Luke 1:1). Far from arguing that a written account cannot communicate the revelation of God, Luke tells Theophilus, "It seemed good to me to write unto thee in order [literally, to write out in order for you] . . . that thou mightest know the certainty of those things, wherein thou hast been instructed" (1:3–4). The idea of faith being a leap in the dark, as Kierkegaard maintained, is completely unbiblical. "In Bible Christianity faith is not a leap in the dark. It is a step into the light."[21]

Although you are probably more likely to meet an outright liberal than an adherent of neo-orthodoxy, there are good reasons for being aware of the dangers of this movement. First, neo-orthodoxy is an example of subtle error. (Indeed, the reason you think you have never met anyone who is neo-orthodox may be that it is so hard to tell.) Jesus warned against wolves in sheep's clothing (Matt. 7:15). The fact that someone uses correct terminology and criticizes other false teachers does not necessarily mean that he or she believes the truths of the Bible.

Furthermore, some supposedly conservative evangelical Christians have embraced neo-orthodoxy. We have mentioned already how noted evangelical writer Bernard Ramm staunchly defended Karl Barth in his book *After Fundamentalism*. Ramm says that Christians should adopt Barth's methodology though not necessarily his conclusions.

Some evangelicals have followed a form of the neo-orthodox teaching about Scripture. For instance, John Woodbridge says Jack Rogers and Donald McKim in their study of inerrancy take a neo-orthodox view of the history of doctrine. He does not accuse Rogers and McKim of being neo-orthodox but of using the neo-orthodox approach to describe inerrancy as a newly invented doctrine.[22] Some evangelicals go further. Theologian Donald Bloesch, although critical of some aspects of neo-orthodoxy, writes, "It can be shown that I stand partly in both neo-evangelicalism and neo-orthodoxy, even though I belong mostly to catholic evangelicalism."[23] Neo-orthodoxy continues to affect the teachers and preachers that Christians hear and read and thereby affects church life in often subtle ways.[24]

THE FACT THAT SOMEONE USES CORRECT TERMINOLOGY AND CRITICIZES FALSE TEACHERS DOES NOT NECESSARILY MEAN THAT HE OR SHE BELIEVES THE TRUTHS OF THE BIBLE.

It is not fair to assume that everyone who says, "The Bible *contains* the Word of God," is neo-orthodox. Some who hold this view believe there is objective revelation from God in the Bible mixed with historical and scientific error. Nevertheless, to discern what in the Bible is really the Word of God, such an individual must rely on human reason (the traditional liberal method) or on intuition (the neo-orthodox approach). In either case, the human mind is permitted to determine what revelation is, rather than allowing revelation to be the authority in their lives.

Even to call neo-orthodoxy a deeply flawed system would probably be too generous, and evangelicals—not to mention fundamentalists—should be wary of it. Perhaps some orthodox believers have been attracted to neo-orthodoxy because of its reputation for scholarly orthodoxy. But the neo-orthodox system, as we concluded about liberalism in the previous chapter, is not biblical Christianity. As one critic put it, neo-orthodoxy is the new modernism.

CHAPTER NINE
EVANGELICALISM

In past chapters we have referred to *evangelicalism* and *new evangelicalism* with only passing reference to the meaning of those terms. Although Americans widely recognize the label *evangelical*, even those who consider themselves evangelical cannot always define exactly what it means. Fundamentalists recognize features they have in common with evangelicalism as well as evident differences. This chapter examines the history and nature of the contemporary evangelical movement, especially in relation to the issue of separation.

HISTORY OF THE TERM *EVANGELICAL*

The word *evangelical* derives from *euangelion*, the Greek word for "good news" or "gospel." From this root we derive other words such as *evangelize* and *evangelist*. During the Reformation, Protestant churches were often called evangelical, and even today in Germany the name Evangelical Church refers to the state Lutheran Church.[1]

In Great Britain and America, the term *evangelical* took on an additional meaning in the 1700s as a result of Britain's Evangelical Awakening (led by John Wesley and George Whitefield) and America's Great Awakening. In English-speaking countries and some other parts of the world, *evangelical* now refers to a Protestant who holds specific beliefs, most commonly including the authority of Scripture alone in religious matters, the importance of the substitutionary atonement of Christ, a focus on the experience of the new birth and individual conversion, an emphasis on good works and holy living after conversion, and the evangelization of non-Christians.[2] Of these tenets, evangelicalism particularly stresses conversion as the central experience of the Christian life.

Based on this description, fundamentalists can be considered evangelicals. In fact, *evangelical* is an older term than *fundamentalist*. But since the 1950s the term *evangelical* has often described a position at odds with fundamentalism. Today the term *evangelical* can be a broad label for conservative Protestants or a narrower catchall for non-fundamentalist conservatives who question fundamentalist separation. The narrower use of the term originated in the 1940s with a movement called the new evangelicalism, whose history and influence are a major theme of this chapter.

RISE OF THE NEW EVANGELICALISM

After the Fundamentalist-Modernist Controversy, fundamentalists developed their own network of independent schools, periodicals, mission boards, and denominations. But with this independence came a loss in national status. No longer were fundamentalists part of the major, or "mainline," denominations that dominated American religious life. Some charged that *fundamentalism* itself had become a negative term, synonymous with bigotry and ignorance. A segment within fundamentalism wanted to reform the movement and return to the less controversial label *evangelical*.

Historian Joel Carpenter notes that fundamentalism might have chosen two courses of "reform" in the 1940s. One would have been to maintain the basic position of fundamentalism but "strengthen" it by raising the intellectual level of fundamentalist apologetics and theological writings and by moderating caustic language that fundamentalists had used in the heat of controversy. The other course of reform hoped to "revise" fundamentalism by taking it in a different direction, especially in regard to separation.[3] This second approach became the philosophy of the new evangelicalism. The spokesman for the movement was Harold J. Ockenga (1905–85), sometimes called the Father of the New Evangelicalism. Ockenga was pastor of the historic Park Street Congregational Church in Boston and the first president of Fuller Theological Seminary. Supporting Ockenga in this effort were several other young evangelical intellectuals, including Carl Henry, the founding editor of *Christianity Today*.[4]

Ockenga was one of the first to use the term *new evangelicalism*, and he outlined the movement's basic beliefs in his foreword to Harold Lindsell's *Battle for the Bible*.[5] Those beliefs, and the fundamentalist reaction to them, sparked a major controversy and division within the fundamentalist ranks.

First, Ockenga spoke of new evangelicalism's "determination to engage itself in the theological dialogue of the day" and the need for "reengagement in the theological debate." The new evangelicals believed that fundamentalism was not conducting biblical study at a sufficiently high level of scholarship. There was a need, they said, for interchange with liberal scholars. As part of that move, some talented young evangelicals began to attend prestigious graduate schools in America and Europe.

Fundamentalism did not oppose scholarship. Christians should use all their abilities and talents for God's glory, and furthermore they need to be aware of all shades of belief and unbelief. But fundamentalists were concerned that scholars might compromise the Christian faith in their attempts to be recognized as scholars. Some new evangelicals protested that they simply wanted to compete with liberals in their own fields of study and to witness to them about Christ.[6] Fundamentalists, however, feared that the new evangelicals intended to recognize liberals as orthodox believers. Nearly thirty years after the fundamentalist break with the new evangelicals,

SINCE THE 1950S THE TERM *EVANGELICAL* HAS OFTEN DESCRIBED A POSITION AT ODDS WITH FUNDAMENTALISM.

Bob Jones Jr. charged that the new evangelical leaders were willing to call liberals "Christian brothers" if the liberals would in turn call the evangelicals "doctor," "professor," and "scholar."[7] Even an apologist for the new evangelicalism notes that critics feared the new evangelicals would absorb liberal beliefs, accommodate liberal ideas, and set bad precedents that would cause later generations to accept liberalism.[8]

Second, Ockenga wrote about the need for "the reexamination of theological problems such as the antiquity of man, the universality of the Flood, God's method of creation, and others." Almost from the beginning, new evangelicals suggested accommodation with evolutionary theory. Some questioned belief in creationism, a young earth, and the Bible's account of Noah and the Flood despite the impact such questions had on the historicity of the Bible and biblical teachings about original sin and Christ's work as the Second Adam (Rom. 5:12–21; 1 Cor. 15:21–22, 45).

Third, Ockenga issued a "summons to social involvement" and a "new emphasis upon the application of the gospel to the sociological, political, and economic areas of life." Ockenga did not adopt the liberal social gospel, but fundamentalists were concerned when Ockenga said things such as, "There need be no disagreement between the personal gospel and the social gospel."[9] The early new evangelicals did not favor the kind of social gospel that downplayed or eliminated personal salvation but rather wanted to apply what the Bible said about social issues by denouncing sin in any form.

Originally, leaders including Harold Ockenga and Carl Henry took stands on social issues that were based on the redemption of the individual through Christ. Henry, for example, wrote in 1947, "Only an anthropology and a soteriology that insists upon man's sinful lostness and the ability of God to restore the responsive sinner is the adequate key to the door of Fundamentalist world betterment."[10] As years passed, however, some younger evangelicals began to stake out positions that threatened to redefine the gospel. In an extensive survey of contemporary Christian attitudes toward social action, Robert Horton warned that many evangelicals viewed social action as a *form of* evangelism rather than a *means to* evangelism, while others made social reform a part of the gospel itself.[11]

Such a position distorts the gospel by adding to it. Fundamentally, the gospel is the redemption of sinners by Jesus Christ through His atonement. "This is a faithful saying, and worthy of all acceptation, that Christ Jesus came into the world to save sinners" (1 Tim. 1:15). While there is a social dimension to Christianity (Matt. 5:13–16; Gal. 6:10), it is a result of the salvation of individuals through the gospel and not part of the gospel itself.

Finally, and most important, Ockenga proclaimed a "ringing call for a repudiation of separation" and aimed for "the recapture of denominational leadership." Rather than pulling out of compromised associations, the new evangelicals wanted to stay in the denominations and even reenter those that fundamentalists had left. From the beginning, fundamentalists protested that the new evangelicalism was leading Christianity toward a close identification with the world system, accommodating not only theological but also scientific and cultural views that rejected Christian truth. Unquestionably, the new evangelicals took the attitude that although false teaching might be wrong, Christians could profitably work with false teachers themselves. The actions of these new evangelical "reformers" led many fundamentalists to break fellowship with fellow Christians who rejected scriptural teaching about separation from false teaching.

In a 1957 press release, Ockenga not only set forth the ideology of the new evangelicalism but also listed its main institutions. These included the National Association of Evangelicals, Fuller Theological Seminary, *Christianity Today* magazine, and the campaigns of evangelist Billy Graham.[12] Because of Graham's high public profile, he became the focus of the movement and its most influential leader.

BILLY GRAHAM AND THE NEW EVANGELICALISM

Born in North Carolina in 1918, Billy Graham was converted as a teenager and attended Bob Jones College, Florida Bible Institute, and Wheaton College. After graduation from Wheaton and a brief pastorate, he entered evangelism. Working as a staff evangelist for Youth for Christ after World War II, Graham built a reputation as a gifted fundamentalist preacher. His 1949 evangelistic crusade in Los Angeles had a remarkable impact that caught the attention of newspapers and national magazines such as *Time*. He then campaigned in Boston and other large US cities before holding a campaign in London in 1954. Conservative Christians rallied to Graham. It appeared to many that he might be leading a national or even worldwide revival that many had prayed for.[13]

Graham, however, became convinced that the new evangelical approach suggested by Ockenga provided wider opportunities for proclaiming the gospel. He lent warm support in 1956 to the founding of *Christianity Today* as a voice for the new evangelicalism, and he agreed in 1958 to join the board of Fuller Theological Seminary, the leading educational institution of the new evangelicalism. The turning point came with his New York campaign in 1957. Declaring that he would "go anywhere, sponsored by anybody, to preach the Gospel of Christ, if there are no strings attached to [his] message," Graham

opened his campaign to liberals, invited liberal ministers to participate, and sent converts from his crusade into liberal churches.

Graham's support gave the new evangelicalism a greater impact
than it ever could have had through the theorizing of men such as
Ockenga and Henry. American Christians cherished evangelism and
revival. They were far more willing to follow a successful evangelist
than an assembly of seminary professors. Quite rightly Ockenga said
that Graham "on the mass level is the spokesman of the convictions
and ideals of the New Evangelicalism."[14]

Graham's activities brought evangelicals into cooperation with
liberals, but his actions split conservative Christianity. Separatist fundamentalists had already protested the ideas of the new evangelical
intellectuals, but Graham's actions sparked a final separation.

In short, fundamentalists said the Graham crusades treated
liberals as fellow Christians. Millard Erickson, a defender of the new
evangelicalism, aptly summarizes the fundamentalist position when
he says that fundamentalists argued "that Graham, by cooperating
with liberal churches and ministers, and having even such men as
Norman Vincent Peale sit on the platform with him, is tacitly approv-
ing of the liberalism which they represent. He is failing to distinguish,
for the public, the spiritual value of nurture in a conservative church
from that of a liberal church. He is sending converts back into liberal
churches, where their spiritual zeal will be confused and they will be
given stones instead of bread."[15]

Erickson then asks whether fundamentalists did not think that
liberals needed to hear the gospel and whether converts sent back
into liberal churches would "become leavening influences" there.[16]
Fundamentalists replied that they would be delighted to see liberals
confronted with the gospel but that presenting them as sponsors of
an evangelistic campaign would instead persuade believers that false
teachers were true Christians. Likewise sending converts back into
false churches was less a preserving and light-giving influence than
sending lambs into a wolf pack.

BROAD EVANGELICALISM

We need to be careful not to make our generalizations too broad.
Not all evangelicals fit in with Ockenga's characteristics of the new

evangelicalism. Some contemporary evangelicals are young-earth creationists who have little interest in interaction with liberal scholars and who are suspicious of church involvement in political affairs. Thus the label *new evangelical* does not accurately describe all evangelicals. But these Christians still accept the methods and ministry of Billy Graham and those who follow his pattern, which fundamentalists reject.

Today, virtually the only people who use the term *new evangelical* are fundamentalists who want to distinguish between the two positions. Most of the people fundamentalists consider new evangelicals see themselves as simply evangelical without anything "new" about it. Although John Stackhouse suggests using the phrase *generic evangelicalism* as an inclusive term for all who identify themselves as evangelical,[17] we will use David Beale's term *broad evangelicalism*,[18] which reflects the

> IT SOON BECAME APPARENT THAT SOME EVANGELICALS WERE DENYING THE INERRANCY OF SCRIPTURE.

inclusivism and breadth of the movement in both numbers and theology, though, as appropriate, we will continue to use the terms *evangelical* and *new evangelical* when they better fit the context.

Broad evangelicalism has had its share of controversies since the 1950s. Abandoning fundamentalism did not save the movement from conflict. The first great battle among broad evangelicals concerned the inerrancy of the Bible. Although early new evangelicals spoke of "a re-opening of the subject of biblical inspiration," they meant a fuller defense of biblical infallibility against the teachings of neo-orthodoxy.[19] Nevertheless, it soon became apparent that some evangelicals were denying the inerrancy of Scripture. In 1976, new evangelical leader Harold Lindsell published *The Battle for the Bible*, which detailed examples of how evangelicals were abandoning inerrancy. One of the most controversial chapters was the one on Fuller Theological Seminary, the flagship school of new evangelicalism, where Lindsell had formerly taught.[20] Lindsell demonstrated that some FTS professors had annually signed a creed saying they believed in inerrancy, when in reality they did not. Fuller eventually dropped inerrancy from its creed altogether.

CULTURAL ACCOMMODATION AND YOUNG EVANGELICALS

Also in the 1970s, two books by Richard Quebedeaux unsettled the broad evangelical world concerning its rising younger generation. In *The Young Evangelicals* (1974) and *The Worldly Evangelicals* (1978), Quebedeaux reported a liberalization of theological and social views among younger evangelicals.[21] Theologically, he noted an increased rejection of inerrancy, an openness to discussions with liberals and Marxists as a means of furthering the gospel, an acceptance of theistic evolution over biblical creationism, and an embrace of some points of neo-orthodoxy.[22] On moral issues, he cited a greater tolerance for divorce and remarriage, acceptance of abortion, defense of masturbation, more prevalent use of profanity, and acceptance of practicing homosexuals as believers.[23] Significantly, Quebedeaux titled the last chapter of his second book "Today's Evangelicals, Tomorrow's Liberals?"

Still, defenders of evangelicalism could argue that Quebedeaux's evidence was anecdotal, representing "horror stories" from only a fringe of the movement, not its mainstream. A weightier report came in James Davison Hunter's *Evangelicalism: The Coming Generation* (1987). Surveying students in nine evangelical colleges and seven evangelical seminaries, Hunter documented a shift in views.[24] Hunter's conclusions were less shocking than Quebedeaux's. Attitudes of evangelical students were still more conservative than those of secular students. But Hunter documented a drift in the evangelical movement. About half the students surveyed believed the Bible could err on matters of science or history.[25] About a third believed that those who never heard of Christ or the gospel could still go to heaven.[26] Hunter also documented significant change regarding issues of personal morality. In a 1951 survey, 46 percent of the students questioned thought that attending Hollywood movies was always morally wrong; in 1982 only 7 percent thought attending R-rated movies was always morally wrong. In 1951, fully 98 percent of the students thought drinking alcohol was wrong whereas in 1982 only 17 percent did.[27] Hunter also revealed that the faculty in such schools were generally more liberal than their students.[28] So concerned were some evangelical leaders about the ramifications of Hunter's work that they held a conference to discuss it.[29]

We should quickly note that cause-and-effect is not necessarily at work here. In other words, we cannot say that the new evangelicalism necessarily led to these shifting beliefs among the younger generation. In fact, a larger problem than shifting cultural attitudes among evangelical youth is the shrinking number of young people who acknowledge any kind of biblical worldview at all. The Barna Group, which specializes in researching religious attitudes, published the results of a survey in 2009 concerning how many Americans hold a "biblical worldview." The survey measured the worldview by whether respondents affirmed ideas such as belief in moral absolutes, the reality of Satan, the sinlessness of Christ, the impossibility of getting to heaven by good works, and God as the Creator and Ruler of the universe. The survey concluded that only 9 percent of Americans had a biblical worldview according to this definition. However, the survey also found that among Americans 18 to 23 years old, only one-half of one percent possessed a biblical worldview.[30] Throughout history various groups have faced the challenge of passing their beliefs and practices to the next generation, from the Pilgrims to the baby boomer generation following World War II. Neither fundamentalists nor evangelicals are immune to this problem.[31]

CONCERNS ABOUT DOCTRINAL DRIFT

The career of theologian Clark Pinnock (1937–2010) is a case study in how evangelicalism has drifted doctrinally. In the 1960s and early 1970s, Pinnock staunchly defended biblical inerrancy and wrote persuasively on the subject.[32] Then in the mid-1970s, he abandoned that position on inerrancy and said there were historical and scientific errors in Scripture.[33] Pinnock also experienced a charismatic awakening and began supporting charismatic teaching.[34] Pinnock abandoned the doctrine of hell, teaching instead that sinners were annihilated after death.[35] Although a Baptist, he suggested that a form of papal primacy could be a means to ecumenical unity.[36] Eventually Pinnock embraced open theism, the idea that God is not omniscient, knowing all things past, present, and future, because for God to be omniscient would limit human freedom. Instead, God knows the past and present but can know only future possibilities.[37]

Not all evangelicals have changed as much as Pinnock did. Some new evangelical leaders such as Lindsell and Ockenga opposed this drift. But there is little question that the theological positions of many evangelicals have moved leftward. A particularly surprising example is a greater openness toward the possibility of salvation apart from Christ. Even Billy Graham, long considered one of the more theologically conservative evangelicals, supported such a position. In a 1997 television interview, Graham said that God was "calling people out of the world for His name, whether they come from the Muslim world, or the Buddhist world, or the Christian world or the nonbelieving world, they are members of the Body of Christ because they've been called by God. They may not even know the name of Jesus but they know in their hearts that they need something that they don't have, and they turn to the only light that they have, and I think that they are saved, and that they're going to be with us in heaven."[38]

EVANGELICALS CAN ACCUSE FUNDAMENTALISTS—SOMETIMES WITH GOOD REASON—OF DIVIDING OVER NONESSENTIALS. YET THE EVANGELICAL MOVEMENT HAD ITS OWN DIVISIONS.

Evangelicals can accuse fundamentalists—sometimes with good reason—of dividing over nonessentials. Yet the evangelical movement had its own divisions. When Zondervan published a book on the current state of American evangelicalism in 2011, the editors found it necessary to present three different evangelical views but only one by a fundamentalist.[39] New evangelicalism rejected fundamentalist separatism, which had produced a multiplicity of independent fundamentalist institutions, in favor of a strategy of infiltrating the American religious mainline. Yet evangelicalism ultimately ended up only creating a different set of independent institutions.

Furthermore the new evangelicals have more than justified fundamentalist concerns that their openness to liberalism and their desire for respectability would lead evangelical Christianity into theological error. The split between fundamentalism and the new evangelicalism began as a dispute over ecclesiastical separation.[40] Increasingly, it has become a divide over foundational doctrines. For example, some evangelicals have questioned even such key doctrines as Christ suffering for the sins of others in His vicarious atonement.[41] Today fundamentalists often separate from other evangelicals not simply over disobedience but over false teaching as well.

CONSERVATIVE EVANGELICALISM

One subgroup within broad evangelicalism, conservative evangelicalism, presents a particular challenge to fundamentalists. The label is applied to a variety of Christian leaders, such as conference speaker John Piper, Southern Baptist pastor Mark Dever, Bible teacher and pastor John MacArthur, seminary professors Charles Ryrie and D. A. Carson, seminary president R. Albert Mohler, and popular Reformed theologian and writer R. C. Sproul.[42] One problem is the definition of the term. Just the people listed above have diverse views on a number of doctrines and practices. What is the overall nature of conservative evangelicalism?

Another problem with definition is that people use the phrase *conservative evangelical* differently in different contexts. In Great Britain the term fundamentalist is not nearly so widely used as in America, so *conservative evangelical* in the United Kingdom can designate Christians ranging from those who resemble fundamentalists to those who are more like broad evangelicals in general.[43]

We will define a conservative evangelical as an evangelical who does not accept the classic new evangelical idea of interaction and cooperation with liberals and who does not tolerate the doctrinal aberrations that have emerged in broad evangelicalism, such as denying inerrancy. Yet, as shown by their cooperation with broader evangelicals and their own practices, conservative evangelicals do not accept the pattern of biblical separation that we have described in this book.[44]

It is important that we do not view this difference concerning separation as merely fundamentalists being miffed that others do not accept their views. The burden of this book is to set out the nature of the Bible's teaching on separation and to stress its importance. Those who undervalue separation are missing an important element concerning Christian sanctification and the proper administration and preservation of the church.

One could perhaps cite specific problems with the views of some conservative evangelicals.[45] Many involved in what has been called the "new Calvinism" practice the charismatic gifts, such as speaking in tongues, prophecies, and healings. However, not all conservative evangelicals hold such views. A better approach is to identify characteristics true of this general position. In fact, our topic of separation is a key point. Let us look at one major figure and one major movement associated with conservative evangelicalism and see how they compare to what we have been teaching about separation.

CASE STUDY: JOHN PIPER

One major leader has been John Piper, an influential writer, pastor, and speaker known especially through his Desiring God website and ministry. As with conservative evangelicals in general, there is much to commend in Piper's ministry. A fundamentalist critiquing some of Piper's views nonetheless notes the creditable aspects of Piper's career: his overall doctrinal soundness on key issues such as inerrancy, his restoration of the idea of the need for right affections (not just right doctrine and practice) in the Christian life, his emphasis on missions, and his overall stress on the glory and enjoyment of God.[46] In spite of some significant differences with fundamentalists, such as his promotion of the charismatic gifts (discussed in the next chapter), there is much to appreciate.

Furthermore, unlike many evangelicals, Piper acknowledges merit in the fundamentalist position. He writes that fundamentalism's "great gift to the church is precisely the backbone to resist compromise and to make standing for truth and principle a means of love rather than an alternative to it." He affirms the helpfulness of the movement's emphasis on the doctrine of biblical separation because he thinks very few evangelicals even consider it. Piper concludes, "So I thank God for fundamentalism, and I think that some of the whining about its ill effects would have to also be directed against the black-and-white bluntness of Jesus."[47]

Despite this appreciation, Piper does not agree with fundamentalists on the specific application of separation issues. He shows his view perhaps most clearly in discussing the controversy over Billy Graham, in many ways the event that defined the fundamentalist protest against new evangelicalism. Piper's father was a fundamentalist evangelist who left the board of Bob Jones University over the Graham issue. In a recent interview, Piper commented that he approves of the decision his father made. He said that even though his father disagreed with some of Billy Graham's methods just as Bob Jones did, he refused to go so far as to deny God's working through the Graham crusades or to say they were a tool of Satan. Asked how this controversy has affected his own practice, Piper replied that his father's approach was definitely a factor: "I can go into a conference and I might say, 'I don't like this music,' or 'I don't like some of the slapstick that's happening on the platform,' 'I don't like all the things the other speakers are saying,' but they're going to let me talk to a lot of people here about the supremacy of God in all things for the joy of all peoples through Jesus, and that's what I'm called to do. Probably my approach to be willing to lift up my vision of God in places where it might not be completely shared has been influenced by my father's choices."[48]

Yet, as we saw earlier, the issues with Graham's methodology were not merely matters of musical taste or decorum on the platform. The Graham methodology embodied the new evangelical idea of cooperation with liberalism and the refusal to identify liberals as false teachers. In that approach is a very real danger to the spiritual health and discipline of Christ's church as "the pillar and ground of the truth" (1 Tim. 3:15). When we recall that Piper is actually more sympathetic to fundamentalists than many evangelicals on separation issues, his position indicates a key problem in the conservative evangelical approach.

CASE STUDY: THE SOUTHERN BAPTIST CONVENTION

Another, even more public example of conservative evangelicalism is the "conservative resurgence" in the Southern Baptist Convention (SBC). In the late 1970s, conservatives in the SBC, worried about theological drift in the convention, rallied to elect conservative presidents. These presidents in turn used their appointive powers to select other conservatives for the boards of SBC seminaries, mission boards, publishing houses, and other organizations. In 2000, SBC members also voted to strengthen the convention's doctrinal statement, the Baptist Faith and Message, and the leadership began to apply the statement as a condition for employment in SBC ministries, such as the Foreign Mission Board. The conservatives tightened standards and forced out a number of liberals. An alliance of liberals and tolerant conservatives (usually calling themselves "moderates") railed at the "fundamentalists" who took control of the convention, but their use of the label *fundamentalist* had less to do with the identity of the conservatives than the moderates' desire to pin an unpopular label on their opponents.[49]

Christians should always be thankful for the defense of truth and the refutation of error. Many trends in the SBC have been for the good and are encouraging. Along with the good that has been done, however, some serious concerns remain. For example, although the seminaries of the SBC now have more conservative faculty and boards, the majority of Southern Baptist colleges and universities have escaped convention control. From these schools have arisen new moderate seminaries and divinity schools that are outside direct convention supervision. Newer schools such as George W. Truett Theological Seminary at Baylor University, Baptist Theological Seminary at Richmond in Virginia, McAfee School of Theology at Mercer University, and Gardner-Webb University School of Divinity in North Carolina continue to turn out moderate pastors with questionable views who end up in SBC pulpits.[50]

> **TODAY FUNDAMENTALISTS OFTEN SEPARATE FROM OTHER EVANGELICALS NOT SIMPLY OVER DISOBEDIENCE BUT OVER FALSE TEACHING AS WELL.**

A larger structural question is the nature of the convention itself. A church, and by extension a denomination, should maintain and defend the truth. As mentioned above, the SBC revised and strengthened its statement of faith and began to apply that statement as a standard of belief for those who serve in SBC ministries. However, the SBC has retained fairly unrestricted standards for membership by its constituent churches. One historian describes the SBC's standards for membership. First, member churches must donate a certain amount to the Cooperative Program, the SBC's system for gathering and distributing funds for its outreaches. Second, in the 1990s the SBC changed its bylaws so that no church could send representatives to the national convention if that church ordained or married homosexuals. The writer comments wryly that "all a Baptist church has to do to affiliate with the SBC is send a few hundred dollars to Nashville [to the Cooperative Program] and refrain from ordaining or marrying homosexuals."[51] Noting this situation, one fundamentalist writes, "I question the value of affiliating with a convention that will not respect at least the fundamentals as a test of fellowship."[52] The guarantee of the convention's orthodoxy is a general consensus among member churches, not a structural protection. The system has worked up to this point for the SBC in pursuing its reform, but what guarantee is there for the future if the rank and file begin to shift their beliefs, as has happened in most other major American denominations?

In short, a serious concern with conservative evangelicalism is an inadequate approach in upholding the proper doctrinal discipline of the church. Conservative evangelicals care about this matter of the nature of the church and its doctrinal stance, unlike liberals or even some others in the broad evangelical camp. But they need to consistently apply protections that will safeguard the testimony and effectiveness of the church.

CONCLUSION

By no means have all evangelicals allowed theological drift to take place without protest. We have already mentioned Harold Lindsell's *Battle for the Bible* and his call for the defense of inerrancy. Shortly before his death, evangelical writer and apologist Francis Schaeffer warned in *The Great Evangelical Disaster* against the increased accommodation of evangelicalism to worldliness. Likewise, although on a more scholarly level, David Wells has warned against theological compromise that threatens the theological and intellectual underpinnings of evangelicalism.[53] Furthermore, some evangelical writers soundly criticized particular doctrinal deviations. John MacArthur challenged the charismatic movement, for example, and both he and R. C. Sproul spoke out against accommodations evangelicals made with Roman Catholicism.[54]

Although fundamentalists may read such critiques with profit, they should also use discernment. Paul counsels us to evaluate the moral quality of what we think about and meditate on (Phil. 4:8). Everything we read should be passed through the filter of God's Word. If a writer takes a commendable stand against error but does not embrace the biblical pattern of ecclesiastical or personal separation, we can appreciate the first stand while rejecting the latter. In short, we must take to heart Paul's simple yet far-reaching command: "Prove all things; hold fast that which is good" (1 Thess. 5:21). It is a frequent mistake to assume that common opposition to certain dangers provides a basis for unity. On a pragmatic level, as in politics, such alliances sometimes work. But the basis for Christian unity must not be common opposition to error but a common commitment to truth.

The new evangelicals thought they could make a greater impact on the world by creating a more intellectually credible presentation of orthodox Christianity. But as one writer notes, liberals and secularists do not reject Christianity because it is poorly presented but because it is *Christian*.[55] The new evangelicals thought they could make greater inroads for the gospel by cooperating with liberals in evangelism, but by doing so they made partners of the very people who were supposed to be the objects of evangelism. The new evangelicals thought that by lowering standards of personal separation they might make more contacts with the world and increase the impact of their testimony. Yet Scripture warns, "Others save with fear, pulling them out of the fire; hating even the garment spotted by the flesh" (Jude 1:23). As one observer says, "We cannot rescue a man sinking in quicksand by jumping in with him."[56] The theological and cultural accommodation of the original new evangelical initiative has carried over into broad evangelicalism and even conservative evangelicalism to an extent. Blurring distinctions that God has made is never a legitimate means of advancing the Christian faith.

> **IT IS A FREQUENT MISTAKE TO ASSUME THAT COMMON OPPOSITION TO CERTAIN DANGERS PROVIDES A BASIS FOR UNITY.**

Finally, we should remember that fundamentalists and evangelicals are fellow Christians. Therefore, in opposing the teachings or practices of various evangelicals, the fundamentalist must bear in mind Paul's command to "count him not as an enemy, but admonish him as a brother" (2 Thess. 3:15). The goal of separation from evangelicalism is not only purity but also the restoration of Christian brothers and sisters. Admittedly, few evangelicals return to the biblical position on separation. But just as obedient Christians must practice biblical separation whatever the circumstances, so they must seek to admonish and win the erring Christian regardless of the discouragements they may face. They should always demonstrate genuine Christian love.

CHAPTER TEN
THE CHARISMATIC MOVEMENT

Before the 1960s, the adjective *charismatic* usually meant having charm, magnetism, and popular appeal, as when newspapers described the young John F. Kennedy as the "charismatic" Democratic candidate for president. But since the 1960s *charismatic* has often meant someone who speaks in tongues. The word comes from the Greek *charis* ("grace") and *charisma* ("gift"). The charismatic movement is a worldwide, interdenominational Christian movement that has grown enormously since the 1960s. Its major emphasis is on spiritual gifts—supernatural abilities said to be bestowed by the Holy Spirit, the most significant of which is an ability to speak in tongues as a sign of the Holy Spirit's blessing. Because of its influence, the charismatic movement presents serious problems for those Christians who wish to practice biblical separation.

HISTORY OF THE CHARISMATIC MOVEMENT

The charismatic movement emerged from a movement born early in the twentieth century known as Pentecostalism. To understand the charismatic movement, then, we must first understand the Pentecostal movement.[1]

THE DEVELOPMENT OF PENTECOSTALISM
Pentecostalism arose out of the nineteenth-century Holiness Movement, mentioned briefly in Chapters 1 and 6. Holiness Christians emphasize the need for a devout, upright life. Methodist Holiness Christians teach that the Holy Spirit eliminates the sinful

nature in the believer through a second work of grace after conversion; Keswick Holiness advocates teach that the power of the Holy Spirit suppresses the sinful nature. Both agree that the Christian can live in victory over conscious sin. This idea of a "second blessing" after salvation led many people to search for further spiritual gifts.

Among these searchers was Charles Parham, a Holiness preacher who headed a small Bible college in Topeka, Kansas. Parham reported that on December 31, 1900, a student named Agnes Ozman asked him to lay hands on her and pray that she might receive the Holy Spirit. Parham did so, and as he prayed, she suddenly began to speak in another language, allegedly Chinese. This event has traditionally marked the birth of Pentecostalism.

There had been occasional examples of tongues speaking in earlier church history. The Montanists (active ca. AD 150–350) prophesied and spoke in tongues. Likewise, during a time of intense persecution by the Catholic Church in the 1700s, a group of French Protestants engaged in tongues speaking. In the nineteenth century other groups such as the Shakers and the Mormons in America and the Irvingites in England also practiced tongues speaking.[2] Unlike the earlier examples, however, the events associated with Parham sparked a movement that has continued to grow until the present.

One who heard Parham teach on the gift of tongues and joined his cause was black Holiness preacher William J. Seymour, who held a series of meetings on Azusa Street in Los Angeles from 1906 to 1909. Word of the displays of faith healing and tongues speaking soon spread, and crowds thronged to the "Azusa Street Revival." The fame of Azusa Street gave momentum to the young movement, which took the name *Pentecostal* in reference to the filling of the Holy Spirit on the day of Pentecost (Acts 2:4). Pentecostals claim that, as at Pentecost, the sign of the baptism of the Holy Spirit is to speak in tongues.

Today there are many Pentecostal bodies, including the Church of God in Christ, the Assemblies of God, the United Pentecostal Church, the Church of God (Cleveland, Tennessee), and the Pentecostal Holiness Church. African Americans made a considerable contribution to Pentecostalism, such as the Church of God in Christ, founded by C. H. Mason, who joined the Pentecostal movement after visiting Seymour's Azusa Street meeting. The Church of God in Christ is the most important predominantly black Pentecostal group and one of the largest and fastest-growing Pentecostal denominations.

RISE OF THE CHARISMATIC MOVEMENT

The transformation of Pentecostalism into Neo-Pentecostalism—or as it is better known, the charismatic movement—was the result of several factors. Although Pentecostals reached out to mainstream American religion and culture, what really launched the movement was the mainstream reaching out to Pentecostalism.

The first Pentecostal outreach toward the mainstream was Pentecostal interest in the ecumenical movement. The career of David DuPlessis, a man often called "Mr. Pentecost," illustrates this trend. Born in South Africa in 1905, DuPlessis became a Pentecostal minister after his conversion and eventually moved to the United States. In 1951, he approached the World Council of Churches (WCC) to promote both recognition of Pentecostalism and involvement by Pentecostals in the ecumenical movement. DuPlessis appeared as an observer in many ecumenical meetings, such as the WCC gatherings at Evanston, Illinois (1954) and New Delhi (1961) as well as the Roman Catholic Vatican Council of the 1960s.

MUCH LIKE FUNDAMENTALISTS AFTER THE 1920S, CHARISMATICS BUILT THEIR OWN NETWORK OF SCHOOLS, PERIODICALS, AND FELLOWSHIPS.

A second outreach was the effort of Oral Roberts to move into the mainstream. An evangelist in the Pentecostal Holiness Church, Roberts became one of the best-known Pentecostal preachers in the nation during the 1950s and 1960s through his tent meetings and television program. He eventually expanded his ministries to include non-Pentecostals by founding the nondenominational, but charismatic, Oral Roberts University (1965) and by joining the United Methodist Church (1968).

A third outreach involved improving the social perception of Pentecostalism. From its beginning, Pentecostalism was strongest in rural areas and among the urban working classes, creating a popular bias against it as a "lower-class" religion. A conscious effort to change this image began with the founding of the Full Gospel Business Men's Fellowship International in 1951 by Demos Shakarian. The FGBMFI demonstrated that Pentecostals could appeal to white-collar workers of the upper middle class. Also, although the FGBMFI was at first composed only of Pentecostals, it was independent of any denomination and could therefore appeal to converts of all denominations.

A significant event that sparked more mainstream acceptance of Pentecostalism occurred in 1960 when Dennis Bennett, pastor of Saint Mark's Episcopal Church in Van Nuys, California, began to speak in tongues. Significantly, Bennett did not leave the Episcopal Church to join a Pentecostal group but remained within his own denomination.

Pentecostal teaching then began to move into other mainstream denominations. Tongues speaking spread like wildfire, and charismatics appeared among Baptists, Lutherans, Methodists, and even Catholics. The first huge gathering of Pentecostals and charismatics was held in 1977 in Kansas City. Fifty thousand people attended, representing some fifty million Pentecostals and charismatics around the world. Fully half of those attending were Roman Catholics.[3]

Much like fundamentalists after the 1920s, charismatics built their own network of schools, periodicals, and fellowships, and they attracted public attention through television broadcasting. Oral Roberts paved the way, but it was a charismatic Southern Baptist, Pat Robertson, who achieved greater renown. Starting with just one television station in 1961, Robertson built an enormous television empire. The popularity of his program *The 700 Club* helped create his Christian Broadcasting Network (CBN). CBN in turn helped launch other institutions, such as Regent University. Television success also gave Robertson a political platform. He ran unsuccessfully for the Republican presidential nomination in 1988 and later founded the Christian Coalition, a political-action organization that replaced Jerry Falwell's Moral Majority as the major voice of the religious right. Robertson was only the most visible of a number of charismatic ministers and television personalities.

RECENT TRENDS

It is difficult today to see much distinction between Pentecostalism and the charismatic movement, but there are differences. Pentecostals remained in their distinctive denominations such as the Pentecostal Holiness Church or the Assemblies of God. Charismatics often continued membership in major denominations. Pentecostals usually insist that speaking in tongues is the mark of the Holy Spirit's baptism, but charismatics are sometimes open on this question.[4] Historically, Pentecostals have been stricter than charismatics in personal and ecclesiastical separation. Pentecostal Ray Hughes notes that "one of the most painful concerns among some traditional Pentecostals is the lifestyle of some who profess the baptism in the Spirit. Most of the traditional Pentecostals believe in a 'separated life,' and many of the new Pentecostals do not."[5] Despite these differences, the two movements generally cooperate, and the terms *Pentecostal* and *charismatic* are almost interchangeable in popular usage.

The Third Wave

The 1980s saw the emergence of what is known as the "third wave" or the "signs and wonders" movement, often called "neo-charismatic."[6] Just as Pentecostalism was the first wave of the Holy Spirit and the charismatic movement was the second wave, so the signs and wonders supposedly represent a third wave of spiritual blessing. The third wave appeals to evangelicals who want to be neither Pentecostal nor charismatic but seek the same kind of spiritual gifts. Supporters of this position claim that miraculous signs and wonders are necessary to proclaim the gospel. They advocate "power evangelism," in which alleged miracles such as healings and exorcisms of demons accompany the preaching of the gospel. Among the leaders of this third wave were John Wimber and his Vineyard Christian Fellowship.[7]

Charismatics in Reformed Circles

Surprisingly, charismatic teaching has also found a place among groups that traditionally have opposed it. An example is the acceptance of charismatic gifts by some Reformed Christians. Historically, the Reformed have rejected continuation of these sign gifts. John Calvin, the Father of Reformed Theology, is typical, arguing that "it is more probable that miracles were promised only for a time, in order to give lustre to the gospel, while it was new and in a state of obscurity." Calvin also said, "I think that the true design for which miracles were appointed was, that nothing which was necessary proving the doctrine of the gospel should be wanting at its commencement. And certainly we see that the use of them ceased not long afterwards, or, at least, that instances of them were so rare as to entitle us to conclude that they would not be equally common in all ages."[8]

However, some contemporary Reformed teachers and writers have accepted these practices. A leading example is John Piper (discussed in the previous chapter), who says, "I am one of those . . . who believes that 'signs and wonders' and all the spiritual gifts of 1 Corinthians 12:8–10 are valid for today and should be 'earnestly desired.'"[9] He represents a segment of a Reformed movement that accepts charismatic gifts, sometimes called the "new Calvinism" or the "young, restless, Reformed" movement (after the title of a popular book).[10] This loosely organized movement includes both practitioners of charismatic gifts and other Calvinists who at least tolerate their practice. A prominent network in this movement goes under the name Sovereign Grace (originally Sovereign Grace Ministries and later named Sovereign Grace Churches) founded by Larry Tomczak and C. J. Mahaney. In addition to building an alliance of churches committed to uniting Reformed theology with a belief in continuing spiritual gifts, the leaders also established Sovereign Grace Music. By publishing Christian music, often with a contemporary Christian music sound, Sovereign Grace Music reached beyond the confines of its own alliance of ministries to affect a wide range of churches through their worship styles.

> **THE BASIS OF CHRISTIAN UNITY FOR MANY CHARISMATICS IS NOT SO MUCH AN AGREEMENT ON THE ESSENTIAL TRUTHS OF CHRISTIANITY BUT A SHARED SPIRITUAL "EXPERIENCE."**

Among Southern Baptists

There is likewise a branch of the charismatic movement among Southern Baptists, a group that traditionally has resisted charismatic teaching. As conservatives have firmed up their control of the SBC, they have had to deal with a pro-charismatic faction within their ranks. Although it appears that the majority of Southern Baptists have registered strong disapproval of their presence, the charismatics remain a force.[11] Recognizing this growing trend, the International

Mission Board of the SBC decided in 2015 to remove speaking in tongues as a disqualification for mission candidates even though the board still prohibited teaching that these gifts are normative and also prohibited any practice of the gifts that disrupted mission work.[12]

The growth of Pentecostal and charismatic teaching has been even more spectacular outside the United States. D. B. Barrett reported in 2002 that Pentecostalism and its offshoots numbered 523 million adherents worldwide. Of this number, Barrett said, 65 million were Pentecostals, 175 million were charismatics, and 295 million belonged to the third wave.[13] Unquestionably Pentecostalism and the charismatic movement are among the most influential worldwide religious movements of the twentieth and twenty-first centuries.

FUNDAMENTALISM AND PENTECOSTALISM

Some writers, such as Robert Mapes Anderson and Virginia Brereton, view early Pentecostalism as another form of fundamentalism.[14] They stress characteristics such as Pentecostalism's biblical literalism, opposition to modernism, belief in premillennialism, and willingness to practice both personal and ecclesiastical separation.

Early fundamentalists generally opposed the movement, however. For example, the World's Christian Fundamentals Association, fundamentalism's first large interdenominational body, refused membership to Pentecostals.[15] Perhaps part of the fundamentalist resistance was the lower social status of Pentecostalism and its extremist reputation at that time. Fundamentalists did not want to be identified with "holy rollers." But the heart of the disagreement was—and remains—fundamentalist rejection of Pentecostal doctrinal distinctives.[16]

ARGUMENTS AGAINST CHARISMATIC TEACHING

Fundamentalists rejected the most prominent Pentecostal teaching, that speaking in tongues is a sign of the baptism of the Holy Spirit. Fundamentalists are usually cessationists, Christians who believe that some spiritual sign gifts, such as speaking in tongues and special acts of healing, ceased at the close of the New Testament era.[17] (The quotation from Calvin earlier in the chapter represents the cessationist position.) They therefore reject one of the most basic Pentecostal teachings and argue that all believers are baptized by the Spirit (without speaking in tongues) when they are converted.

Even if they allow that speaking in tongues might be possible today, fundamentalists usually reject the Pentecostal practice of tongues as unscriptural. For example, in 1 Corinthians 14:26–32, Paul sets down rules for speaking in tongues in church: there should be no more than two or three people speaking in tongues in a service, and no one should do it if an interpreter is not present. Those who speak should do so in order and not simultaneously. Fundamentalists argue that Pentecostals often do not follow these instructions in their services.

Another major concern to fundamentalists is the tendency of some who speak in tongues to consider their utterances a special revelation from God. Fundamentalists (and many other evangelicals) reject the idea of special revelation apart from the Bible. Paul teaches in 2 Timothy 3:15–17 that the Scriptures provide *everything* needed for salvation and Christian living. No extra revelation can bind the conscience of a believer. Long before the Pentecostal movement ever arose, John Wesley (whom Pentecostals see as one of their forerunners) warned,

> Give no place to a heated imagination. Do not hastily ascribe things to God. Do not easily suppose dreams, voices, impressions, visions, or revelations to be from God. They may be from him. They may be from nature. They may be from the devil. Therefore "believe not every spirit, but try the spirits whether they be of God." Try all things by the written word, and let all bow down before it. You are in danger of enthusiasm every hour, if you depart ever so little from Scripture; yea, or from the plain literal meaning of any text, taken in connexion with the context. And so you are, if you despise or lightly esteem reason, knowledge, or human learning; every one of which is an excellent gift of God, and may serve the noblest purposes.[18]

Finally, fundamentalists reject the implication of spiritual superiority in Pentecostal teaching, that Pentecostalism has the "full gospel" lacked by other Christians. Such an idea is unscriptural. Paul told the Colossian believers, "Ye are complete in him, which is the head of all principality and power" (Col. 2:10). The salvation of Christ through the gospel is perfect, lacking nothing. Christians should grow in grace (2 Pet. 3:18), but this growth is the realizing of what Christ has already granted to the believer. As Paul wrote, "I follow after, if that I may apprehend that for which also I am apprehended of Christ Jesus" (Phil. 3:12).

But at least a few fundamentalists are willing to regard some Pentecostal beliefs as matters of interpretation and to suggest a basis for fellowship with conservative Pentecostals. For instance, Bob Jones Jr. cited an independent Pentecostal who withdrew from his denomination in protest over its participation in the charismatic movement and declared that he "is as much of a fundamentalist as I am." Jones also referred to other independent, old-line Pentecostal churches that withdrew from the major Pentecostal denominations in protest against the charismatic movement. He argued that there was a place for fellowship with such believers. Still, he drew the line at accepting new revelation, tongues, and the gift of healing, which he believed exceeded the bounds of mere difference of interpretation and precluded fellowship in worship and service.[19]

Various excesses of both Pentecostalism and the charismatic movement have offended other observers as well. A former Pentecostal describing the "dark side" of Pentecostalism cites its anti-intellectualism, the sexual and financial irregularities by a few key figures, and the tolerance of exaggerated and dishonest claims by its leaders.[20] A loyal charismatic writes, "I have to be honest—when I've read about the latest angel sightings, gold dust sprinklings, teeth fillings and crazy revival antics, it's felt more like *National Enquirer* material than New Testament experience."[21] But charismatic proponents argue that these extremes are not typical.

THE CHARISMATIC MOVEMENT AND BIBLICAL SEPARATION

An indisputable difference between fundamentalists and charismatics (and those Pentecostals who go along with the charismatics) is the question of separation. In a few cases the point of dispute is personal separation, such as athletes and entertainers who claim some kind of charismatic experience but whose worldly lifestyles hardly "shew forth the praises of him who hath called [them] out of darkness into his marvellous light" (1 Pet. 2:9). To be fair, however, many charismatics and Pentecostals do uphold biblical standards of personal behavior and criticize worldliness.

Far more often the problem is ecclesiastical separation. The basis of Christian unity for many charismatics is not so much an agreement on the essential truths of Christianity but a shared spiritual "experience" and good will. Leading Catholic charismatic Edward O'Connor writes, "When the charismatic renewal, after having been confined for decades to the Pentecostal denominations, began to penetrate into the established churches, it naturally tended to create bonds among all those who embraced it. These were not, however, bonds of doctrinal agreement; for it is not the spread of *ideas* about the Holy Spirit that constitutes the Pentecostal movement, but the *experience* of the Spirit's power action."[22] Michael Harper, in advocating unity among charismatics, evangelicals, and Catholics, writes, "What if Luther had drunk a good pint of German beer with the papal nuncio? Or if John Wesley had been invited to share his views with a group of Anglican bishops? Or if the early Pentecostals had been invited to 'talk things over' with other leaders? Or if the early fundamentalists had gone off for a week of prayer and fasting with their liberal 'enemies'? It makes one think."[23]

By no means are all charismatics and Pentecostals so flexible with doctrine. Ray Hughes, a traditional Pentecostal, says that a common experience cannot build unity where there is no agreement on doctrine. He points out that non-Christians, even Satanists, have spoken in tongues and that therefore the experience of tongues by itself cannot provide a basis for unity.[24] Jack Hayford likewise argues that Christians must agree on the person and work of Christ as Creator, Redeemer, God's Son, and Savior, in addition to spiritual gifts, before they can know true unity. Yet Hayford says that "biblical unity is discovered not as a resolution of doctrinal differences, but as a revelation of the Living Word—Jesus."[25] Although W. Dennis Pederson argues that God "will unify His body through those who are open to His Spirit," he urges

> **TRULY, THERE CAN BE NO SPIRITUAL UNITY WHERE THERE IS NO SALVATION THROUGH THE WORK OF THE HOLY SPIRIT, AND LIKEWISE THERE CAN BE NO UNITY OF THE SPIRIT WHERE TRUTH IS SACRIFICED.**

charismatics to remain in their churches in the compromised main-line denominations.[26]

We could cite other examples, such as the doctrinal errors of Catholic charismatics who try to reconcile Catholic and Pentecostal teaching.[27] Truly, there can be no spiritual unity where there is no salvation through the work of the Holy Spirit, and likewise there can be no unity of the Spirit where truth is sacrificed. Jesus said of the Holy Spirit, "When he, the Spirit of truth, is come, he will guide you into all truth" (John 16:13). When a movement embraces error, it is not being guided by the Holy Spirit, despite declarations of its adherents.

CONCLUSION

There are many extremes in the charismatic movement that give fundamentalists pause. Furthermore, we have seen important doctrinal disagreements between fundamentalists and charismatics. These matters alone may give fundamentalists sufficient reason to distance themselves from the movement, but the greatest danger in the charismatic movement is its ecumenicity—its willingness to embrace all sorts of doctrinal deviations in the name of Christian unity and under the supposed leading of the Holy Spirit. When the charismatic movement blurs the distinction between truth and error, it promotes false unity.

Some unregenerate people may be deceived into thinking they are Christians because they have had a charismatic experience. Many other charismatics and Pentecostals are genuine Christians, sincere in their desire to serve God. Jesus told the woman of Samaria that "true worshippers shall worship the Father in spirit and in truth: for the Father seeketh such to worship him" (John 4:23). To worship and serve in the power of the Holy Spirit is essential to Christian living, but not all worship and service claimed to be in the power of the Spirit will also always be in truth.

CHAPTER ELEVEN
ROMAN CATHOLICISM

Before the 1960s, virtually all Protestants in the United States thought it was obvious that they should keep their distance from Roman Catholicism. In 1946, noted liberal Protestant Charles Clayton Morrison had written in *Christian Century*,

> Catholicism is more than a way of salvation. Seen whole, it presents itself as a system of power—a kind of power which no human institution should presume to possess and exercise, a power which is radically incompatible with both Christianity and democracy, and which carries within itself the seeds of corruption. The Roman Church is a monarchical and feudal institution. . . . The hierarchy, with the pope at its head, is the counterpart (or should I say the prototype?) of the fascist or nazist or communist "party" with the dictator at its head.[1]

Today the situation has drastically changed. We have looked at several theological systems in the historical order in which they emerged: liberalism, neo-orthodoxy, the new evangelicalism, and the charismatic movement. Roman Catholicism is older than all of these combined, but only within the relatively recent past have some evangelicals accepted Catholics and even joined hands with them in political and religious efforts.

THE HEART OF CATHOLICISM

ORIGINS

Probably one of the most asked—and least answerable—questions
about church history is when the Roman Catholic Church began.
People have offered various ideas contrasting with the Catholic
claim that it is simply the true church since New Testament times.
The Protestant reformers generally believed that when the popes
(the bishops of Rome) assumed the overlordship of the church, they
corrupted it into the Roman Catholic Church. Suggestions as to
which bishop of Rome initiated this corruption include Leo the Great
(440–61), Gregory the Great (590–604), and Gregory II (715–31). The
papacy alone, however, cannot bear the blame for all the problems of
Catholicism.

Another suggestion is that the Roman Catholic Church began when
the Roman emperor Constantine embraced Christianity in AD 313
and his conversion encouraged many unbelievers to join the church.
These non-Christians brought their pagan superstitions with them and
thereby corrupted the church. Although there is certainly an element
of truth to this theory, some distinctive Catholic teachings were already
current before Constantine's time, and others developed later.

Others hold that the Council of Trent (1545–63) marked the
establishment of the Roman Catholic Church by expressly rejecting
the teachings of the Protestant Reformation and demanding submission to all teachings required by the Catholic hierarchy. Again, there
is much truth to this idea. Trent drew hard lines between Catholicism
and Protestantism and forced all who held Protestant ideas either to
submit or to leave the Church. Nevertheless, the beliefs required of
Catholics by the Council of Trent had previously existed in one form
or another even though not all not been recognized as official dogma.

AUTHORITY AND SALVATION

Actually, the Roman Catholic Church diverged from biblical
Christianity over a period of centuries. We will focus on two major
issues: the authority of Scripture and the nature of salvation.[2]

The Protestant reformers argued that the Bible alone was the authority in religious matters. The Catholic Church replied that Scripture
and tradition were both religious authorities. By *tradition* Catholics

meant a body of oral teaching given by Christ to the apostles along with the written Scriptures. This oral tradition is the authority for many nonbiblical Catholic teachings rejected by Protestants.

Karl Keating, a Catholic apologist writing to warn Catholics against fundamentalism, notes that some Catholics "are dismayed to discover there is no clear mention of auricular confession, infant baptism, or the Immaculate Conception in any book from Matthew to Revelation."[3] Later, dealing with the assumption of Mary (the dogma that Mary was bodily taken to heaven at the end of her life), he writes, "Still, fundamentalists ask, where is the proof from Scripture? Strictly, there is none. It was the Catholic Church that was commissioned by Christ to teach all nations and to teach them infallibly. The mere fact that the Church teaches the doctrine of the Assumption as something definitely true is a guarantee that it is true."[4]

As Keating indicates, not only do Catholics view tradition as an authority, but they also believe that the Church, under the leadership of the popes and bishops, is the only interpreter of what Scripture and tradition actually teach. The practical effect is that there are not two sources of authority, Scripture and tradition, but only one, a Church that interprets both Scripture and tradition.[5] In 1870, the First Vatican Council strengthened this idea by declaring that the pope was preserved from all error when pronouncing official Church teaching. Pope Pius XII invoked this authority when he declared in 1950 that all Catholics must believe in the assumption of Mary.

The doctrine of salvation is another essential difference. The Bible teaches that believers are justified by faith alone. God declares them righteous by crediting the righteousness of Christ to them. Roman Catholicism, however, teaches that a person is justified by both faith and works. In an effort to build bridges between Catholics and evangelicals, Alister McGrath attacks those evangelicals who "continue to insist that the Roman Catholic Church officially teaches justification by works [even though] that is simply not true"[6] McGrath is partly correct. Catholics do not believe that anyone can be saved without faith. Nevertheless, they equally believe that no one will be saved without works. In Catholic teaching, both are necessary.

Catholicism confuses justification with sanctification. In justification God declares the Christian righteous on the basis of Christ's atonement, not on any merit of the believer. By the process of sanctification and as a *result* of justification, a Christian becomes more righteous in thought and action. Catholics, however, say that in the process of justification righteousness is infused into the believer so that he or she really becomes more righteous. Salvation then becomes a process in which a Catholic, on the basis of faith, strives to be righteous enough to merit heaven. In other words, instead of being declared righteous, a person actually becomes more righteous.

Chief among Catholic attempts to become more righteous is receiving the seven sacraments: baptism, confirmation, holy orders (ordination), matrimony, penance, eucharist (the Lord's Supper), and anointing of the sick (formerly known as extreme unction or last rites). By participating in these sacraments, Catholics believe they receive grace from God, which in turn enables them to perform meritorious works to secure their salvation.

Catholics believe that God graciously gives them the ability to perform good works, and then God graciously accepts these good works as sufficient for earning merit even though humans can actually do nothing truly meritorious before God. Paul, to the contrary, says, "To him that worketh is the reward not reckoned of grace, but of debt" (Rom. 4:4). Later he says of "the election of grace" that "if by grace, then is it no more of works: otherwise grace is no more grace. But if it be of works, then is it no more grace: otherwise work is no more work" (Rom. 11:6).

CATHOLICISM CONFUSES JUSTIFICATION WITH SANCTIFICATION.

In effect, the Catholic Church lifts up human merit at the expense of Christ's merit. For example, in Catholic teaching, Christ's death for sin is sufficient to pay the penalty for eternal punishment and save a person from hell. Christ's sacrifice is not sufficient, however, to pay for the "temporal" punishment that Catholics believe they must satisfy by performing good works or by suffering in purgatory before entering heaven. In contrast, Paul says, "There is therefore now no condemnation to them which are in Christ Jesus" (Rom. 8:1)—neither eternal nor temporal condemnation.

Other nonbiblical teachings of the Catholic Church include the glorification of the virgin Mary, the intercession of Mary and the saints for Christians, the idea that in the mass (celebration of the eucharist) the body of Christ is actually offered in an "unbloody sacrifice"—all of these teachings clash with those of Scripture. But the root of these errors is the refusal of the Roman Catholic Church to be bound by the authority of Scripture. If the Church were bound by Scripture instead of its own authority, it would not hold these teachings because they have no scriptural support.

VATICAN II AND CATHOLIC CHANGE

If the dogma of Roman Catholicism is unbiblical, then why would any evangelical Christian want closer ties with the Catholic Church? Undoubtedly, part of the reason is the weakening doctrinal stance of mainline denominations and many evangelical and charismatic churches as well. Another major reason is a popular perception of change in Catholicism since the Second Vatican Council (1962–65), commonly called Vatican II.

Vatican II did introduce significant changes. It encouraged Bible study and authorized new translations of the Bible. It revised the Church's liturgy and dropped Latin in favor of the common languages. Catholic liberals perceived a new openness toward liberalism. Most significantly, the Catholic Church began to call non-Catholics "separated brethren" instead of heretics and claimed that both sides had sinned in the Reformation controversy. The council's decree "Catholic Principles on Ecumenism" also encouraged discussions about unity between Catholics and non-Catholics.[7]

Although the tone was friendlier, these changes did not modify the doctrinal differences that have divided Catholics and Protestants since the Reformation. The decree on ecumenism, for example, still teaches, "All those justified by faith through baptism are incorporated into Christ" (sect. 3). The decree calls non-Catholics "separated brethren" but chides those who "have not preserved the genuine and total reality of the Eucharist mystery" (sect. 22), that is, who do not believe in the physical presence of Christ's body in the eucharist or that a real sacrifice of Christ's body is offered in the mass.

Just how little Catholicism had changed was illustrated some thirty years after Vatican II. In 1994, the Catholic Church published a new catechism summarizing official church teaching, the first such official summary since the Reformation.[8] This catechism, although maintaining the friendly tone of Vatican II, made no major change in doctrine.

On authority, for example, the catechism says that "the Church, to whom the transmission and interpretation of Revelation is entrusted, 'does not derive her certainty about all revealed truths from the holy Scriptures alone. Both Scripture and Tradition must be accepted and honored with equal sentiments of devotion and reverence'" (¶82). The "interpretation" of this revelation belongs to the Church, in particular "to the bishops in communion with the successor of Peter, the Bishop of Rome" (¶85).

On the question of justification, the catechism does not differ from the Council of Trent, but in fact quotes Trent: "Justification is not only the remission of sins, but also the sanctification and renewal of the interior man" (¶1989). "Justification is conferred in Baptism, the sacrament of faith" (¶1992), the catechism says, and "includes the remission of sins, sanctification, and the renewal of the inner man" (¶2019). To the Catholic Church salvation is still partly by Christ's merit and partly by human merit: "No one can merit the initial grace which is at the origin of conversion. Moved by the Holy Spirit, we can merit for ourselves and for others all the graces needed to attain eternal life, as well as necessary temporal goods" (¶2027). Essential to salvation are the Church's sacraments: "The Church affirms that for believers the sacraments of the New Covenant are *necessary for salvation*" (¶1129). Clearly the gulf between Rome and biblical Protestantism has not narrowed but remains as wide as ever.

> **CLEARLY THE GULF BETWEEN ROME AND BIBLICAL PROTESTANTISM HAS NOT NARROWED BUT REMAINS AS WIDE AS EVER.**

EVANGELICALS AND CATHOLICISM

In addition to Vatican II, other factors have promoted closer ties between Catholics and evangelical Christians. For instance, the charismatic movement attracted many Catholic followers. Undoubtedly, some of these Catholics were genuinely converted. But one effect of the growth of charismatic Catholicism was to make Catholics and their church seem more acceptable to Protestants. Because Catholics were apparently receiving the same spiritual gifts as Protestants, charismatic Protestants saw less reason for distancing themselves from the Catholic Church.

Another factor fostering greater unity was what has been called "evangelical cobelligerence," the notion that "there is no inconsistency in evangelicals' forming alliances or coalitions with others to address issues on which they can agree." Evangelicals forming such an alliance would not pass judgment on "the correctness or incorrectness of the outlooks of such other groups."[9] This means evangelicals may form all sorts of temporary alliances with diverse groups as long as they have some common objective. Such alliances were also supported by Vatican II's "Catholic Principles on Ecumenism," which encourages Catholics to work with non-Catholics on behalf of social causes (sect. 12).

This position of cobelligerence has limited validity for Bible-believers. Catholics and Protestants may join political groups to work together to get certain candidates elected. But such cooperation is not in religious activities or dedicated to religious goals. When religious issues become the basis of an organization, then the biblical teaching concerning religious fellowship must guide its activities. Religious unity that is not based on the essential truths of Scripture can lead only to the compromise of those truths.

One troubling example of Protestant accommodation to Catholicism is an initiative known as "Evangelicals and Catholics Together" (ECT). This effort takes its name from a document signed in 1994 by a number of Catholics and evangelicals, led by Richard John Neuhaus, a former Lutheran turned Catholic priest, and Charles Colson, a former member of President Richard Nixon's staff who was converted after his involvement in the Watergate scandal. Several leading evangelicals endorsed the original document, including Pat Robertson, charismatic broadcaster; Bill Bright, leader of Campus Crusade (also known as Cru); Richard Mouw, president of Fuller Theological Seminary; and J. I. Packer, theologian and professor at Regent College in Canada.[10]

The document presents evangelicalism and Catholicism as equally valid expressions of the Christian faith. For example, it condemns "proselytizing" to convert Catholics to evangelical Protestantism or vice versa.[11] Although it lists "points of difference" between Catholics and evangelicals, such as the nature of the church and the authority of

Scripture,[12] the document does not consider these points significant enough to prevent their cooperation.

The leaders of ECT addressed other issues in further statements. In 1997, several of the Catholics and evangelicals involved in ECT issued a second document, "The Gift of Salvation."[13] The statement declares that both sides agree that "justification is not earned by any good works or merits of our own" and that "the New Testament makes it clear that the gift of justification is received through faith alone."[14] However, the document also says that one of the questions Catholics and evangelicals still need to discuss is "the historic uses of the language of justification as it relates to imputed or transformative righteousness,"[15] which is the key distinction between the Protestant and Catholic views of justification.

In a third document, "Your Word Is Truth" (2002), the signers declared that both sides agreed on the authority of Scripture with tradition apparently placed in a subordinate role.[16] "Tradition is not a second source of revelation alongside the Bible but must ever be corrected and informed by it, and Scripture itself is not understood in a vacuum apart from the historical existence and life of the community of faith."[17] Finally, in 2003 the signers issued "The Communion of Saints."[18] Taking its title from the closing words of the Apostles' Creed, the document discussed communion with God and among Christians in matters such as the sacraments. Building on the previous statements, "The Communion of Saints" did not provoke as much controversy, except in such matters as a qualified acceptance of the Catholic sense of the word *saint*.[19]

Reaction to ECT was not uniformly positive. A number of evangelicals, fundamentalists, and even Roman Catholics criticized the document.[20] A sympathetic critic from the Eastern Orthodox Church observed that neither side was consistent in maintaining its heritage. The Protestant belief in *sola scriptura* means that "Scripture alone" is authoritative and not, as the statement says, authoritative in connection with something else such as the church or "the community of faith." Catholic signers must wrestle with their historic belief that the church stands over the Bible. "One who accords priority and final authority to the written canon must be a Protestant; one who accords priority and final authority to the Church cannot be a Protestant."[21] Another writer criticized the literary structure of the statements because a clear statement of belief includes not only affirmations but also clarifying denials of what is rejected. By omitting the denials, the ECT documents allows signers on both sides more latitude in interpreting the statements.[22]

Most important, the ECT documents underestimate the significance of doctrinal differences between Catholicism and evangelical Christianity. "The Gift of Salvation" admits that there is a gap between the biblical Protestant idea that in justification God declares the sinner righteous on the basis of Christ's righteousness and the Catholic teaching that in justification (which includes sanctification) a person becomes more righteous.[23] "Your Word Is Truth" admits there are still differences over issues such as purgatory, the role of Mary, transubstantiation, and the intercession of the saints.[24] Even if a group of Catholics such as those involved in ECT should accede to biblical definitions of justification or the authority of Scripture, their agreement would not change the official Catholic teaching as expressed in the Canons and Decrees of the Council of Trent, *The Catechism of the Catholic Church*, and other official Catholic documents.

> ONE CRITIC OBSERVED THAT NEITHER SIDE WAS CONSISTENT IN MAINTAINING ITS HERITAGE.

Sadly, the acceptance of Catholicism by evangelicals represented by ECT illustrates a trend. Looking back on a generation of Catholic-evangelical encounters, Mark Noll and Carolyn Nystrom published *Is the Reformation Over?* in 2005 to suggest an evangelical reassessment of Catholicism that would allow greater fellowship and cooperation. But *is* the Reformation over? Considering the issues involved, asking this question is tantamount to asking, "Is the gospel still central to the church and Christian life?" Insofar as the Protestant Reformation represents the promotion of the true gospel of Jesus Christ and as long as others reject that gospel, the Reformation will never be over.

CATHOLICISM AND BIBLICAL SEPARATION

The biblical response to Roman Catholicism is the same as for any form of false teaching: Christians are to resist it, expose its teachings, and refuse to have fellowship with it. Catholic error is in some ways subtler than that of other systems we have looked at. Liberalism, for example, subtracts from Scripture's teachings by discarding doctrines such as the inerrancy of the Bible and the deity and resurrection of Christ. Roman Catholicism by contrast *adds* to the Scriptures' teaching—the authority of Scripture *and* tradition, salvation by faith *and* works.

J. Gresham Machen once argued that with all of its serious flaws, Roman Catholicism is not as bad as liberalism: "The Church of Rome may represent a perversion of the Christian religion; but naturalistic liberalism is not Christianity at all."[25] This is probably true, although it is unlikely that Machen viewed this "perversion" as a basis for unity between Protestants and Catholics. We do not associate with a movement because it is less far from the truth than some other movement. Rather we associate with those persons and movements that actively hold to the truth. One writer notes, "There is enough gospel in Romanism to save a soul who trusts Jesus Christ alone. However, there is also enough of the poison of false presumption leading to damnation for the soul who accepts the promise that none are lost who die in communion with the institutional church."[26]

Biblical divergence from Catholicism reveals that there is more to orthodox Christianity than the lists of fundamentals that emerged from the Fundamentalist-Modernist Controversy. Justification by faith alone is also an essential of the gospel. We should hold to it along with the deity of Christ, the virgin birth, and the other teachings that early fundamentalists defended.[27] We could rightly copy the Reformation pattern and say that we believe in the inerrancy and authority of Scripture alone. Otherwise, human tradition can open the church to unscriptural teachings such as purgatory and the veneration of Mary.

What about genuine Christians who belong to the Catholic Church? Alister McGrath tries to reassure evangelicals who resist cooperating with Roman Catholics because of Catholic teachings such as prayers for the dead and the veneration of Mary, arguing, "This reaction . . . rests on the assumption that individual Roman Catholics accept the authority of all the official teachings of their church. The empirical evidence available suggests that large numbers of them simply do not." He cites widespread Catholic disobedience to the church's pronouncements on contraception as an example of how Catholics select what they will believe and what they will reject.[28]

Christians, however, are bound not only by biblical doctrine about false teaching but also by its doctrine about disobedient Christians. Since Roman Catholicism is a system of false teaching, then genuine Christians who are members of that system should obey the Bible's commands concerning separation from false doctrine. "The often-suggested exception of 'a good Christian in the Roman Catholic Church' is a misnomer. Such a person is either ignorant or disobedi-ent—ignorant of what Rome teaches or of what the Bible teaches, or disobedient to what Rome teaches or to what the Bible teaches. None of these conditions fits either a 'good Roman Catholic' or a 'good Christian.'"[29] Christians who refuse to abide by commands to separate from false teaching are themselves walking in disobedience.

> SINCE ROMAN CATHOLICISM IS A SYSTEM OF FALSE TEACHING, THEN GENUINE CHRISTIANS WHO ARE MEMBERS OF THAT SYSTEM SHOULD OBEY THE BIBLE'S COMMANDS CONCERNING SEPARATION FROM FALSE DOCTRINE.

But as we have noted elsewhere, we do not treat disobedient Christians the same way we treat false teachers. Our goal in main-taining religious separation from genuine believers who are still part of the Catholic Church is to "gain" them, to "provoke [them] unto love and good works" (Heb. 10:24). Perhaps we have here another application of Jude 1:23. Catholic believers we are to "save with fear, pulling them out of the fire," all the while "hating even the garment spotted by the flesh," the false teaching of Catholicism. It may be that such Christians will not understand or appreciate our position. But as we have repeatedly stressed, our duty is to obey God and leave the consequences to Him.

CHAPTER TWELVE
EXAMPLES OF SEPARATION IN HISTORY

When discussing the separatism espoused by American fundamentalism, some writers have argued that its roots lay in the movement's theological and historical framework, rather than biblical command. They contend that dispensationalism, which influenced fundamentalist theology, promoted a belief in the apostasy of the visible church, which in turn caused fundamentalists to view the major denominations with suspicion. Thus fundamentalists used their dispensationalist bias to justify, even urge, separation.[1] Added to this theological factor, the historical reality that the United States has always been a religious free market of competing churches and sects only intensified the separatist impulse.

The inadequacy of this theory is demonstrated by one episode in the history of the Fundamentalist-Modernist Controversy. Even J. Gresham Machen, who was not a dispensationalist and in fact criticized dispensationalism,[2] led the fight against theological liberalism that climaxed in the formation of what became known as the Orthodox Presbyterian Church, a separatist group without a dispensationalist framework. Furthermore, we have surveyed at length biblical evidence that demonstrates that separation is rooted in the teaching of Scripture.

The following pages describe several separatist movements in history. Sometimes the separation was a sudden event but at other times a slow withdrawal; sometimes it entailed the expulsion of false teachers. Some efforts were relatively successful, and others saw at best limited gains. Yet all assumed that fidelity to the Bible required separation.

THREE MARKS OF THE CHURCH IN THE REFORMATION

The Protestant Reformation was obviously a significant separation, a split between the Roman Catholic Church and the Protestant churches. To illumine this discussion of separation, it is helpful to focus on one idea from the Reformation debates, the marks of the true church.

Because the reformers sought to demonstrate the scriptural basis of their rift with the Roman Catholic Church, they engaged in debates with Catholics about the method of distinguishing a true church from a false one. Catholics used historical arguments, tracing their church back through historical succession to the apostles. The reformers replied with arguments based on the Bible. Early in the Reformation, the Lutherans identified two marks of the true church in Article 7 of their Augsburg Confession of Faith, which said that the characteristics of a true church were that "the Gospel is rightly taught" and "the Sacraments rightly administered."[3] Other reformers adopted these marks and added a third—church discipline rightly practiced.

What do these marks mean precisely? The gospel rightly preached is the simplest to understand. A true church will be correct in its doctrinal teaching; specifically it will correctly proclaim the gospel of salvation through Christ alone. The sacraments (or ordinances, as most fundamentalists would say) rightly administered means first that the church practices the proper number—two (baptism and the Lord's Supper) and not seven as the Catholic Church does. Also the meaning of those sacraments must be biblical, as in the Protestant rejection of the Catholic idea of transubstantiation.[4] Church discipline in the third mark is more than just punishment. It entails proper corrective procedures for dealing with sin (the way we normally think of church discipline) and also formative discipline (the pattern for teaching and mutual edification in the church).

Martin Bucer, the reformer of Strasbourg, was the first to write and teach extensively on this third mark.[5] A contemporary of Martin Luther and a mentor of John Calvin, Bucer helped spread the idea of church discipline as a mark of the true church. John Knox, who was exposed to Bucer's teaching during his exile in Strasbourg, included the idea in the First Scots Confession (1560). Likewise Article 29 of the Belgic Confession, the creed of the Dutch Reformed Church, says, "The marks by which the true Church is known are these: If the pure doctrine of the gospel is preached therein; if she maintains the pure administration of the sacraments as instituted by Christ; if church discipline is exercised in punishing of sin."[6]

Bucer's ideas likely influenced English-speaking Christians after he and other Protestant reformers were invited to teach in England during the reign of King Edward VI (1547–53). Later on, English Protestants stressed the idea of church discipline as a necessary mark of the true church.

CATHOLICS USED HISTORICAL ARGUMENTS, TRACING THEIR CHURCH BACK THROUGH HISTORICAL SUCCESSION TO THE APOSTLES. THE REFORMERS REPLIED WITH ARGUMENTS BASED ON THE BIBLE.

The Puritans (those who wanted to purify the Church of England from Catholic ceremonies and practices) and the Separatists (those who believed they should separate from the Church of England) both emphasized the place of church discipline. The Puritans who settled New England established a system of church government that required testimony to a conversion experience, agreement with biblical teaching, and the evidence of an upright life as prerequisites for membership in the church and participation in the Lord's Supper.[7]

The Separatists went even further, making church discipline a major point in their arguments for separation from the Church of England.[8] Perhaps the most famous Separatists in American history were the Pilgrims of Plymouth Colony. Their pastor, John Robinson, wrote extensively to defend Separatist practice based on arguments about the nature of the church.[9] Separatist arguments also influenced other contemporary groups, notably the English Baptists.

This heritage of identifying the true church by doctrine and discipline did not fade with the close of the Reformation. Others appealed to these principles in controversies after that time. For example, after the mainline Presbyterian church defrocked J. Gresham Machen, he and his supporters viewed the launching of their new denomination as establishing a church genuinely grounded in the gospel and proper practice. Saying that "the hopes of many long years were realized," Machen declared those gathered in the new church "became members, at last, of a true Presbyterian Church; we recovered, at last, the blessing of true Christian fellowship."[10]

HENRY COOKE'S WAR AGAINST UNITARIANISM

Beginning in the 1600s, many Scots settled in the northern counties of Ireland, commonly called the province of Ulster, bringing with them their Presbyterianism. To understand controversies among Presbyterians, we need to explain the terms *presbytery* and *subscription*. A Presbyterian church consists of presbyteries, districts that are usually geographical in nature, and *subscription* refers to the promise of a candidate for the ministry to subscribe to (i.e., promise to believe and uphold) the Westminster Standards: the Westminster Confession (the major Presbyterian creed), the Shorter and Larger Catechisms, and other documents of the church. Normally, if a candidate refuses to subscribe to the standards, he is denied ordination.

In the early 1700s, however, the Irish Presbyterian Church decided not to reject candidates who would not fully subscribe. Instead the church put all nonsubscribing ministers into the same presbytery, the presbytery of Antrim. Unsurprisingly this presbytery became a center of controversy. By the beginning of the 1800s, serious false doctrine flourished in the Antrim presbytery. The biggest challenges were Unitarianism (teaching that Christ was just a man) and Arianism (teaching that Christ, although an exalted being, was not equal to the Father).

This situation disturbed Irish Presbyterian Henry Cooke.[11] He launched what came to be known as a "seven years' war" to eliminate Arianism from the church. Beginning in 1822, he campaigned in the church's annual synod meetings to purge Arian teaching. Initially he was almost alone in these clashes, leading a modern historian to call Cooke "the Athanasius of Irish Presbyterianism," after the church father who fought the Arian heresy in the fourth century.[12] Although the majority of the church was orthodox, many conservatives feared causing a split. Nevertheless, Cooke persevered and slowly swung the majority to his side. Finally, in 1827 he pressed the church to test all ministers using Question 6 of the Shorter Catechism, "How many persons are there in the Godhead?" The next year the church adopted his position, and the following year the Arians withdrew to form their own church.

After the withdrawal of the protesting party, the Irish Presbyterian Church entered a period of prosperity. In 1835, the church required all ministers to subscribe fully to the Westminster Standards. Impressed by the stand against heresy, another Presbyterian group in Ulster merged with the Irish Presbyterian Church, making up for the loss of the Arian party. Later the church benefited from the '59 Revival, a widespread awakening in the British Isles. Although we cannot prove that purging heretics contributed to the revival, many Ulster Christians viewed the awakening as God's blessing on the church's stand for truth.[13] Unquestionably the Irish Presbyterian Church had the greatest growth among all Ulster churches as a result of the '59 Revival.

THE GREAT DISRUPTION

In the nineteenth century, Scotland, the original homeland of Presbyterianism, endured its largest and most famous division, called the Great Disruption.[14] Two major parties had formed within the Presbyterian Church of Scotland (often called simply the Church of Scotland because it was the established church). The group dominating the leadership of the church, its schools, and other institutions was the moderates. Influenced by the Enlightenment, they stressed reason, emotional restraint, and propriety. Most moderates were "ostensibly if tepidly orthodox,"[15] but some were rationalistic in theology. The other party, probably more numerous, was the evangelicals. They were strongly orthodox in theology, and their sermons focused on the Bible and its application. The evangelicals supported revivals, evangelistic work, and foreign missions, but the moderates were lukewarm about such matters.

The actual cause of the break was government interference in the affairs of the church. A major source of conflict was lay patronage, the right of wealthy landowners within a parish to choose the minister of the church. Patrons could impose on a church any minister they liked, regardless of the wishes of the congregation. Because congregations sometimes had unworthy men foisted on them, they desired at least a say in whether to accept the patron's candidate. Therefore, the

Church of Scotland adopted a policy of allowing the heads of household in each congregation to register their opinions. If the congregation rejected the patron's candidate, the presbytery could reject him as
minister.

Patrons and their nominees obviously resented this change. They
took the issue to the church and civil courts, appealing as high as the
House of Lords. The government rejected the congregational veto,
ruling that the Church of Scotland was a creation of the state and
subject to state control even in internal matters. Displeased by this
decision, the evangelical opposition, led by minister and professor
Thomas Chalmers, walked out of the annual meeting of the church's
General Assembly and formed the Free Church of Scotland in 1843.

By leaving the Church of Scotland, ministers lost their salaries
and congregations lost their property. The Free Church had to begin
from scratch, raising money from voluntary offerings to build church
buildings and schools, to support missionaries, and to provide for all
the other ministries they had left behind in the established church.
Furthermore, the government and many newspapers were hostile to
the Disruption, and patrons refused to let Free Church congregations
buy land to construct new buildings. In spite of many difficulties,
over a third of the ministers and laity left the Church of Scotland, and
those who left tended to be those who had been most active in the
Church of Scotland.

Despite the obstacles, the Free Church grew and flourished. At
the same time, new forces moved the church toward reunion with
the Church of Scotland. The Free Church did not oppose an established church as such and was willing to return if spiritual autonomy
were guaranteed. Legislative changes such as eliminating lay patronage removed many of the causes of the Disruption. Furthermore, the
Free Church, though strongly evangelical at first, began to drift in a
liberal direction. New professors in the Free Church schools brought
in liberal ideas from their study in universities on the continent of
Europe, and their students spread those teachings in the churches.[16]
Finally in 1929, the Free Church reunited with the Church of
Scotland, although a minority resisted and continued separately as
the Free Church of Scotland.[17]

THE DOLEANTIE

Abraham Kuyper (1837–1920) was a major religious leader in the Netherlands at the turn of the twentieth century, influencing not only theology but also politics, education, and culture in general. In 1880, he founded the Free University of Amsterdam, a Christian institution independent of government control. He became the leader of the Anti-Revolutionary Party (so-called because it opposed humanistic policies founded in the ideology of the French Revolution), and he served as prime minister of the Netherlands (1901–1905). Many contemporary Christians affirm ideas he advocated, such as the need for believers to form a Christian worldview and his concept of the cultural mandate, that God commands Christians to subdue all creation to bring every area of legitimate culture in subjection to Christ. As Kuyper himself famously declared, "There is not a square inch in the whole domain of our human existence over which Christ, who is Sovereign over *all*, does not cry: 'Mine!'"[18]

Yet Abraham Kuyper was also an ecclesiastical separatist. Converted from liberalism after he entered the ministry of the Dutch Reformed Church, Kuyper became an implacable foe of modernism and called for a new reformation to return the church to its biblical and historical roots.[19] Amsterdam, where Kuyper ministered, became a center of the conservative opposition to liberal trends. Kuyper and his followers protested in 1883 when the state church relaxed the doctrinal standards that protected the church's orthodoxy. The conservative faction clashed with church authorities two years later when the conservatives refused to recognize certificates of profession of faith from liberal members issued by liberal clergy. In the ensuing conflict, the state church suspended Kuyper and other ministers and elders.[20]

The protesters first formed the *Doleantie* church (from the Latin word for "sorrow" or "mourning") and in 1892 merged with an earlier secession group to form the Reformed Churches in the Netherlands. Kuyper's actions were not rash. Only two years before the break, he had published a pamphlet calling for "the ecclesiastical return to obedience to God and His Word because the church was disobedient to God and His Word." Kuyper wrote, "Each child of God must refuse to do anything, to have a part in anything, or to cooperate in anything which is disobedience to God . . . even though men forbid him, hinder him, or try to make it impossible."[21]

THE DOWNGRADE CONTROVERSY

One of the closest parallels to the Fundamentalist-Modernist Controversy in the United States occurred in England in the late 1800s.[22] The central figure was English Baptist Charles Haddon Spurgeon (1834–92), pastor of the Metropolitan Tabernacle in London, a church with a regular attendance of five thousand. His sermons not only attracted many hearers but in printed form they also reached many thousands more around the world. Spurgeon oversaw a number of ministries, including a pastor's college, an orphanage, and a religious periodical (*The Sword and Trowel*), and he wrote numerous devotional and practical works. He was probably the best-known evangelical in Britain, perhaps in the world.

In the 1880s, Spurgeon became concerned about liberal teaching within the Baptist Union, a major fellowship of British Baptists to which Spurgeon belonged. Spurgeon warned of the "downgrade" of biblical doctrine, and he and other writers published a series of exposés in *Sword and Trowel*. Spurgeon corresponded privately with the organization's secretary, S. H. Booth, who was also concerned about the doctrinal drift and provided Spurgeon with documentation of the errors. The articles in *Sword and Trowel* revealed that some Baptists denied teachings such as Christ's atonement, the plenary inspiration of the Bible, the personality of the Holy Spirit, and justification by faith.[23] He urged the union to adopt a doctrinal statement to make it impossible for liberals to hide their views. Spurgeon said belief in baptism by immersion, the only requirement for membership in the Baptist Union, was an insufficient creedal test.

In October 1887, Spurgeon and his church withdrew from membership in the Baptist Union, but this withdrawal did not end the controversy. The council of the Baptist Union confronted him about having not approached the group with his charges before publishing them. In his earlier correspondence with the secretary of the Union, Spurgeon had promised not to reveal Booth's involvement. When the council censured Spurgeon, that promise prevented him from vindicating himself.

After leaving the Baptist Union, Spurgeon did not attempt to form a new group but simply made the Metropolitan Tabernacle an independent church. This bitter fight had exhausted Spurgeon and may have contributed to his early death four years later. During the controversy and its aftermath, Spurgeon encouraged Christians with words that fundamentalists in America would echo a few years later: "The bounden duty of a true believer towards men who profess to be Christians, and yet deny the Word of the Lord, and reject the fundamentals of the gospel, is to come out from among them."[24] He declared, "To pursue union at the expense of truth is treason to the Lord Jesus," and he concluded, "Fellowship with known and vital error is participation in sin."[25]

D. MARTYN LLOYD-JONES AND "EVANGELICAL UNITY"

Our final example of historical separatism occurred after the Fundamentalist-Modernist Controversy in America. British minister D. Martyn Lloyd-Jones (1899–1981) was an influential figure among evangelical Christians in the United Kingdom.[26] During his long pastorate at the Westminster Chapel in London, Lloyd-Jones set a high standard for expository preaching. He also renewed interest in the theology and piety of the Puritans by sponsoring annual conferences and reprinting numerous Puritan works.

Lloyd-Jones was one of the first in Britain to see problems in the drift of Billy Graham. When Graham invited him to chair a congress on evangelism, Lloyd-Jones replied that he would "make a bargain," that if Graham "would stop the general sponsorship of his campaigns—stop having liberals and Roman Catholics on the platform," he would support him. Lloyd-Jones specifically noted the presence of liberal John Sutherland Bonnell on the committee for Graham's New York campaign in 1957. When Graham said he had "more fellowship with John Sutherland Bonnell than with many evangelical ministers," Lloyd-Jones replied, "Now it may be that Bonnell is a nicer chap than Lloyd-Jones—I'll not argue that. But real fellowship is something else: I can genuinely fellowship only with someone who holds the same basic truths that I do."[27]

Even more important to Lloyd-Jones was the rising challenge of the ecumenical movement. Evangelicals in the British churches, notably the Church of England, had long argued that as long as the official doctrinal beliefs of a church were sound, then the church was sound and evangelicals could belong to it in good conscience. The ecumenical movement, however, changed the situation. Evangelicals found themselves asked to enter into union with other bodies on the basis of vague doctrinal statements. Lloyd-Jones had no confidence in such ecumenical unity. When one minister told Lloyd-Jones that "when so many churches are coming together in a World Council of Churches, revival must be on the way," he replied, "You seem to be arguing that if you succeed in bringing together a sufficient number of dead bodies they will come alive!"[28]

The climax came in 1966 when the Evangelical Alliance asked Lloyd-Jones to address its gathering. In that address, later titled "Evangelical Unity: An Appeal," Lloyd-Jones called for evangelicals to consider leaving their compromised denominations to form a new church, faithful to the Scriptures.[29] The appeal immediately sparked controversy. As soon as Lloyd-Jones finished, the chair of the meeting, Anglican minister John Stott, stood up and disagreed with his position. In the years that followed, British evangelicals divided over the positions advocated by Lloyd-Jones and Stott, whether to leave or to stay in the major British denominations.

Like Spurgeon in the Downgrade Controversy, Lloyd-Jones was unwilling to lead a new church himself. He did persuade his own church to pull out of the Congregational Union when that group prepared to join a new ecumenical denomination, and he traveled all over Britain to speak for ministers who agreed with his separatist argument. But only a small number followed his path.

CONCLUSION

These examples of separatist movements in history certainly cannot prove the practice of separation to be correct. As we said at the beginning of the book, the only authority for the believer is Scripture. Nevertheless, these examples do demonstrate that biblical separation is not an invention of twentieth-century American fundamentalists but a teaching that Christians throughout history have viewed as a practice commanded in God's Word.

AFTERWORD

In these few pages we have attempted to understand and to apply the teaching of biblical separation. We have seen that it is a part of the Christian's sanctification to separate from worldliness, from false teaching, and from disobedient Christians. Remember that like the quality of holiness of which it is an expression, separation begins internally. It is an attitude of heart that is demonstrated by outward actions. You do not become holy by practicing separation; you practice separation as a testimony to the change that has taken place in your heart through the power of the Holy Spirit.

We can give you no better exhortation for practicing separation than to determine the lines that Scripture lays down for believers and to resolve by God's grace to abide by His standards. The Christian practicing biblical separation may have to leave a church or perhaps break a friendship in order to obey God's Word. Jesus put all such sacrifices in their proper perspective in the light of eternal values: "Verily I say unto you, There is no man that hath left house, or parents, or brethren, or wife, or children, for the kingdom of God's sake, who shall not receive manifold more in this present time, and in the world to come life everlasting" (Luke 18:29–30).

One of the major goals of this book is to demonstrate that separation is a biblical teaching, not just the practice of the modern fundamentalist movement. Nonetheless, you will find that in today's religious scene, fundamentalism presents the major viable option for those who seek to practice separation. You should seek above all to be biblical, not simply to be part of some movement. But do not let any reluctance to be associated with a movement affect your desire to be obedient to God.

As you seek to practice separation, you will undoubtedly be challenged by many, including other Christians, who argue that your practice is wrong. Some may protest that separation is unloving. Remind them that Jesus said, "If ye love me, keep my commandments" (John 14:15). We must direct our love first toward God, then toward others, and always in obedience to Him. Others may point to the Bible's commands for Christian unity. For them, recall the lesson of Romans 16:17 that the path to Christian unity involves putting away false teaching, not ignoring it. Always keep the *whole* of Scripture in mind.

As we said earlier in the book, we cannot anticipate every situation you may encounter as you attempt to practice biblical separation. We can only help lay out the principles you should follow in those situations. Determine to be obedient in all circumstances, and prayerfully seek God's guidance through His Word. Treasure the counsel of godly advisers, but always test such counsel by Scripture. If you have a heart regenerated by the Holy Spirit and dedicated to true holiness and biblical love and if you maintain a devotion to God's Word, you have the foundation for practicing biblical separation in a manner that will both honor and glorify your Lord Jesus Christ.

ENDNOTES
ENDNOTES

PREFACE

[1] See also, for example, John Ashbrook, *The New Neutralism II* (Mentor, OH: Here I Stand Books, 1992); and Douglas R. McLachlan, *Reclaiming Authentic Fundamentalism* (Independence, MO: American Association of Christian Schools, 1993).

[2] See, for example, Mark Noll, *The Scandal of the Evangelical Mind* (Grand Rapids: Eerdmans, 1994), 47, 52, 140-41, 188.

[3] Edward M. Panosian, "Roman Catholicism: A Philosophy," *Focus on Missions*, Spring 1992, [1].

CHAPTER 1: DEFINING OUR TERMS

[1] Rolland McCune, "Separation: An Important Benchmark of True Fundamentalism," *Frontline*, May–June 1993, 16.

[2] An example of separation from a brother as part of ecclesiastical separation is Rolland D. McCune, "The Self-Identity of Fundamentalism," *Detroit Baptist Theological Seminary Journal* 1 (1996): 28–32. Examples of treating separation from a brother independently are Douglas R. McLachlan, *Reclaiming Authentic Fundamentalism* (Independence, MO: American Association of Christian Schools, 1993), 121–37 and Fred Moritz, "*Be Ye Holy*": *The Call to Christian Separation* (Greenville, SC: Bob Jones University Press, 1994), 47–87. There is merit to both positions. In Chapters 3–5, we will use the three categories, in part because separation from fellow Christians is such a sensitive matter that it needs separate attention.

[3] John R. Rice, *Come Out or Stay In* (Nashville: Thomas Nelson, 1974), 217–35.

[4] Peter Masters, *Stand for the Truth* (London: Sword and Trowel, 1996), 16–20.

[5] Rolland McCune, *Ecclesiastical Separation* (Allen Park, MI: Detroit Baptist Theological Seminary, n.d., 5–6.

[6] See, for example, Ernest D. Pickering, *The Biblical Doctrine of Separation* (Clarks Summit, PA: Baptist Bible College, 1976), 13–14; McCune, "The Self-Identity of Fundamentalism," 28.

[7] *Epistle to Diognetus* (trans. J. B. Lightfoot), sect. 5.

[8] Tertullian, *De Spectaculis*, Loeb Classical Library (1960; trans. T. R. Glover), sect. 15.

[9] *Tertullian: Disciplinary, Moral and Ascetical Works*, trans. R. Arbesmann, E. J. Daly, and E. A. Quain, vol. 40 of *The Fathers of the Church* (1959; repr.,Washington, DC: Catholic University of America Press, 2008), 99.

[10] John Wesley, "A Plain Account of Christian Perfection" in *The Works of John Wesley,* vol. 11 of *Thoughts, Addresses, Prayers, Letters* (1872; repr., Grand Rapids: Zondervan, n.d.), 444. On history and teaching of the Holiness Movement, see Charles Edwin Jones, *Perfectionist Persuasion: The Holiness Movement and American Methodism, 1867–1936* (Metuchen, NJ: Scarecrow Press, 1974); Delbert Rose, *Vital Holiness: A Theology of Christian Experience,* 3rd ed. (Minneapolis: Bethany Fellowship, 1975); and Wallace Thornton, *Radical Righteousness: Personal Ethics and the Development of the Holiness Movement* (Salem, OH: Schmul Publishing, 1998).

[11] Rousas Rushdoony, *Foundations of Social Order* (Fairfax, VA: Thoburn Press, 1978), 19. Lloyd-Jones makes this same point: "The great concern of the [early church councils] was doctrine: definition of doctrine and denunciation of error and heresy." D. Martyn Lloyd-Jones, "The Basis of Christian Unity," in *Knowing the Times* (Edinburgh: Banner of Truth, 1989), 154.

[12] One excellent study of biblical separation devotes several pages to these various separatist groups, notably the Donatists. See Ernest Pickering and Myron J. Houghton, *Biblical Separation: The Struggle for a Pure Church,* 2nd ed. (Schaumburg, IL: Regular Baptist Press, 2008), 15-45. This work is more cautious than many writings in treating these groups, and one cannot deny that they were separatists, whatever else they might have been. But one must be careful not to ignore serious doctrinal deviation simply because a person or group is separatistic; the authors warn against this tendency (33). On the theological problems with these early and medieval separatist groups, see James Edward McGoldrick, *Baptist Successionism: A Crucial Question in Baptist History* (Metuchen, NJ: Scarecrow Press, 1994.)

CHAPTER 2: SEPARATION IN THEOLOGICAL CONTEXT

[1] Cohen, for example, points out how Robert O. Ferm resorts to false antitheses in his criticism of separatism in *Cooperative Evangelism: Is Billy Graham Right or Wrong?* (Grand Rapids: Zondervan, 1958). See Gary G. Cohen, *Biblical Separation Defended: A Biblical Critique of Ten New Evangelical Arguments* (Philadelphia: Presbyterian and Reformed, 1966), 59. Moritz notes how *Christian Life* magazine in 1956 made a dichotomy between evangelism and contending for the faith. Fred Moritz, *"Be Ye Holy": The Call to Christian Separation* (Greenville, SC: Bob Jones University Press, 1994, 47.

[2] D. Martyn Lloyd-Jones, "The Basis of Christian Unity," in *Knowing the Times* (Edinburgh: Banner of Truth, 1989), 118–63.

[3] Ibid., 122.

[4] Ibid., 123.

[5] Ibid., 160.

[6] Ibid.

[7] D. Martyn Lloyd-Jones, "'Consider Your Ways': The Outline of a New Strategy," in *Knowing the Times*, 186.

[8] Ibid., 187.

[9] Peter Masters, *Stand for the Truth* (London: Sword and Trowel, 1996), 31.

[10] Although he was often critical of fundamentalism, Vernon Grounds offers a good distinction between separation and schism; see Vernon Grounds, "Separation Yes, Schism No," *Eternity*, August 1963, 17–22.

[11] L. Nelson Bell, "On 'Separation,'" *Christianity Today*, 8 October 1971, 26.

[12] The other verses are 3:17, 3:19, 6:14, 10:36, 11:27, 12:46, 16:28, and 18:37.

[13] One of Fred Moritz's themes is that evangelism is in fact a major purpose of separation. See Moritz, *"Be Ye Holy,"* 29–30, 47–48, 63–65, 91–92. Masters points out that this outreach can extend to those ensnared by false teaching: "We may show love to people who are in error by trying to win them to the Truth. . . . We may endeavour to reach them as *outsiders*, but we must never condone and recognize their teaching, for this is a high crime against the Word of God," *Stand for the Truth*, 14.

[14] Ronald Nash, *The New Evangelicalism* (Grand Rapids: Zondervan, 1963), 96. See also Donald Grey Barnhouse, "One Church," *Eternity*, July 1958, 20–21; and Walter R. Martin, "Love, Doctrine, and Fellowship: How Can We Put Them Together?" *Eternity*, November 1960, 22, 56. Martin does criticize love that "is not accompanied by confession of sound doctrine," but he accuses the "ultra-fundamentalists" of having forgotten "the bounds of Christian love" (56).

[15] Moritz, 64.

[16] The ideas discussed from this point in the chapter are examined more fully in Randy Leedy, "The Ethic of Love," *Biblical Viewpoint* 30, no. 1 (1996): 5–14.

[17] Ernest Pickering and Myron J. Houghton, *Biblical Separation: The Struggle for a Pure Church,* 2nd ed. (Schaumburg, IL: Regular Baptist Press, 2008), 205.

[18] D. G. Hart, *Defending the Faith: J. Gresham Machen and the Crisis of Conservative Protestantism in Modern America* (Baltimore: Johns Hopkins University Press, 1994), 166. Likewise Runia speaks of "an unscriptural perfectionism that looks for the 'pure' church." Klaas Runia, "When Is Separation a Christian Duty?" *Christianity Today*, 7 July 1967, 7.

[19] James B. Hunt, "The Faith Journey of Frederick Douglass, 1818–1895," *Christian Scholar's Review* 15 (1986): 235. A contrast to Douglass's situation is that of Richard Allen (1760-1831). He too was born a slave and was converted while still a slave. Allen's master, however, was deeply troubled by slavery, and he made a way for Allen to purchase his freedom. See *The Life Experience and Gospel Labors of the Rt. Rev. Richard Allen* (Nashville: Abingdon, 1960), 16–18.

²⁰ See Howard Edgar Moore, "The Emergence of Moderate Fundamentalism: John R. Rice and *The Sword of the Lord*" (PhD diss., George Washington University, 1990), 99–100, 131–32.

²¹ See Barry Hankins, *God's Rascal: J. Frank Norris and the Beginnings of Southern Fundamentalism* (Lexington: University Press of Kentucky), 127–30.

²² Randy Leedy notes that this reversal of love for God with love for others is the "basic problem" of the new evangelicals. "By failing to love God first and foremost, they misdefine the interests of men, or else ignore them entirely." "The Ethic of Love," 12.

CHAPTER 3: SEPARATION FROM THE WORLD

¹ For a thorough discussion of the question of worldliness in the Christian life, see Randy Leedy, *Love Not the World: Winning the War Against Worldliness* (Greenville, SC: Bob Jones University Press, 2012). See 68–69 in particular for a discussion of the definition of *world*.

² Ibid., 104–5.

³ Ibid., 55–56. Leedy suggests that these three descriptions in 1 John refer not to three categories of worldly temptations "but rather the aspects of fallen human nature that worldly things appeal to."

⁴ Earl Nutz, "Important Lessons: 1 John 2," *Biblical Viewpoint* 27, no. 1 (1993): 35.

⁵ Fred Moritz, *"Be Ye Holy": The Call to Christian Separation* (Greenville, SC: Bob Jones University Press, 1994), 53–54.

⁶ Ibid., 50.

⁷ See, e.g., Elton M. Eenigenburg, "Separatism Is Not Scriptural," *Eternity*, August 1963, 20; Donald Grey Barnhouse, "One Church," *Eternity*, July 1958, 20; and Walter R. Martin, "When Is Separation Necessary?" *Eternity*, January 1961, 30.

⁸ Eenigenburg, 20; see also Paul Barnett, *The Message of 2 Corinthians: Power in Weakness*, The Bible Speaks Today (Downers Grove, IL: InterVarsity Press, 1988), 130–31.

⁹ Klaas Runia, "When Is Separation a Christian Duty?" *Christianity Today*, 23 June 1967, 4.

¹⁰ It is worth noting that Charles Hodge, writing well before modern controversies over separation, thinks it wrong to limit the 2 Corinthians passage to just idolatry. He writes, "The principle applies to all the enemies of God and children of darkness. It is intimate voluntary association with the wicked that is forbidden." *An Exposition of the Second Epistle to the Corinthians* (1859; repr., Grand Rapids: Eerdmans, 1950), 166.

¹¹ Chester Tulga, *The Doctrine of Separation in These Times* (Chicago: Conservative Baptist Fellowship, 1952), 42.

¹² Ibid., 10.

¹³ Charles Hodge, *A Commentary on the Epistle to the Ephesians* (1856; repr., Grand Rapids: Baker, 1980), 292.

¹⁴ D. Edmond Hiebert, *The Thessalonian Epistles: A Call to Readiness* (Chicago: Moody Press, 1971), 67.

¹⁵ A good discussion of worldliness in Old Testament teaching is found in Leedy, 13–33. His argument rests particularly on this idea that desire to be like the nations is the common Old Testament expression of worldliness.

¹⁶ See Edward John Carnell, *The Case for Orthodox Theology* (Philadelphia: Westminster Press, 1959), 121.

¹⁷ See John W. V. Smith, *The Quest for Holiness and Unity: A Centennial History of the Church of God (Anderson, Indiana)* (Anderson, IN: Warner Press, 1980), 194–204.

¹⁸ Hiebert, 68.

CHAPTER 4: SEPARATION FROM FALSE TEACHERS

¹ Douglas R. McLachlan, *Reclaiming Authentic Fundamentalism* (Independence, MO: American Association of Christian Schools, 1993), 125.

² Rolland D. McCune, "Doctrinal Non-Issues in Historic Fundamentalism," *Detroit Baptist Theological Seminary Journal* 2 (1996): 171–85.

³ F. F. Bruce, *The Epistle to the Galatians: A Commentary on the Greek Text,* New International Greek Testament Commentary (Grand Rapids: Eerdmans, 1981), 81.

⁴ J. Gresham Machen, *Machen's Notes on Galatians* (Philadelphia: Presbyterian and Reformed, 1972), 47.

⁵ Martin Luther, "Preface to the Epistles of St. James and St. Jude," in *Word and Sacrament I,* ed. E. Theodore Bachmann, vol. 35 of *Luther's Works,* ed. Helmut T. Lehmann (Philadelphia: Muhlenburg Press, 1960), 396.

⁶ Machen, 49–50.

⁷ James Montgomery Boice, "Galatians," in *Romans Through Galatians,* Expositor's Bible Commentary, ed. Frank E. Gaebelein (Grand Rapids: Zondervan, 1976), 10:429.

⁸ D. Edmond Hiebert, *The Epistles of John: An Expositional Commentary* (Greenville, SC: Bob Jones University Press, 1991), 306.

⁹ For the interpretation of this passage as referring to the Second Coming, see R. W. Orr, "The Letters of John" in *A New Testament Commentary,* ed. G. C. D. Howley (Grand Rapids: Zondervan, 1969), 623. Dodd discusses the evidence for this view but ultimately concludes that the passage refers to Christ's incarnation. C. H. Dodd, *The Johannine Epistles,* Moffatt New Testament Commentary (New York: Harper and Brothers, 1946), 149.

¹⁰ Peter Masters, *Stand for the Truth* (London: Sword and Trowel, 1996), 11–12.

¹¹ Leon Morris, *The Epistle to the Romans* (Grand Rapids: Eerdmans, 1988), 539.

¹² Irenaeus, *Against Heresies*, 1.16.3. Irenaeus also claims that they were followers of the Nicolas who was one of the first deacons chosen by the church at Jerusalem (Acts 6:5), but this claim is disputed.

¹³ Sketching a hypothetical picture of complete apostasy, Hodge says that "a member may forsake his church or denomination" in such circumstances but warns, "Before a man leave of his own accord, let him be terribly sure the Lord Himself has removed that church's lampstand." Elton M. Eenigenburg, "Separatism Is Not Scriptural," *Eternity*, August 1963, 22.

¹⁴ Klaas Runia, "When Is Separation a Christian Duty?" *Christianity Today*, 23 June 1967, 4.

¹⁵ Ronald Nash, *The New Evangelicalism* (Grand Rapids: Zondervan, 1963), 94.

¹⁶ Runia, 4. Some might debate his use of the term *church* for Judaism, but his point is worth noting. Although many converted Jews continued to worship for a time in the synagogues (see, e.g., Acts 13:14–42; 17:1–4, 10, 17; 18:4, 19, 24–26), there was by the end of the first century a clear separation of Christianity from Judaism. This would be an example of withdrawal, but we should acknowledge that the Jews were also expelling the Christians.

¹⁷ See, e.g., Eenigenburg, 20.

¹⁸ Early American religious leader Roger Williams (ca. 1603–83) followed this interpretation of the parable of the tares in his controversy with the authorities of the Massachusetts Bay Colony. See Roger Williams, *The Bloudy Tenet of Persecution*, vol. 3 of *The Complete Writings of Roger Williams* (1963; repr., Eugene, OR: Wipf and Stock, 2007), 97–119. Noting Christ's identification of "the field" as "the world," he applied the passage not to the composition of the church but to the Christian's place in the state, particularly the Christian's lack of coercive power against non-Christians. Williams likewise notes the fact that no one may rightly use the parable to invalidate the Bible's commands concerning church discipline (110).

¹⁹ One example is the poignant testimony of a Christian led astray by liberalism in John P. Jewell, *The Long Way Home* (Nashville: Nelson, 1982).

²⁰ Admittedly there is a textual variant here. Some manuscripts do not have the phrase "from such turn away." However, the teaching is consistent with Paul's counsel to "flee these things" (1 Tim. 6:11) as well as other passages in his writings (Rom. 16:17; 2 Thess. 3:6).

CHAPTER 5: SEPARATION FROM DISOBEDIENT CHRISTIANS

[1] Fred Moritz, *"Be Ye Holy": The Call to Christian Separation* (Greenville, SC: Bob Jones University Press, 1994), 71.

[2] Edward John Carnell, *The Case for Orthodox Theology* (Philadelphia: Westminster Press, 1959), 130. Italics in original.

[3] What we describe here is more precisely called *corrective* church discipline, which concerns restoring an erring church member. There is also *formative* church discipline, which describes the church's process of education and discipleship that nurtures the believer in the faith. Christians hope that a proper formative discipline can reduce the likelihood of having to practice corrective discipline.

[4] See Charles Hodge, *Commentary on the First Epistle to the Corinthians* (1857; repr., Grand Rapids: Eerdmans, 1994), 85.

[5] Moritz, 76.

[6] Leon Morris, *The First and Second Epistles to the Thessalonians*, New International Commentary on the New Testament (Grand Rapids: Eerdmans, 1959), 251.

[7] For a discussion of the meaning of *disorderly*, see D. Edmond Hiebert, *The Thessalonian Epistles: A Call to Readiness* (Chicago: Moody Press, 1971), 235.

[8] John R. Rice, *Come Out or Stay In* (Nashville: Thomas Nelson, 1974), 206–10, 224–25; Jack Van Impe, *Heart Disease in Christ's Body* (Royal Oak, MI: Jack Van Impe Ministries, 1984), 158–61. Van Impe likewise argues for a narrow interpretation of 1 Corinthians 5:11 (156–58).

[9] See Brian S. Rosner, "'Drive Out the Wicked Person': A Biblical Theology of Exclusion," *Evangelical Quarterly* 71 (1999): 25–36. Not only does Rosner survey the Old Testament's teaching concerning exclusion from the congregation of Israel, but he also notes how New Testament passages on church discipline, such as 1 Corinthians 5, draw directly on Old Testament language and images.

[10] J. Gresham Machen, *Christianity and Liberalism* (1923; repr., Grand Rapids: Eerdmans, 1981), 50.

[11] Douglas R. McLachlan, *Reclaiming Authentic Fundamentalism* (Independence, MO: American Association of Christian Schools, 1993), 134.

[12] Donald Grey Barnhouse, "Thanksgiving and Warning," *Eternity*, September 1957, 9. Italics in original.

[13] Donald Grey Barnhouse, "One Church," *Eternity*, July 1958, 20.

[14] Walter R. Martin, "When Is Separation Necessary?" *Eternity*, January 1961, 30–31.

[15] Ernest Pickering and Myron Houghton also point out that in 1 Timothy 1:20 Paul uses the same language for the exclusion of Hymenaeus that he

uses in 1 Corinthians 5:5 of the immoral man in Corinth. Because 2 Timothy 2:17–18 describes Hymenaeus's error as saying that the resurrection is already past, this certainly seems to be another case of exclusion of a believer over doctrinal error. Ernest Pickering and Myron J. Houghton, *Biblical Separation: The Struggle for a Pure Church,* 2nd ed. (Schaumburg, IL: Regular Baptist Press, 2008), 265.

[16] See Rice, 217–35.

[17] Robert Lightner, "A Biblical Perspective on False Doctrine," *Bibliotheca Sacra* 142 (1985): 20–21.

[18] Bob Jones, *Scriptural Separation: "First and Second Degree"* (Greenville, SC: Bob Jones University Press, 1971), 1.

[19] Rolland McCune, "An Inside Look at Ecclesiastical Separation," Detroit Baptist Theological Seminary website, 7.

[20] Ibid., 6.

[21] John Ashbrook, *Axioms of Separation* (Mentor, OH: Here I Stand Books, n.d.), 22. Likewise McLachlan writes, "While Christian separation is an indispensable ingredient in the recipe for an authentic Christian life, it is not the single or only ingredient. No recipe for life is really palatable if it consists of only one ingredient" (139).

[22] For more on this idea, see David R. Shumate, "Separation Versus Limited Participation: Is There a Difference?" *Frontline,* May/June 2009, 12–16.

CHAPTER 6: FUNDAMENTALISM

[1] The best introduction to the history of fundamentalism, particularly for the lay Christian, is David O. Beale, *In Pursuit of Purity: American Fundamentalism Since 1850* (Greenville, SC: Unusual Publications, 1986); the book provides a clear narrative overview from a fundamentalist perspective. An older fundamentalist work, still helpful on some points, is George Dollar, *A History of Fundamentalism in America* (Greenville, SC: Bob Jones University Press, 1973). Useful interpretive studies of fundamentalism are found in two works by George Marsden: *Fundamentalism and American Culture: The Shaping of Twentieth-Century Evangelicalism, 1870–1925,* 2nd ed. (New York: Oxford University Press, 2006), and *Understanding Fundamentalism and Evangelicalism* (Grand Rapids: Eerdmans, 1991). A pioneering work on fundamentalist history still worth noting is Ernest Sandeen, *The Roots of Fundamentalism: British and American Millenarianism, 1800–1930* (Chicago: University of Chicago Press, 1970). A collection of short biographies of fundamentalist leaders is C. Allyn Russell, *Voices of American Fundamentalism* (Philadelphia: Westminster, 1976), though Russell is sometimes critical of fundamentalism. An interesting broad overview of the movement is John Fea, "Understanding the Changing Facade of Twentieth-Century American Protestant Fundamentalism:

Toward a Historical Definition," *Trinity Journal* 15 (1994): 181–99; Fea uses a chronological scheme similar to the one adopted in this chapter.

[2] This approach is probably best represented by the Fundamentalism Project sponsored by the University of Chicago, which has published several hefty volumes, such as Martin E. Marty and R. Scott Appleby, ed., *Fundamentalisms Observed* (Chicago: University of Chicago Press, 1991). An introduction to this approach is found in Marty and Appleby's *The Glory and the Power: The Fundamentalist Challenge to the Modern World* (Boston: Beacon Press, 1992). Critiques of this approach can be found in D. G. Hart, "Fundamentalism(s) Redux," *Evangelical Studies Bulletin*, Spring 1993, 2–4; and Mark Sidwell, "Defining Fundamentalism: A Question of Theology or Sociology?" *Biblical Viewpoint* 30, no. 2 (1996): 73–83.

[3] I wish to acknowledge my debt to my former teacher Edward Panosian for helping me to understand the church's progressive understanding of revealed truth. A brief summary of these ideas is found in Mark Sidwell, "Progressive Illumination in Church History," in *The Providence of God in History* by Edward M. Panosian, et al. (Greenville, SC: Bob Jones University Press, 1996), 37–43.

[4] For a good discussion of the historical place of inerrancy in Christian belief, see John D. Woodbridge, *Biblical Authority* (Grand Rapids: Zondervan, 1982).

[5] For a critique of George Marsden's position on this point, see John D. Woodbridge, "Is Biblical Inerrancy a Fundamentalist Doctrine?" *Bibliotheca Sacra* 142 (1985): 292–305.

[6] See Marsden, *Fundamentalism and American Culture*, 132–35.

[7] See Betty A. DeBerg, *Ungodly Women: Gender and the First Wave of American Fundamentalism* (Minneapolis: Fortress Press, 1990); and the more moderate Margaret Bendroth, *Fundamentalism and Gender, 1875 to the Present* (New Haven, CT: Yale University Press, 1993).

[8] Kirsopp Lake, *Religion of Yesterday and Tomorrow* (Boston: Houghton Mifflin, 1925), 61–62. One observer cautions against the use of this quotation by several fundamentalists (including the first edition of this book) as potentially oversimplified. See Kevin T. Bauder, "Fundamentalism: Whence? Where? Whither? Part 2," *In the Nick of Time*, SharperIron, http://sharper-iron.org/article/fundamentalism-whence-where-whither-part-2 (accessed 1 June 2015). The warning is well taken, particularly because Lake means no compliment. However, I use the quotation to illustrate that regardless of whatever particular historical and cultural features fundamentalism possesses, the movement does stand at its core in continuity with historic orthodoxy as expressed in the creeds, confessions, and other significant doctrinal affirmations of the Christian church.

[9] For an overview of this "establishment," see Martin Marty, *Righteous Empire: The Protestant Experience in America* (New York: Dial Press),

1970; Timothy L. Smith, *Revivalism and Social Reform in Mid-Nineteenth-Century America* (New York: Abingdon, 1957); and Mark Noll, *A History of Christianity in the United States and Canada* (Grand Rapids: Eerdmans, 1992), 163–90, 219–44, 286–309. David Beale views the Prayer Meeting Revival and related movements such as Britain's '59 Revival as the primary progenitor of fundamentalism (13–33).

[10] For an overview of the division of Protestant thought in this period, see Marsden, *Understanding Fundamentalism*, 9–61; Ferenc Morton Szasz, *The Divided Mind of Protestant America*, 1880–1930 (Tuscaloosa: University of Alabama Press, 1982); and Martin E. Marty, *The Irony of It All*, vol. 1 of *Modern American Religion* (Chicago: University of Chicago Press, 1986), 208–47.

[11] On the development and impact of premillennialism, see Timothy P. Weber, *Living in the Shadow of the Second Coming: American Premillennialism 1875–1982* (Grand Rapids: Zondervan, 1983).

[12] On the history of the Bible conference movement, see Sandeen, 132–61; and Mark Sidwell, "Come Apart and Rest a While: The Origin of the Bible Conference Movement in America," *Detroit Baptist Seminary Journal* 15 (2010): 75–98. The text of Niagara's creed is found in Beale, Appendix A, 375–79.

[13] On the history of fundamentalist Bible schools, see Virginia Brereton, *Training God's Army: The American Bible School, 1880–1940* (Bloomington: Indiana University Press, 1990).

[14] One critical history is C. Norman Kraus, *Dispensationalism in America: Its Rise and Development* (Richmond, VA: John Knox Press, 1958). A favorable, more theologically oriented work from within the movement is Charles Ryrie, *Dispensationalism* (Chicago: Moody Press, 1995). For an interesting liberal view of dispensationalism, see Marty, *The Irony of It All*, 218–32. On Scofield and the impact of his reference Bible, see R. Todd Mangum and Mark S. Sweetnam, *The Scofield Bible: Its History and Impact on the Evangelical Church* (Colorado Springs: Paternoster Publishing, 2009).

[15] On the influence of Holiness teaching on fundamentalism, see Marsden, *Fundamentalism and American Culture*, 72–101. For a history and critique of Keswick theology, see Andrew David Naselli, "Keswick Theology: A Survey and Analysis of the Doctrine of Sanctification in the Early Keswick Movement," *Detroit Baptist Seminary Journal* 13 (2008): 17–67.

[16] On Princeton and its influence, see Mark Noll, ed., *The Princeton Theology: 1812–1921* (Grand Rapids: Baker, 1983).

[17] R. A. Torrey, A. C. Dixon, et al., *The Fundamentals: A Testimony to the Truth*, 4 vols. (1917; repr., Grand Rapids: Baker, 1988). On the background of the pamphlets, see Gerald L. Priest, "A. C. Dixon, Chicago Liberals, and *The Fundamentals*," *Detroit Baptist Seminary Journal* 1 (1996): 113–34.

[18] On the Presbyterian struggles, see Beale, 113–51; for a liberal viewpoint on this topic, see Lefferts Loetscher, *The Broadening Church* (Philadelphia: University of Pennsylvania Press, 1954).

[19] There is no satisfactory history of the entire Fundamentalist-Modernist Controversy. See the relevant sections in Beale for a survey. For an interesting liberal overview, see Martin E. Marty, *The Noise of Conflict 1919–1941*, vol. 2 of *Modern American Religion* (Chicago: University of Chicago Press, 1991), 155–214.

[20] On the WCFA, see Nathan V. Lentfer, "A History of the World's Christian Fundamentals Association (1919–1952)" (PhD diss., Bob Jones University, 2011); and Beale, 97–109. On Riley, see William Vance Trollinger, *God's Empire: William Bell Riley and Midwestern Fundamentalism* (Madison: University of Wisconsin Press, 1991).

[21] Quoted in Beale, 195.

[22] Quoted in Beale, 206.

[23] For an overview of the Baptist controversies, probably the best source is Kevin Bauder and Robert Delnay, *One in Hope and Doctrine: Origins of Baptist Fundamentalism 1870–1950* (Schaumburg, IL: Regular Baptist Books, 2014). See also Beale, 173–242, and Dollar, 145–72.

[24] On the history of the BBU, see Robert Delnay, *A History of the Baptist Bible Union* ([Winston-Salem]: Piedmont Bible College, 1974); see also Bauder and Delnay, *One in Hope and Doctrine*. On Norris, see Barry Hankins's critical but perceptive biography, *God's Rascal: J. Frank Norris and the Beginnings of Southern Fundamentalism* (Lexington: University Press of Kentucky, 1996).

[25] On the Presbyterian controversy, see Bradley Longfield, *The Presbytery Controversy: Fundamentalists, Modernists, and Moderates* (New York: Oxford University Press, 1991); also still useful is Edwin Rian, *The Presbyterian Conflict* (1940; repr., Philadelphia: Committee for the Historian of the Orthodox Presbyterian Church, 1992). On Machen, see D. G. Hart, *Defending the Faith: J. Gresham Machen and the Crisis of Conservative Protestantism in Modern America* (Baltimore: Johns Hopkins University Press, 1994).

[26] A fairly evenhanded study of the Scopes Trial is Edward J. Larson, *Summer for the Gods: The Scopes Trial and America's Continuing Debate over Science and Religion* (New York: Basic Books, 1997).

[27] The best overview of this period is Joel Carpenter, *Revive Us Again: The Reawakening of American Fundamentalism* (New York: Oxford University Press, 1997). For an earlier and much more critical survey of the same period, see Louis Gasper, *The Fundamentalist Movement 1930–1956* (1963; repr., Grand Rapids: Baker, 1981). For the rise of independent missions in particular, see the four essays in Joel Carpenter and Wilbert R. Shenk, ed., *Earthen Vessels: American Evangelicals and Foreign Missions, 1880–1980* (Grand Rapids: Eerdmans, 1990), 29–132.

[28] On fundamentalist's use of mass media, see Douglas Carl Abrams, *Selling the Old-Time Religion: American Fundamentalists and Mass Culture, 1920–1940* (Athens: University of Georgia Press, 2001) and Carpenter, *Revive Us Again*, 139.

[29] See William G. McLoughlin, "Is There a Third Force in Christendom?" in *Religion in America*, ed. William G. McLoughlin and Robert N. Bellah (Boston: Houghton Mifflin, 1968), 45–72.

[30] Ernest Pickering and Myron J. Houghton, *Biblical Separation: The Struggle for a Pure Church*, 2nd ed. (Schaumburg, IL: Regular Baptist Press, 2008), 112–15. The authors note that this difference in philosophy also marked the organizations that gave rise to the GARBC and CBA, the BBU and the Fundamentalist Fellowship, respectively (108–10).

[31] Billy Graham, "The Lost Chord of Evangelism," *Christianity Today*, 1 April 1957, 26.

[32] On this conference, see Howard Edgar Moore, "The Emergence of Moderate Fundamentalism: John R. Rice and 'The Sword of the Lord'" (PhD diss., George Washington University, 1990), 274–76. The actual pledge with its signatories is "Resolutions on Evangelism," mimeograph, December 26–27 [1958], Folder: Jones, Bob, 1883–1968, Fundamentalism File, Mack Library, Bob Jones University.

[33] On the split in the CBA, see Beale, 289–301, for a fundamentalist perspective, and Bruce Shelley, *A History of Conservative Baptists* (Wheaton: Conservative Baptist Press, 1971, 1981), 69–102, for the majority perspective.

[34] On this congress, see Elmer L. Rumminger, "Special Report: World Congress of Fundamentalists," *Faith for the Family*, September/October 1976, 3–10.

[35] Carl Henry, "Wavering Evangelical Initiative," *Christianity Today*, 16 January 1976, 33.

[36] This section on history since the 1970s focuses on the internal struggles within fundamentalism. Other forces in evangelicalism and the religious world in general also challenged the movement. For a good survey of these external forces since the 1970s, see Chapter 10 in Pickering and Houghton, *Biblical Separation*, 165–87.

[37] On Rice's position, see John R. Rice, "Separation from Infidels, Not from Good Christians," *Sword of the Lord*, 2 September 1969, 1, 9–10, and "The Problem of Secondary Separation," *Sword of the Lord*, 2 March 1973, 1, 14–15. On McIntire's criticisms, see Carl McIntire, "The World Congress of Fundamentalists," *Christian Beacon*, 4 March 1976, 3–4, 7, and "The New Fundamentalism," *Christian Beacon*, 11 March 1976, 3–4, 7.

[38] It is difficult to find a balanced history of the KJV-only movement. Compact and more evenhanded than most, although still critical, is Jeffrey P.

Straub, "Fundamentalism and the King James Version: How a Venerable English Translation Became a Litmus Test for Orthodoxy," *Southern Baptist Journal of Theology* 15, no. 4 (2011): 44–62. In defense of the pro-KJV position, see Edward F. Hills, *The King James Version Defended: A Christian View of the New Testament Manuscripts* (Des Moines, IA: Christian Research Press, 1956); and David Otis Fuller, ed., *Which Bible?* 5th ed. (Grand Rapids: Institute for Biblical Textual Studies, 1990). For critiques, see James R. White, *The King James Only Controversy: Can You Trust the Modern Translations?* (Minneapolis: Bethany House, 1995); J. B. Williams, ed., *From the Mind of God to the Mind of Man: A Layman's Guide to How We Got Our Bible* (Greenville, SC: Ambassador-Emerald International, 1999); and Roy E. Beacham and Kevin T. Bauder, ed., *One Bible Only? Examining Exclusive Claims for the King James Bible* (Grand Rapids: Kregel Publications, 2001). An attempt to balance the discussion, written by advocates of the eclectic and Majority texts, respectively, is Sam Schnaiter and Ron Tagliapietra, *Bible Preservation and the Providence of God* ([Philadelphia]: Xlibris, 2002).

[39] See, e.g., the statement on "Scriptures" by the Independent Baptist Fellowship of North America, which states a preference for the KJV in its conferences but allows liberty to individuals and congregations. http://www.ibfna.org/v2/index.php/founding-documents/articles-of-faith (accessed 29 May 2015). On the other side, see the statement of Heartland Baptist Bible College on "The Scriptures" which affirms the superiority of the KJV as a doctrinal marker. http://heartlandbaptist.edu/about/doctrinal-statement/ (accessed 29 May 2015).

[40] Earle Cairns, *Christianity Through the Centuries*, 3rd ed. (Grand Rapids: Zondervan, 1996), 485.

[41] Bob Jones, "Pseudo-Fundamentalists: The New Breed in Sheep's Clothing," *Faith for the Family*, January 1978, 7, 16. Jones says that the term *pseudo-fundamentalism* was apparently coined by fundamentalist pastor Rod Bell.

[42] See George Marsden, *Understanding Fundamentalism and Evangelicalism* (Grand Rapids: Eerdmans, 1991), 76–81; and C. T. McIntire, "Fundamentalism" in *Evangelical Dictionary of Theology*, ed. Walter Elwell (Grand Rapids: Baker, 1984), 433–36. The terminology is not always exact. Jack Van Impe, for example, accuses militant fundamentalists of being neo-fundamentalist because they represent, he claims, a change from historic fundamentalism. Jack Van Impe, *Heart Disease in Christ's Body* (Royal Oak, MI: Jack Van Impe Ministries, 1984), 25–26. When fundamentalists began to use the term *pseudo-fundamentalism*, some neo-fundamentalists retorted that the militants were the pseudo-fundamentalists. See Ed Dobson and Ed Hindson, "Who Are the 'Real' Pseudo-Fundamentalists?" *Fundamentalist Journal*, June 1983, 10–11; and Daniel R. Mitchell, "The Siege-Mentality of Pseudo-Fundamentalism" *Fundamentalist Journal*, February 1987, 59.

[43] The basic position of neo-fundamentalism is set out in Jerry Falwell, Ed Dobson, and Ed Hindson, *The Fundamentalist Phenomenon: The Resurgence of Conservative Christianity* (Garden City, NY: Doubleday-Galilee, 1981); and Edward Dobson, *In Search of Unity: An Appeal to Fundamentalists and Evangelicals* (Nashville: Thomas Nelson, 1985). Also numerous articles in Falwell's periodical *Fundamentalist Journal* (published 1982–89) set forth the neo-fundamentalist position.

[44] Falwell, et al., *The Fundamentalist Phenomenon*, 24–25.

[45] Ibid., 139–40, 158-59; Dobson, *In Search of Unity*, 63–64.

[46] Falwell, et al., *The Fundamentalist Phenomenon*, 167–72, 221–23; Dobson, *In Search of Unity*, 136–39.

[47] For a sample of fundamentalist objections to the Moral Majority, see Bob Jones III, "The Moral Majority," *Faith for the Family*, September 1980, 3, 27–28.

[48] Bob Jones III, "The Ultimate Ecumenism," *Faith for the Family*, September 1985, 3, 9–10.

[49] Falwell states his opposition to the charismatic movement and to having charismatic students at Liberty in "Open Letter from Jerry Falwell," *Journal Champion*, 18 August 1978, 2. On his reversal, see Stephen Strang, "Revival in Lynchburg?" *Charisma*, October 1997, 122.

[50] Fundamentalist reports of Van Impe's sympathy to Catholicism are found in "The Capitulation of Dr. Jack Van Impe to Roman Catholicism and the One World Ecumenical Movement," *Fundamentalist Digest,* July–August 1995, 7–17; and Frank McClelland, "Van Impe's TV Attack on Dr. Paisley," *Revivalist*, November 1995, 3–4.

[51] C. T. McIntire, "Fundamentalism," 435.

[52] Fea, 195, cites two sources that estimate the number fundamentalists to be between 4 and 4.5 million.

[53] Millard Erickson, *The New Evangelical Theology* (Westwood, NJ: Revell, 1968), 203–4.

[54] Robert L. Sumner, review of *In Pursuit of Purity: American Fundamentalism Since 1850*, by David O. Beale, *The Biblical Evangelist*, 1 December 1986, 2, 4–5.

[55] Harold O. J. Brown, *Heresies: The Image of Christ in the Mirror of Heresy and Orthodoxy from the Apostles to the Present* (Garden City, NY: Doubleday, 1984), 29–30. He also likens fundamentalism to heresy in stressing only selected doctrines (30). John W. Sanderson, although more sympathetic to fundamentalism, makes the same charge of reductionism in "Fundamentalism and Its Critics," *Sunday School Times*, 21 January 1961, 66.

[56] Ronald Nash, *The New Evangelicalism* (Grand Rapids: Zondervan, 1963), 91.

[57] Fred Moritz, *"Be Ye Holy": The Call to Christian Separation* (Greenville, SC: Bob Jones University Press, 1994), 97.

⁵⁸ "Christian liberty" was one of the causes of the division in 1937 between the Orthodox Presbyterian Church and the Bible Presbyterian Church. See George Marsden, "Perspectives on the Division of 1937," in *Pressing Toward the Mark: Essays Commemorating Fifty Years of the Orthodox Presbyterian Church*, ed. Charles G. Dennison and Richard C. Gamble (Philadelphia: Orthodox Presbyterian Church, 1986), 295–328.

⁵⁹Arie den Hartog, "Fundamentalism and Our Reformed Heritage," *Standard Bearer*, 1 January 1977, 159. See also Andrew Sandlin, "The Truncated Vision of Modern Fundamentalism: A Review Essay," *Chalcedon Report*, January 1997, 27–30.

⁶⁰ Milton L. Rudnick, *Fundamentalism and the Missouri Synod* (St. Louis: Concordia, 1966), 84–85. One of Rudnick's complaints is that some fundamentalists remain in denominations containing liberals despite the Bible's teaching in Romans 16:17, 2 Corinthians 6:14–16, Galatians 5:9, and Titus 3:9–11 (85).

⁶¹ David E. Gonnella, "Why I Am Not a Fundamentalist," *Baptist Challenge*, July 1990, 6.

CHAPTER 7: LIBERALISM

¹ Quoted in J. H. Merle d'Aubigné, *The Triumph of Truth: A Life of Martin Luther* (Greenville, SC: Bob Jones University Press, 1996), 327. Italics in original.

² René Descartes, *A Discourse on the Method,* trans. Ian Maclean (Oxford: Oxford University Press, 2006), 34.

³ Immanuel Kant, *Religion Within the Limits of Reason Alone,* trans. Theodore M. Greene and Hoyt H. Hudson (1934; repr., New York: Harper Torchbooks, 1960), 123. For a survey of the philosophical background of liberalism, see Justo L. González, *A History of Christian Thought* (Nashville: Abingdon, 1975), 3:290–318.

⁴ For a conservative overview of biblical criticism, see David S. Dockery, Kenneth A. Mathews, Robert B. Sloan, ed., *Foundations for Biblical Interpretation* (Nashville: Broadman and Holman, 1994), 187–231, 396–453.

⁵ R. A. Torrey, "Methods of Bible Study," in *The New Topical Textbook,* rev. ed. (Chicago: Revell, 1897), xii.

⁶ Adolf von Harnack, *What Is Christianity?* trans. Thomas Bailey Saunders (London: Williams and Norgate, 1901), 51–77.

⁷ A brief history of liberal theology up to the twentieth century is Bernard Ramm, "The Fortunes of Theology from Schleiermacher to Barth and Bultmann," in *Tensions in Contemporary Theology*, ed. Stanley N. Gundry and Alan F. Johnson (Chicago: Moody, 1976), 15–41.

⁸ For an overview of the growth of liberalism among American Protestants, see David O. Beale, *In Pursuit of Purity: American*

Fundamentalism Since 1850 (Greenville, SC: Unusual Publications, 1986), 70–86; Ferenc Morton Szasz, *The Divided Mind of Protestant America, 1880–1930* (Tuscaloosa: University of Alabama Press, 1982), 1–55; and Martin E. Marty, *The Irony of It All*, vol. 1 of *Modern American Religion* (Chicago: University of Chicago Press, 1986), 15–43. A standard liberal work on the topic is Kenneth Cauthen, *The Impact of American Religious Liberalism*, 2nd ed. (Washington, DC: University Press of America, 1983). Also very helpful are three volumes by Gary Dorrien: *The Making of American Liberal Theology: Imagining Progressive Religion, 1805–1900* (Louisville: Westminster John Knox Press, 2001); *The Making of American Liberal Theology: Idealism, Realism, and Modernity, 1900–1950* (Louisville, KY: Westminster John Knox Press, 2003); and *The Making of American Liberal Theology: Crisis, Irony, and Postmodernity 1950–2005* (Louisville: Westminster John Knox Press, 2006).

[9] See Gerald L. Priest, "A. C. Dixon, Chicago Liberals, and *The Fundamentals*," *Detroit Baptist Seminary Journal* 1 (1996): 113–34.

[10] Rauschenbusch summarizes his views in *A Theology for the Social Gospel* (New York: Macmillan, 1917).

[11] H. Richard Niebuhr, *The Kingdom of God in America* (1935; repr., Hamden, CT: Shoe String Press, 1956), 193.

[12] For a survey of the various schools of modern theology, see David L. Smith, *A Handbook of Contemporary Theology* (Wheaton: BridgePoint, 1992); William Hordern, *A Layman's Guide to Protestant Theology*, rev. ed. (1968; repr., Eugene, OR: Wipf and Stock, 2002); and Paul Enns. *The Moody Handbook of Theology*, 3rd ed. (Chicago: Moody Press, 2014). In many ways, the best critique of liberalism is still J. Gresham Machen, *Christianity and Liberalism* (1923; repr., Grand Rapids: Eerdmans, 1981).

[13] Good introductory critiques of postmodernism are Douglas Groothuis, *Truth Decay: Defending Christianity Against the Challenges of Postmodernism* (Downers Grove, IL: InterVarsity Press, 2000); and Gene Edward Veith, Jr., *Postmodern Times: A Christian Guide to Contemporary Thought and Culture* (Wheaton: Crossway Books, 1994).

[14] *Proslogion* (trans. Sidney Norton Deane), Chap. 1.

[15] For a popularly written example of liberalism's continued rejection of orthodox Christianity, see John Shelby Spong, *Rescuing the Bible from Fundamentalism* (San Francisco: Harper, 1991), a best-selling summary of modern liberal views of the Bible.

[16] See Clarence Macartney, "Shall Unbelief Win? An Answer to Dr. Fosdick" in *Sermons That Shaped America: Reformed Preaching from 1630 to 2001*, ed. William S. Barker and Samuel T. Logan Jr. (Phillipsburg, NJ: P&R Publishing, 2003), 323–43.

[17] Machen, 160.

CHAPTER 8: NEO-ORTHODOXY

[1] William Hordern, *The Case for a New Reformation Theology* (Philadelphia: Westminster Press, 1959), 161.

[2] Ibid., 17.

[3] The best introduction to neo-orthodoxy from within the movement is Hordern's *Case for a New Reformation Theology*. The best scholarly critique of neo-orthodoxy is probably Cornelius Van Til, *The New Modernism: An Appraisal of the Theology of Barth and Brunner*, 3rd ed. (N.p.: Presbyterian and Reformed, 1973). A good popular-level critique is Charles Caldwell Ryrie, *Neo-Orthodoxy* (Chicago: Moody Press, 1956). See also Robert L. Reymond, *Introductory Studies in Contemporary Theology* (Philadelphia: Presbyterian and Reformed, 1968), 73–153.

[4] Barth's own writings are enormously complex. Perhaps the most accessible works by Barth (which are not a systematic review of his views, however) are *Evangelical Theology: An Introduction*, trans. Grover Foley (New York: Holt, Rinehart and Winston, 1963); and *Dogmatics in Outline*, trans. G. T. Thompson (London: SCM Press, 1949).

[5] Donald Grey Barnhouse, "An Interview with Karl Barth," *Eternity*, April 1984, 20. This article is a reprint of the original interview.

[6] Carl F. H. Henry, *Confessions of a Theologian: An Autobiography* (Waco: Word Books, 1986), 210–11. To Barth's comment about "Christianity *Today* or Christianity *Yesterday*," Henry replied, "*Yesterday, today, and forever.*"

[7] Bernard Ramm, *After Fundamentalism: The Future of Evangelical Theology* (San Francisco: Harper and Row, 1983), 76–79.

[8] See, e.g., Van Til, 405–7, 418–20.

[9] A typical, if early, statement of Brunner's views is *The Mediator*, trans. Olive Wyon (New York: Macmillan, 1934).

[10] Hordern, 68–69.

[11] The most readable introduction to Reinhold Niebuhr is his memoir, *Leaves from the Notebook of a Tamed Cynic* (San Francisco: Harper and Row, 1929); for a sample of his more substantial works, see *An Interpretation of Christian Ethics* (New York: Harper and Brothers, 1935). For important works of H. Richard Niebuhr, see *The Kingdom of God in America* (1935; repr., Hamden, CT: Shoe String Press, 1956); and *Christ and Culture* (New York: Harper, 1951).

[12] Ryrie, 12.

[13] Charles W. Kegley and Robert W. Bretall, ed., *Reinhold Niebuhr: His Religious, Social, and Political Thought* (New York: Macmillan, 1956), 11. In fairness to Niebuhr, we should note that he is here criticizing the liberals' view of sin, saying that they excuse their denial of human sinfulness by rejecting the story of Adam. Niebuhr does not believe in the story of Adam either, but he affirms human sinfulness.

[14] Reinhold Niebuhr, *Beyond Tragedy* (New York: Charles Scribner's Sons, 1937), 30.

[15] Probably the most famous works by Bonhoeffer are *The Cost of Discipleship*, trans. R. H. Fuller (New York: Macmillan, 1959); and *Letters and Papers from Prison*, ed. Eberhard Bethge, rev. ed. (New York: Macmillan, 1967).

[16] Hordern, 62.

[17] Ryrie, 62.

[18] Bonhoeffer, *The Cost of Discipleship*, 36.

[19] Van Til, 2.

[20] Alan Cairns, *Apostles of Error* (Greenville, SC: Faith Presbyterian Church, 1989), [11].

[21] Ibid., [12].

[22] See John D. Woodbridge, "A Neoorthodox Historiography Under Siege," *Bibliotheca Sacra* 142 (1985): 3–15; and "The Rogers and McKim Proposal in the Balance," *Bibliotheca Sacra* 142 (1985): 99–113. Rogers and McKim present their view of the history of inerrancy in *The Authority and Interpretation of the Bible: An Historical Approach* (San Francisco: Harper and Row, 1979).

[23] Donald G. Bloesch, *The Future of Evangelical Christianity: A Call for Unity amid Diversity* (Garden City, NY: Doubleday, 1983), 165. Some of his criticisms of neo-orthodoxy are found on 48. Bloesch identifies the school where he teaches, University of Dubuque Theological Seminary, as one of the few schools still reflecting "motifs associated with neo-orthodoxy" (48). He lists numerous mainline and evangelical theologians, denominations, periodicals, and publishing houses that he says "maintain the salient emphases of neo-orthodoxy" (46–47).

[24] Cairns, [12–13], warns about the influence of neo-orthodox ideas in even "Fundamentalist and Bible-believing churches." He is particularly concerned about faith being based on a decision or series of decisions "rather than on the Person and work of the Lord Jesus Christ."

CHAPTER 9: EVANGELICALISM

[1] For a brief history of the use of the word *evangelical*, see Alister McGrath, *Evangelicalism and the Future of Christianity* (Downers Grove, IL: InterVarsity Press, 1995), 19–23.

[2] On the definition of *evangelicalism*, see Grant Wacker, *Augustus H. Strong and the Dilemma of Historical Consciousness* (Macon: Mercer University Press, 1985), 17; David Bebbington, *Evangelicalism in Modern Britain* (Grand Rapids: Baker, 1989), 4–17; and Harold John Ockenga, "Resurgent Evangelical Leadership," *Christianity Today*, 10 October 1960, 11.

[3] Joel Carpenter, *Revive Us Again: The Reawakening of American Fundamentalism* (New York: Oxford University Press, 1997), 195–204.

[4] On the history of the new evangelical movement, a perceptive analysis is George Marsden, *Reforming Fundamentalism: Fuller Seminary and the New Evangelicalism* (Grand Rapids: Eerdmans, 1987); see also Marsden's *Understanding Fundamentalism and Evangelicalism* (Grand Rapids: Eerdmans, 1991), 62–82. Also helpful, although openly favorable toward new evangelicalism, is Garth M. Rosell, *The Surprising Work of God: Harold John Ockenga, Billy Graham, and the Rebirth of Evangelicalism* (Grand Rapids: Baker, 2008). An early apologetic for the movement, highly critical of fundamentalism, is Ronald Nash, *The New Evangelicalism* (Grand Rapids: Zondervan, 1963). A helpful fundamentalist critique of the new evangelicalism is Ernest Pickering, *The Tragedy of Compromise: The Origin and Impact of the New Evangelicalism* (Greenville, SC: Bob Jones University Press, 1994). Even more exhaustive is Rolland McCune, *Promise Unfulfilled: The Failed Strategy of Modern Evangelicalism* (Greenville, SC: Ambassador International, 2004). Also useful is John Ashbrook, *The New Neutralism II* ([Mentor, OH]: Here I Stand Books, 1992), a sequel to an earlier critique by his father.

[5] The points in the following paragraphs, unless otherwise indicated, are from Harold J. Ockenga, "Foreword" to *The Battle for the Bible* by Harold Lindsell (Grand Rapids: Zondervan, 1976), [11–12].

[6] See "Is Evangelical Theology Changing?" *Christian Life*, March 1956, 19.

[7] Bob Jones, *Cornbread and Caviar: Reminiscences and Reflections* (Greenville, SC: Bob Jones University Press, 1985), 104.

[8] John W. Sanderson, "Neo-Evangelicalism and Its Critics," *Sunday School Times*, 28 January 1961, 82.

[9] "Harold John Ockenga's Press Release on 'The New Evangelicalism,'" Appendix B in Fred Moritz, *"Be Ye Holy": The Call to Christian Separation* (Greenville, SC: Bob Jones University Press, 1994), 118.

[10] Carl F. H. Henry, *The Uneasy Conscience of Modern Fundamentalism* (Grand Rapids: Eerdmans, 1947), 27.

[11] Robert Lon Horton, "The Christian's Role in Society," *Biblical Viewpoint* 15 (1981): 130–37; this article is an abstract of his dissertation. See also McCune, *Promise Unfulfilled*, 231–57. Examples of evangelical writings that take this approach are Ronald J. Sider, ed., *The Chicago Declaration* (Carol Stream, IL: Creation House, 1974); David O. Moberg, *The Great Reversal: Evangelism Versus Social Concern* (Philadelphia: Lippincott, 1972); and Ronald J. Sider, *Rich Christians in an Age of Hunger* (New York: Paulist Press, 1977). Former Senator Mark Hatfield, an evangelical social activist, says that to preach redemption without a stress on social action is to "preach only half the gospel." Mark Hatfield, *Conflict and Conscience* (Waco, TX: Word, 1971), 25.

[12] "Ockenga Press Release," 119.

[13] The standard biography of Graham is William C. Martin, *Prophet with Honor: The Billy Graham Story* (New York: Morrow, 1991). Also interesting is Graham's autobiography, *Just As I Am: The Autobiography of Billy Graham* (Grand Rapids: Zondervan, 1997).

[14] "Ockenga Press Release," 119.

[15] Millard Erickson, *The New Evangelical Theology* (Westwood, NJ: Revell, 1968), 212.

[16] Erickson, 198–99. For further defense of Graham's methodology, see Robert O. Ferm, *Cooperative Evangelism: Is Billy Graham Right or Wrong?* (Grand Rapids: Zondervan, 1958). For responses to Ferm's work, see Gary G. Cohen, *Biblical Separation Defended: A Biblical Critique of Ten New Evangelical Arguments* (Philadelphia: Presbyterian and Reformed, 1966); and John R. Rice, *Earnestly Contending for the Faith* (Murfreesboro, TN.: Sword of the Lord, 1965), 249–309.

[17] John G. Stackhouse Jr., "Generic Evangelicalism," in *Four Views on the Spectrum of Evangelicalism,* ed. Andrew David Naselli and Collin Hansen (Grand Rapids: Zondervan, 2011), 116–42.

[18] David O. Beale, *In Pursuit of Purity: American Fundamentalism Since 1850* (Greenville, SC: Unusual Publications, 1986), 261, 267.

[19] "Is Evangelical Theology Changing?" 18–19.

[20] Lindsell, 106-21.

[21] Richard Quebedeaux, *The Young Evangelicals: Revolution in Orthodoxy* (New York: Harper and Row, 1974); and *The Worldly Evangelicals* (New York: Harper and Row, 1978).

[22] See *The Young Evangelicals*, 37, 39; and *The Worldly Evangelicals*, 100.

[23] See *The Young Evangelicals*, 106; and *The Worldly Evangelicals*, 16, 17, 119, 128–30.

[24] James Davison Hunter, *Evangelicalism: The Coming Generation* (Chicago: University of Chicago Press, 1987). He lists the sixteen participating schools on 9.

[25] Ibid., 24.

[26] Ibid., 36.

[27] Ibid., 59.

[28] Ibid., 174-75.

[29] See "Passing It On: Will Our Kids Recognize Our Faith?" *World,* 11 March 1989, 5–6.

[30] Barna Group, "Barna Survey Examines Changes in Worldview Among Christians over the Past 13 Years," 2009, https://www.barna.org/barna-update/article/21-transformation/252-barna-survey-examines-changes-in-worldview-among-christians-over-the-past-13-years#.VaZ0I6PD9jo (accessed 15 July 2015).

[31] In the early twenty-first century, fundamentalists faced the challenge of what became known as the "young fundamentalists." A survey of fundamentalists conducted in 2005 surveying over a thousand respondents ages 18 to 35 helped popularize this label for this loosely defined movement. As with Hunter's survey of young evangelicals, the survey shows younger fundamentalists to be more conservative than both their secular and evangelicals peers. Yet the survey also shows some differences with the older generation of fundamentalists, such as a greater tolerance of differing music styles and a belief that many personal standards of dress and behavior have no biblical basis. See Jason Janz, *Young Fundamentalists' Beliefs and Personal Life Survey Findings* (Fleetwood, PA: Right Ideas Inc., 2005), available at http://sharperiron.org/downloads/2005%20Young%20Fundamentalists%20Survey%20Results.pdf (accessed 1 June 2015). The young fundamentalists lack a unified agenda but generally share several concerns. They desire more emphasis on expository preaching and argue that some fundamentalist behavioral standards are merely preferences that have degenerated into legalistic standards. They also question whether all fundamentalist standards of personal separation are scripturally valid, and they argue that fundamentalists apply ecclesiastical separation (particularly from other professing Christians) inconsistently and even erroneously. Some fundamentalists have seriously weighed these concerns while others have expressed concern that the young fundamentalists are following the downward path of earlier would-be reformers such as the new evangelicals. For a brief statement of young fundamentalist concerns, see Aaron Blumer, "Toward a Positive Agenda for Young Fundamentalists," SharperIron, http://sharperiron.org/article/toward-positive-agenda-for-young-fundamentalists (accessed 1 June 2015). Blumer says young fundamentalists "are those who still identify with Fundamentalism in some way but want to see what remains of the movement go in a new direction. . . . Most emphasize that more love and unity and better handling of Scripture are desperately needed." Blumer also mentions the inspiration provided to the movement by the publication of Douglas R. McLachlan's *Reclaiming Authentic Fundamentalism* in 1993 as an unusual example of fundamentalist self-criticism. For a fundamentalist critique of the movement see Chris Anderson, "The Young Fundamentalists: Déjà Vu," *The Ohio Bible Fellowship Visitor,* 1 May 2005, available at http://obfvisitor.wordpress.com/2005/05/01/young-fundamentalists-deja-vu/ (accessed 1 June 2015).

[32] See Clark H. Pinnock, *A Defense of Biblical Infallibility* (Philadelphia: Presbyterian and Reformed, 1967); and *Biblical Revelation: The Foundation of Christian Theology* (Chicago: Moody, 1971).

[33] See Rex A. Koivisto, "Clark Pinnock and Inerrancy: A Change in Truth Theory?" *Journal of the Evangelical Theological Society* 24 (1981): 139–51. Pinnock replied to this article but admitted to many of the changes. Clark Pinnock, "A Response to Rex A. Koivisto," *Journal of the Evangelical Theological Society* 24 (1981): 153–55.

[34] See Daniel Strange, "Clark H. Pinnock: The Evolution of an Evangelical Maverick," *Evangelical Quarterly* 71 (1999): 313.

[35] Clark H. Pinnock, "The Destruction of the Finally Impenitent," *Criswell Theological Review* 4 (1990): 243–59.

[36] Clark Pinnock, "Does Christian Unity Require Some Form of Papal Primacy?" *Journal of Ecumenical Studies* 35 (1998): 380–82. He wrote of the pope at that time, "For myself I would say John Paul II is already my pope. I respect him and pray for him" (381).

[37] On Pinnock's views on open theism, see Clark H. Pinnock, *Most Moved Mover: A Theology of God's Openness* (Grand Rapids: Baker Academic, 2001).

[38] Quoted in Robert E. Kofahl, "Billy Graham Believes Catholic Doctrine of Salvation Without Bible, Gospel, or Name of Christ," *Foundation*, May–June 1997, 22. For further discussion of the growth of this teaching among Evangelicals, see Dennis Okholm and Timothy Phillips, ed., *More Than One Way? Four Views on Salvation in a Pluralistic World* (Grand Rapids: Zondervan, 1995).

[39] *Four Views on the Spectrum of Evangelicalism* covers the fundamentalist view plus the confessional evangelical, the generic evangelical, and the post-conservative evangelical views.

[40] Douglas Sweeney notes how the early new evangelicals were similar to the fundamentalists in doctrine and outlook, arguing in part that they were more separatist than later evangelicals. See Douglas Sweeney, "Fundamentalism and the Neo-Evangelicals," *Fides et Historia* 24, no. 1 (1992): 81–96.

[41] See Steve Jeffery, Michael Ovey, and Andrew Sach, *Pierced for Our Transgressions: Rediscovering the Glory of Penal Substitution* (Wheaton: Crossway Books, 2007). Not all of the opponents of penal substitution discussed in this work consider themselves evangelicals, but professed evangelicals are among the critics the book answers. For example, the authors cite works by Joel B. Green of Fuller Theological Seminary, Brian McLaren of the emergent church movement, and books published by Zondervan, a leading evangelical publisher.

[42] This list is selected from Kevin T. Bauder, "Let's Get Clear on This," *Nick of Time*, 5 March 2010, http://www.centralseminary.edu/resources/nick-of-time/in-the-nick-of-time-archive/279-lets-get-clear-on-this (accessed 1 June 2015).

[43] An example of this contrast in contemporary Britain is the difference between evangelical author Iain Murray and Peter Masters, pastor of the Metropolitan Tabernacle in London. Murray has written critically of Billy Graham and the new evangelical movement but distances himself from American fundamentalism. See his *Evangelicalism Divided: A Record of Crucial Change in the Years 1950 to 2000* (Edinburgh: Banner of Truth, 2000). On the other hand, Masters has suggested that conservative

evangelicals in Britain might find it profitable to adopt the term *fundamentalist*. See his *Are We Fundamentalists?* (London: Sword & Trowel, 1995).

[44] R. Albert Mohler, commonly identified as a leading conservative evangelical, prefers the label *confessional evangelical* to stress the doctrinal basis of the position. See R. Albert Mohler, "Confessional Evangelicalism" in *Four Views on the Spectrum of Evangelicalism,* 68–96. Replying to Mohler in the same book, Stackhouse (104) raises the point that *confessional* usually refers to orthodox Christians asserting a particular confessional tradition, such as confessional Lutherans or confessional Presbyterians. He calls Mohler's position "conservative." Also in the same work Kevin Bauder notes that conservative evangelicals retain ties to other evangelicals (99).

[45] For several areas of disagreement between fundamentalists and conservative evangelicals, see Kevin Bauder, "A Fundamentalist Response," *Four Views on the Spectrum of Evangelicalism,* 97–99, especially the bulleted points on 99.

[46] Mike Riley, "On the Ministry of John Piper," *Frontline,* July/August 2005, 16.

[47] John Piper, "Praise God for Fundamentalists," 31 October 2007, http://www.desiringgod.org/blog/posts/praise-god-for-fundamentalists (accessed 2 June 2015). See also John Piper, "20 Reasons I Don't Take Potshots at Fundamentalists," 2 June 2008, http://www.desiringgod.org/articles/20-reasons-i-dont-take-potshots-at-fundamentalists.

[48] John Piper, "Billy Graham's Controversial Ministry," 7 January 2014. http://www.desiringgod.org/interviews/billy-graham-s-controversial-ministry (accessed 2 June 2015).

[49] A relatively balanced analysis of the moderate-conservative conflict in the SBC is Barry Hankins, *Uneasy in Babylon: Southern Baptist Conservatives and American Culture* (Tuscaloosa: University of Alabama Press, 2002).

[50] These schools are all discussed in Nancy L. deClaisse-Walford, "The Changing Face of Baptist Theological Students," *Review and Expositor* 95 (1998): 39–45. In her study she notes that students at these schools affirm central doctrines such as the deity and resurrection of Christ but are less concerned about teachings such as six-day creation, the historicity of Adam and Eve, and whether Jesus actually spoke the words attributed to Him in the New Testament. Another significant moderate seminary is Beeson Divinity School, located at Samford University in Birmingham, Alabama. With the ecumenically oriented conservative Timothy George as its dean, Beeson is a good example of the theologically inclusive moderate approach in the SBC. See "A Reformation & Revival Journal Interview with Dr. Timothy George," *Reformation & Revival Journal* 13 (2004): 133–64.

[51] Hankins, 9.

[52] Kevin Bauder, "Now, About Those Differences, Part Twenty-Four: Fellowship & the Evangelical Spectrum," *In the Nick of Time,* http://seminary

SET APART

.wcts1030.com/resources/nick-of-time/288-now-about-those-differences-pt-24 (accessed 1 June 2015). His point is that the standards for "institutional employment" in the schools and other bodies are good but should be applied to the SBC as a whole.

[53] Francis A. Schaeffer, *The Great Evangelical Disaster* (Westchester, IL: Crossway, 1984). See also John MacArthur, *Ashamed of the Gospel: When the Church Becomes Like the World* (Wheaton: Crossway, 1993). David F. Wells, *No Place for Truth, or Whatever Happened to Evangelical Theology?* (Grand Rapids: Eerdmans, 1992); David F. Wells, *God in the Wasteland: The Reality of Truth in a World of Fading Dreams* (Grand Rapids: Eerdmans, 1994).

[54] For criticism of the charismatic movement, see John MacArthur, *Charismatic Chaos* (Grand Rapids: Zondervan, 1992), and MacArthur's *Strange Fire: The Danger of Offending the Holy Spirit with Counterfeit Worship* (Nashville: Nelson, 2013). For protests against accommodation to Catholicism, see John MacArthur, *Reckless Faith: When the Church Loses Its Will to Discern* (Wheaton: Crossway, 1994), 119–52; and R. C. Sproul, *Faith Alone: The Evangelical Doctrine of Justification* (Grand Rapids: Baker, 1995).

[55] John W. Sanderson, "Purity of Testimony—or Opportunity?" *Sunday School Times*, 11 February 1961, 111.

[56] Jerry Huffman, "Separation—The Big 'S' Word," *Frontline*, January–February 1992, 5.

CHAPTER 10: THE CHARISMATIC MOVEMENT

[1] The most useful work on the history of Pentecostalism is Stanley M. Burgess and Eduard M. Van Der Maas, ed., *New International Dictionary of Pentecostal and Charismatic Movements,* rev. ed. (Grand Rapids: Zondervan, 2002). Also helpful are Stanley M. Burgess, ed., *Encyclopedia of Pentecostal and Charismatic Christianity* (New York: Routledge, 2006); Robert Mapes Anderson, *Vision of the Disinherited: The Making of American Pentecostalism* (New York: Oxford University Press, 1979); Vinson Synan, *The Holiness-Pentecostal Tradition: Charismatic Movements in the Twentieth Century* (Grand Rapids: Eerdmans, 1997); and Donald W. Dayton, *Theological Roots of Pentecostalism* (Metuchen, NJ: Scarecrow, 1987). The history of Pentecostalism presented here follows the traditional outline of events. However, as the writers cited here and elsewhere note, the actual history is much more complex. Even these authors disagree with each other on many points, such as the relative influence of Keswick and Methodist Holiness teaching on Pentecostalism. Some of the disputed points about Pentecostal history are examined in Joe Creech, "Visions of Glory: The Place of the Azusa Street Revival in Pentecostal History," *Church History* 65 (1996): 405–24.

[2] For a critical but extremely helpful survey of tongues speaking in history, see Victor Budgen, *The Charismatics and the Word of God* (Welwyn, England: Evangelical Press, 1985), 113–99.

[3] H. V. Synan, "Kansas City Conference," in *New International Dictionary of Pentecostal and Charismatic Movements*, 816. On the charismatic movement among Roman Catholics, see J. Charles Whitehead, "Catholic Charismatic Movement," *Encyclopedia of Pentecostal and Charismatic Christianity*, 80–84. For a brief but good overall history of the charismatic movement that also analyzes its status among the mainline denominations, see John Dart, "Charismatic and Mainline," *Christian Century*, 7 March 2006, 22–27.

[4] *The New International Dictionary of Pentecostal and Charismatic Movements* identifies the question of denominational association as an *ecclesiastical* difference and the question of the relation of tongues to a second work of grace as a *theological* difference. "Introduction," xxi. Ray Hughes of the Church of God (Cleveland, Tennessee) cites the question of speaking in tongues as a major distinction between Pentecostals and charismatics. He says that Pentecostals believe that tongues is the "normative experience" for the baptism of the Holy Spirit whereas charismatics do not. Ray H. Hughes, "A Traditional Pentecostal Looks at the New Pentecostals," *Christianity Today*, 7 June 1974, 7–8. Kenneth Kantzer notes the results of a *Christianity Today*/Gallup survey indicating that fewer than a fifth of professing charismatics claim to have spoken in tongues. Kantzer notes also that Pentecostal leaders admit that only half to two-thirds of the members of their denominations say they have spoken in tongues, but it is still a much higher percentage among Pentecostals. Kenneth Kantzer, "The Charismatics Among Us," *Christianity Today*, 22 February 1980, 25–26. A more recent survey confirms that about half of Pentecostals in the United States have spoken in tongues. See Ted Olsen, "What Really Unites Pentecostals?" *Christianity Today*, December 2006, 18.

[5] Hughes, 10.

[6] In recent years there has been a trend to subsume "third wave" under "neocharismatic." Under this category would also fall various Pentecostal/charismatic groups outside the western world that have no organic connection to the Pentecostal or charismatic movements in North America. See S. M. Burgess, "Neocharismatics" in *New International Dictionary of Pentecostal and Charismatic Movements*, 928.

[7] See C. Peter Wagner, *The Third Wave of the Holy Spirit* (Ann Arbor, MI: Vine Books, 1988). For a critique of the third wave, see John MacArthur, *Charismatic Chaos* (Grand Rapids: Zondervan, 1992), 128–51.

[8] John Calvin, *Commentary on a Harmony of the Evangelists*, trans. William Pringle, in *Calvin's Commentaries*, 500th Anniversary Edition (repr.; Grand Rapids: Baker, 2009), 2:389.

[9] John Piper, "Signs and Wonders: Then and Now," 1 February 1991, http://www.desiringgod.org/articles/signs-and-wonders-then-and-now (accessed 8 June 2015).

¹⁰ Collin Hansen, *Young, Restless, Reformed: A Journalist's Journey with the New Calvinism* (Wheaton: Crossway, 2008). A fairly evenhanded evaluation and critique of this movement is found in Jeremy Walker, *The New Calvinism Considered: A Personal and Pastoral Assessment* (Darlington, England: Evangelical Press, 2013). Walker discusses the topic of spiritual gifts on 92–98.

¹¹ See Ken Walker, "Shaking the Southern Baptist Tradition," *Charisma*, March 1999, 68–76, 116; Ken Walker, "Charismatic Worship Becoming the Norm in Growing Numbers of SBC Churches," *Baptist Courier*, 18 March 1999, 10–12. On opposition to this trend, see John Pierce, "Phillips: Charismatic-Leaning Baptists Betrayed," *Baptists Today*, March 2006, 12–13.

¹² David Roach, "IMB to Align Missionary Requirements with BF&M," Baptist Press, 15 May 2015, http://www.bpnews.net/44772/imb-to-align-missionary-requirements-with-bfm (accessed 9 June 2015).

¹³ D. B. Barrett, "Global Statistics," in *New International Dictionary of Pentecostal and Charismatic Movements*, 284. A more recent estimate is that Pentecostals and charismatics total over 584 million. Pew Research Center Religion & Public Life, "Global Christianity—A Report on the Size and Distribution of the World's Christian Population," 19 December 2011, http://www.pewforum.org/2011/12/19/global-christianity-exec/ (accessed 11 August 2015).

¹⁴ Anderson, 5–6; Virginia Brereton, *Training God's Army: The American Bible School, 1880–1940* (Bloomington: Indiana University Press, 1990), 166-69.

¹⁵ Nathan V. Lentfer, "A History of the World's Christian Fundamentals Association (1919–1952)" (PhD diss., Bob Jones University, 2011), 132–34. Interestingly, Lentfer notes that the WCFA's leader, W. B. Riley, opposed a 1928 resolution by the association condemning Pentecostalism even though Riley himself rejected Pentecostal teaching. Riley argued that none of Pentecostal teaching contradicted the WCFA's nine-point statement of faith. That resolution was the only one passed that year from which a substantial minority dissented. An overview of fundamentalist-Pentecostal relations from a Pentecostal point of view is H. V. Synan, "Fundamentalism," *New International Dictionary of Pentecostal and Charismatic Movements*, 655–58.

¹⁶ Among the best and most readable critiques of Pentecostalism and the charismatic movement are MacArthur's *Charismatic Chaos* and his *Strange Fire: The Danger of Offending the Holy Spirit with Counterfeit Worship* (Nashville: Nelson, 2013). Also very helpful is Budgen's *Charismatics and the Word of God*. Critiques from an avowedly fundamentalist position are Ernest D. Pickering and Myron J. Houghton, *Charismatic Confusion*, rev. ed. (Schaumburg, IL: Regular Baptist Press, 2006); and two works by O. Talmadge Spence, *Charismatism: Awakening or Apostasy?* (Greenville, SC: Bob Jones University Press, 1978), and *Pentecostalism: Purity or Peril?*

(Greenville, SC: Unusual Publications, 1989). Spence's critiques are particularly interesting in that they are written from a Pentecostal perspective.

[17] For a defense of the idea of the cessation of these spiritual gifts, see Benjamin B. Warfield, *Counterfeit Miracles* (1918; repr., London: Banner of Truth, 1972).

[18] John Wesley, "A Plain Account of Christian Perfection" in *The Works of John Wesley*, vol. 11 of *Thoughts, Addresses, Prayers, Letters* (1872; repr., Grand Rapids: Zondervan, n.d.), 429.

[19] Bob Jones, *Cornbread and Caviar: Reminiscences and Reflections* (Greenville, SC: Bob Jones University Press, 1985), 181–82. For further discussion of Jones's distinction between old-line Pentecostalism and the charismatic movement, see Daniel L. Turner, *Standing Without Apology: The History of Bob Jones University*, rev. ed. (Greenville, SC: Bob Jones University Press, 2001), 242.

[20] Roger E. Olson, "Pentecostalism's Dark Side," *Christian Century*, 7 March 2006, 27–30.

[21] Greg Surratt, "How to Be Charismatic Without Being Crazy," *Charisma and Christian Life*, November 2010, 28. Surratt is referring to alleged miracles among charismatic churches such as inexplicable sprinklings of gold dust falling on worship services and tooth fillings being miraculously changed to gold.

[22] Edward O'Connor, *Pentecost in the Modern World* (Notre Dame, IN: Ave Maria Press, Charismatic Renewal Books, 1972), 33, cited in James Richard Monk, "Bases of Neo-Pentecostal Ecumenicity" (ThM thesis, Dallas Theological Seminary, 1980), 55; italics in original. Monk argues that a shared spiritual experience is the basis of unity in charismatic and Pentecostal circles; see especially his discussion on 54–56.

[23] Michael Harper, *Three Sisters* (Wheaton: Tyndale House, 1979), 96.

[24] Hughes, 8.

[25] Jack Hayford, "No One Like Jesus," *Charisma and Christian Life*, December 1991, 54.

[26] W. Dennis Pederson, "A Time to Mend," *Christian Life*, April 1984, 42, 48.

[27] See Hughes, 9–10, for a summary of how Catholics resolve differences between Pentecostal and Roman Catholic theology.

CHAPTER 11: ROMAN CATHOLICISM

[1] Charles Clayton Morrison, "Roman Catholicism and Protestantism," *Christian Century*, 8 May 1946, 585.

[2] Probably the best popular critique of Catholicism from an evangelical point of view is James G. McCarthy, *The Gospel According to Rome: Comparing Catholic Tradition and the Word of God* (Eugene, OR: Harvest

SET APART

House, 1995). McCarthy's book is balanced in its language and focuses mainly on doctrinal disagreements between Catholicism and the Scripture. McCarthy's use of the *Catechism of the Catholic Church* (1994) makes his work one of the most up to date. A more historical critique is William Webster, *The Church of Rome at the Bar of History* (Edinburgh: Banner of Truth, 1995). Norman L. Geisler and Ralph E. MacKenzie, *Roman Catholics and Evangelicals: Agreements and Disagreements* (Grand Rapids: Baker, 1995) is also a good summary of the differences between Catholicism and Protestantism, but the authors are eager to find grounds of agreement and cooperation between Catholics and evangelicals.

[3] Karl Keating, *Catholicism and Fundamentalism: The Attack on "Romanism" by "Bible Christians"* (San Francisco: Ignatius Press, 1988), 84.

[4] Ibid., 275.

[5] Edward M. Panosian, "Roman Catholicism: A Philosophy," *Focus on Missions*, Spring 1992, [3].

[6] Alister McGrath, *Evangelicalism and the Future of Christianity* (Downers Grove, IL: InterVarsity Press, 1995), 176.

[7] "Catholic Principles on Ecumenism," in *The Documents of Vatican II*, ed. Walter M. Abbott (New York: Guild Press, 1966), 343–66.

[8] *Catechism of the Catholic Church* (Washington, DC: United States Catholic Conference, 1994). References to this catechism in the text are to paragraph numbers, not page numbers.

[9] McGrath, 172. McGrath says that this idea originated with Francis Schaeffer and was expounded by J. I. Packer.

[10] The text of the document, is in "Evangelicals and Catholics Together: The Christian Mission in the Third Millennium," *First Things*, May 1994, 15–22; all quotations are from this version. It is also found in Charles Colson and Richard John Neuhaus, ed., *Evangelicals and Catholics Together: Toward a Common Mission* (Dallas: Word, 1995), xv–xxxiii. For a helpful summary and critique of the ECT initiative, see Leonardo De Chirico, "Christian Unity vis-à-vis Roman Catholicism: A Critique of the *Evangelicals and Catholics Together* Dialogue," *Evangelical Review of Theology* 27 (2003): 337–52. A sympathetic overview of ECT and the controversies it engendered is found in Mark A. Noll and Carolyn Nystrom, *Is the Reformation Over? An Evangelical Assessment of Contemporary Roman Catholicism* (Grand Rapids: Baker, 2005), 151–83.

[11] "Evangelicals and Catholics Together," 21.

[12] Ibid., 17–18.

[13] See "The Gift of Salvation," *Christianity Today*, 8 December 1997, 35–38.

[14] Ibid., 36.

[15] Ibid., 38.

[16] All references from the document are from Charles Colson and Richard John Neuhaus, ed., *Your Word Is Truth: A Project of Evangelicals and*

Catholics Together (Grand Rapids: Eerdmans, 2002), 1–8; it is also found in "Your Word Is Truth," *First Things,* August/September 2002, 38–42.

[17] "Your Word Is Truth," 5.

[18] "The Communion of Saints," *First Things,* March 2003, 26–33.

[19] "The Christian tradition, following the New Testament, also lifts up some persons for special respect and veneration." Ibid., 31.

[20] One thorough response to the ECT discussion of salvation is R. C. Sproul, *Faith Alone: The Evangelical Doctrine of Justification* (Grand Rapids: Baker, 1995).

[21] Eric Grant, "Affirmations and Obfuscations," *First Things,* December 2002, 5.

[22] De Chirico, 348–49.

[23] "The Gift of Salvation," 38.

[24] "Your Word Is Truth," 7.

[25] J. Gresham Machen, *Christianity and Liberalism* (1923; repr., Grand Rapids: Eerdmans, 1981), 52.

[26] Panosian, [2].

[27] See Sproul, 175–92.

[28] McGrath, 178. He discusses the idea of Catholic-evangelical relations on 175–80.

[29] Panosian, [3].

CHAPTER 12: EXAMPLES OF SEPARATION IN HISTORY

[1] Kraus sees a continuity from J. N. Darby through channels such as prophecy conferences and the *Scofield Reference Bible* "to a spirit of separatism and exclusion," which had "devastating effects" on contemporary evangelicalism. C. Norman Kraus, *Dispensationalism in America: Its Rise and Development* (Richmond, VA: John Knox Press, 1958), 99. See also Vern S. Poythress, *Understanding Dispensationalists,* 2nd ed. (Phillipsburg, NJ: P&R Publishing, 1994), 18, and the discussion in Joel Carpenter, *Revive Us Again: The Reawakening of American Fundamentalism* (New York: Oxford University Press, 1997), 38–40.

[2] On Machen's criticism of dispensationalism, see R. Todd Mangum, *The Dispensational-Covenantal Rift: The Fissuring of American Evangelical Theology from 1936 to 1944* (Eugene, OR: Wipf and Stock, 2007), 34–35, 54–63. Mangum notes that Machen was more accommodating to dispensationalism than many of his Reformed counterparts (59).

[3] Philip Schaff, *The Creeds of Christendom* (1931; repr., Grand Rapids: Baker, 1983), 3:11–12.

4 Martin Bucer said that rightly administering the sacraments involved allowing only those to participate who are "holy and blameless according to the Word of the Lord" and that only those who "have evidence of true repentance for sins and a solid faith in Christ the Lord" should receive the Lord's Supper. He also advised that ministers explain the meaning and purpose of the sacraments to the congregation. Martin Bucer, "De Regno Christi," in *Melanchthon and Bucer,* ed. Wilhelm Pauck, vol. 19 of the Library of Christian Classics (Philadelphia: Westminster, 1969), 236–37.

5 See Bucer, "De Regno Christi," 232-47. Most of the literature on the third mark is of a scholarly nature. See Amy Nelson Burnett, *The Yoke of Christ: Martin Bucer and Christian Discipline* (Kirksville: Northeast Missouri State University, 1994); Robert M. Kingdom, "Peter Martyr Vermigli and the Marks of the True Church," in *Continuity and Discontinuity in Church History,* ed. E. Forrester Church and Timothy George. (Leiden: E. J. Brill, 1979), 198–214; and Glenn S. Sunshine, "Discipline as the Third Mark of the Church: Three Views," *Calvin Theological Journal* 33 (1998): 469–80.

6 Schaff, *Creeds of Christendom,* 3:419. See also Article 18 of the First Scots Confession, Schaff, 3:461–62.

7 See Edmund S. Morgan, *Visible Saints: The History of a Puritan Idea* (New York: New York University Press, 1963).

8 See the works of early separatist writer Henry Barrow in *Writings, 1587–1590,* ed. Leland H. Carlson, vol. 3 of Elizabethan Nonconformist Texts (London: Sir Halley Stewart Trust, 1962). Morgan, *Visible Saints,* 21–25, demonstrates how separatists believed in discipline as the mark of a true church.

9 See John Robinson, *A Justification of Separation from the Church of England,* vol. 2 of *The Works of John Robinson, Pastor of the Pilgrim Fathers* (1851; repr., Harrisonburg, VA: Sprinkle Publications, 2009). See also Timothy George, *John Robinson and the English Separatist Tradition* (Macon, GA: Mercer University Press, 1982), 137–59, on the importance of discipline as a mark of the church for Robinson and other separatists.

10 J. Gresham Machen, "A True Presbyterian Church at Last," *Presbyterian Guardian,* 22 June 1936, 110, http://www.opc.org/cfh/guardian/Volume_2/1936-06-22.pdf (accessed 10 June 2015).

11 The best source on Cooke is J. L. Porter, *The Life and Times of Henry Cooke* (1871; repr., Belfast: Ambassador, 1999), a very favorable work written by his son-in-law. For short surveys of the Irish conflict, see Thomas Hamilton, *History of the Irish Presbyterian Church* (Edinburgh: T. & T. Clark, 1886), 148–58; and John M. Barkley, *A Short History of the Presbyterian Church in Ireland* (Belfast: Presbyterian Church in Ireland, 1959), 44–48.

12 R. F. G. Holmes, "Dr. Henry Cooke: The Athanasius of Irish Presbyterianism," in *Religious Motivation: Biographical and Sociological*

Problems for the Church Historian, vol. 15 of *Studies in Church History,* ed. Derek Baker (Oxford: Basil Blackwell, 1978), 367–80.

[13] For example, "the purging of the Presbyterian Church from the errors of Arianism under the leadership of Dr. Cooke, and the Arian withdrawal in 1829, laid the foundation for the union with the Seceders in 1840 and thus prepared the way for the Ulster Revival of 1859." Stanley Barnes, *A Pictorial History of the 1859 Revival and Related Awakenings in Ulster* (Belfast: Ambassador, 2008), 47.

[14] See Hugh Watt, *Thomas Chalmers and the Disruption* (Edinburgh: Thomas Nelson and Sons, 1943).

[15] John H. S. Burleigh, *A Church History of Scotland* (New York: Oxford University Press, 1960), 303.

[16] A description of this drift is found in Iain Murray, *A Scottish Christian Heritage* (Edinburgh: Banner of Truth, 2006), 369–96. See also Burleigh, 358–61, for a discussion of the growth of liberal theology as a factor in the move toward reunion, although Burleigh, unlike Murray, approves of the shift.

[17] In 1900, the Free Church had merged with another group to form the United Free Church. It was this body from which the minority seceded and which ultimately merged with the Church of Scotland.

[18] Abraham Kuyper, "'Sphere Sovereignty,'" in *Abraham Kuyper: A Centennial Reader,* ed. James D. Bratt (Grand Rapids: Eerdmans, 1998), 488; italics in original. An example of evangelical writers who hold up Kuyper as a model of cultural engagement is Richard J. Mouw. See Mouw's *Abraham Kuyper: A Short and Personal Introduction* (Grand Rapids: Eerdmans, 2011); "Abraham Kuyper: A Man for This Season," *Christianity Today,* 26 October 1998, 86–87; and "Culture, Church, and Civil Society: Kuyper for a New Century," *Princeton Seminary Bulletin,* 28 (2007): 48–63.

[19] On his conversion, see Abraham Kuyper, "Confidentially," in *Abraham Kuyper: A Centennial Reader,* 45–61. On his opposition to theological modernism, see Abraham Kuyper, "Modernism: A Fata Morgana in the Christian Domain," in *Abraham Kuyper: A Centennial Reader,* 87–124.

[20] On the history of the *Doleantie* conflict, see James Edward McGoldrick, *God's Renaissance Man: The Life and Work of Abraham Kuyper* (Darlington, England: Evangelical Press, 2000), 87–97; Frank Vandenberg, *Abraham Kuyper* (Grand Rapids, Eerdmans, 1960), 128–61; and Ron Cammenga, "The *Doleantie,*" *Standard Bearer,* 15 October 1998, 33–35. For the sermon Kuyper preached after his dismissal, see Abraham Kuyper, "'It Shall Not Be So Among You,'" in *Abraham Kuyper: A Centennial Reader,* 125–40.

[21] Abraham Kuyper, "A Pamphlet Concerning the Reformation of the Church," *Standard Bearer,* 15 October 1982, 31–32. The pamphlet was originally published in 1883. This translation was published as a multipart series in the *Standard Bearer* between 1 November 1977 and 15 December 1986.

[22] There are several useful works on the Downgrade Controversy. For primary sources, see Charles Haddon Spurgeon, *The "Down Grade" Controversy* (Pasadena, TX: Pilgrim Publications, n.d.), a compilation of the major articles from Spurgeon's *Sword and Trowel* dealing with the controversy; Susannah Spurgeon and Joseph Harrald, ed., *C. H. Spurgeon's Autobiography* (1899; repr., Pasadena, TX: Pilgrim Publications, 1992), 4:253–64 (vols. 3 and 4 are bound together as vol. 2 in this edition); and Iain H. Murray, ed., *Letters of Charles Haddon Spurgeon* (Edinburgh: Banner of Truth, 1992), 179–97. For secondary works, see Iain H. Murray, *The Forgotten Spurgeon*, 2nd ed. (Edinburgh: Banner of Truth, 1973), and R. J. Sheehan, *C. H. Spurgeon and the Modern Church* (London: Grace Publications, 1985).

[23] This list comes from C. H. Spurgeon, "A Fragment upon the Down-Grade Controversy," *Sword and Trowel,* November 1887, 558; see *The "Down Grade" Controversy,* 34.

[24] "Notes," *Sword and Trowel,* October 1888, 562; see *The "Down Grade" Controversy,* 66.

[25] C. H. Spurgeon, "A Fragment upon the Down-Grade Controversy," *Sword and Trowel,* November 1887, 558, 559; see *The "Down Grade" Controversy,* 34, 35.

[26] The best biography of Lloyd-Jones is the one by Iain Murray. See particularly the second volume, *David Martyn Lloyd-Jones: The Fight of Faith* (Edinburgh: Banner of Truth, 1990), 425–567, on his battle for separatism. See also Mark Sidwell, "Call to Separation and Unity: D. Martyn Lloyd-Jones and 'Evangelical Unity,'" *Detroit Baptist Seminary Journal* 3 (1998): 35–62.

[27] "Martyn Lloyd-Jones: From Buckingham to Westminster," interview by Carl F. H. Henry, *Christianity Today,* 8 February 1980, 29, 32.

[28] G. N. M. Collins, "The Friend," in Christopher Catherwood, ed., *Martyn Lloyd-Jones: Chosen by God* (Westchester, IL: Crossway Books, 1986), 262–63. For Lloyd-Jones's views on Christian unity and the ecumenical movement, see D. Martyn Lloyd-Jones, "The Basis of Christian Unity," in *Knowing the Times* (Edinburgh: Banner of Truth, 1989), 118–63.

[29] D. Martyn Lloyd-Jones, "Evangelical Unity: An Appeal," in *Knowing the Times,* 246–57.

GLOSSARY OF TERMS

apostasy: In its biblical sense, apostasy is the repudiation of the Christian faith by persons or organizations, even though they may maintain the name "Christian." The term *apostate* is sometimes applied to an individual who himself has not personally repudiated Christian truth but who belongs to groups characterized by apostasy and holds to teachings characteristic of apostasy.

cessationist: One who believes that special spiritual gifts such as speaking in tongues ceased with the close of the New Testament era.

charismatic movement: Also known as neo-Pentecostalism, the charismatic movement is a variant of ***Pentecostalism*** (q.v.). Emerging in the 1960s, the movement is similar to Pentecostalism in stressing the exercise of spiritual gifts, notably speaking in tongues. The differences with Pentecostalism are that charismatics remain members in major denominations and hold to looser standards of ecclesiastical separation.

conservative evangelical: Although this term can be variously defined, here it is used for an evangelical who does not cooperate with liberals or tolerate serious doctrinal aberrations but who in cooperating with broader evangelicals does not follow the pattern of biblical separation.

discipline in the church: Church discipline can take one of two forms. *Formative* church discipline is the church's process of education and discipleship to nurture believers in the faith. *Corrective* church discipline is action taken by a body of believers to correct the disobedience of one of its members. The goal of corrective discipline is to preserve the purity of the church and to reclaim the disobedient Christian.

disobedient believer: A professing Christian who, despite admonition, deliberately refuses to modify some aspect of his conduct or belief to conform to the clear teaching of Scripture.

dispensationalism: A system of biblical interpretation named for the different ages, or dispensations, seen in history. It teaches that in each of these dispensations, God tests mankind in some way, and each age ends with man's failure and God's judgment. Central to dispensationalism is a distinction between Israel and the church.

Certain parts of the Bible, including a great deal of prophecy, apply only to the Jews, and other parts apply only to Christians. Among the distinctive dispensationalist teachings is the **Rapture** (q.v.).

Doleantie: A separation from the Reformed Church in the Netherlands in the late nineteenth century led by Abraham Kuyper.

Downgrade Controversy: A conflict within Great Britain's Baptist Union in the late nineteenth century over the inclusion of liberal views within the Union. The conflict led to the withdrawal of C. H. Spurgeon and his church from the Union.

ecclesiastical separation: Essentially the application of the principles of **personal separation** (q.v.) practiced on the level of an assembly of believers. It involves a refusal to align with false doctrine or unbelief and a rejection of the willful practice of disobedience. **Discipline in the church** (q.v.) is a form of ecclesiastical separation.

ecumenical movement: Since ecumenical means "universal" or "worldwide," this phrase refers to the attempt to unite all Christian churches, usually on a liberal basis that downplays important doctrinal matters.

evangelical: During the Reformation the term *evangelical* was virtually synonymous with *Protestant*. As a result of the awakenings of the 1700s, the term evangelical came to refer to Protestants who stress teachings such as the authority of Scripture alone, the substitutionary atonement of Christ, the new birth, the importance of holy living, and evangelism. Today, the term is used mainly for "any non-Fundamentalist conservative who does not accept or practice the principle of ecclesiastical separation" (David Beale). See also **new evangelicalism**.

evangelical cobelligerence: An idea credited to Reformed apologist Francis Schaeffer, the concept of evangelical cobelligerence is that evangelicals may work in temporary alliances with religious groups they disagree with as long as they share a common goal, such as a particular political or moral reform

exclusivism: The belief that a religious body such as a church or denomination should exclude all religious teaching contrary to the doctrinal standards of the church or denomination. In the

Fundamentalist-Modernist Controversy, for example, the fundamentalists were the exclusivist party. See also *inclusivism*.

existentialism: The philosophy that maintains that every person must face the inescapable fact that existence is the basic truth of life. Meaning in life comes not from some authority but from a person's own decisions and actions. Life itself has no purpose or meaning, so the individual must create his own meaning by his actions. At its most extreme, existentialism holds that truth is completely subjective. Because there is often no rational basis for committing to a certain course of action, an individual must take a "leap of faith" and commit himself to such a course apart from or even in spite of rational considerations.

false teacher: Someone who professes to be a Christian but who attempts to deceive the church by false doctrine. Regardless of his personal standing with God, such a person teaches doctrine that threatens the eternal well-being of souls.

first-degree separation: Used by some Christians in reference to ecclesiastical separation, this term refers to refusing to cooperate with false teachers in religious activities; it is also known as primary separation. See also *second-degree separation*.

fundamental doctrine: A clear scriptural teaching that the Bible itself indicates is an important truth of Christianity; a teaching so essential to Christianity that it cannot be denied without destroying Christianity. Among the fundamental doctrines are the inspiration and authority of the Bible, the virgin birth of Christ, His deity, His absolute sinlessness, His substitutionary death on the cross, His bodily resurrection, His personal return, and the reality of heaven and hell.

fundamentalism: The view that there are certain truths so essential to Christianity that they cannot be denied without destroying Christianity and that these essentials are the basis of Christian fellowship. The term *fundamentalism* is often used to refer to the militant form of orthodox Protestantism espousing this view, a movement that emerged in the United States in the late nineteenth and early twentieth centuries.

Great Disruption: A major division in the Church of Scotland in the 1840s that led to the formation of the Free Church of Scotland under Thomas Chalmers.

heresy: A dangerously false teaching (from the Greek word *hairesis*, which often has the meaning of "division" or "faction"; 1 Cor. 11:19; Gal. 5:20). *Heresy* came to mean "false doctrine" probably because false teachings create divisions.

higher criticism: The study of the content of the Bible, dealing with questions of the authorship, date, and literary structure of the books of the Bible. The term is often viewed with suspicion by conservative Christians because liberal higher critics with faulty assumptions about the Bible's nature undermine the authority of Scripture by their conclusions. Reverent scholars with a high view of the Bible's inspiration, however, can also practice higher criticism. See also **lower criticism.**

holiness: In the biblical sense of the word, holiness is essentially uniqueness or "differentness." The difference is fundamentally moral (e.g., difference between good and evil or between God and Satan). The Bible expresses this uniqueness as moral purity and separation from that which is unclean. It is not primarily an external attribute but an internal one expressing itself externally.

inclusivism: The belief that a religious body such as a church or denomination should include a wide range of theological beliefs, despite how those beliefs may clash with the traditional standards of belief for that body or church. In the Fundamentalist-Modernist Controversy, for example, the modernists were the inclusivist party. See also **exclusivism.**

Keswick Holiness: A system of teaching (named for a conference site in England) that stresses the need for personal holiness through the power of the Holy Spirit. Among its distinctive ideas are the "victorious" or "abundant" life, the existence of two distinct natures in the believer (a corrupt old nature and a regenerate new nature), and a special experience following conversion (often called "surrender") when a Christian moves to a higher level of spiritual development and maturity.

legalism: The theological heresy of trying to earn merit with God by performing good works. As commonly used, however, *legalism* means requiring Christians to follow standards of behavior that have no basis in the Bible.

liberalism, religious: Broadly speaking, religious liberalism is an approach to the Christian faith based on the presuppositions of the Enlightenment. It assumes that reason and science are sure roads to truth and that human reason or experience is the test of the validity of religious ideas.

love: Defined biblically, love is a disposition to act in the highest interests of the one who is loved, regardless of the cost to the one who loves. Such a disposition may or may not involve an emotional attachment to the loved object, but it will unquestionably involve a self-sacrificial commitment.

lower criticism: The study of the surviving manuscripts of the Bible (also called textual criticism). Textual critics endeavor to determine the exact reading of the original Scripture by a careful study of all available manuscripts. See also **higher criticism**.

modernism: A form of **religious liberalism** (q.v.) that was influential in the United States in the late 1800s and early 1900s.

neo-fundamentalism: A movement that emerged in the 1970s in an effort to reform fundamentalism by modifying fundamentalism's practice of separation and by involving conservative Christians in right-wing political causes. It differed initially from **new evangelicalism** (q.v.) in its reluctance to build bridges to theological liberals.

neo-liberalism: A post-1920s revision of American modernism that stresses greater realism and less optimism concerning the nature of humanity and progress in world affairs.

neo-orthodoxy: A view that arose after World War I as an attempt to correct the excesses of theological liberalism by returning to such orthodox biblical ideas as the pervasiveness of sin, God's transcendence, and the need for redemption. Critics charge, however, that neo-orthodoxy redefines such terms in an unbiblical manner, taking a subjective view of revelation (i.e., that the Bible is not itself God's Word but is a channel of revelation as the Holy Spirit speaks to the individual). Neo-orthodoxy borrows from **existentialism** (q.v.) and is sometimes called "the theology of crisis" because commitment to truth is often viewed as a leap of faith resulting from an inner crisis.

neo-Pentecostalism: See **charismatic movement.**

new evangelicalism: A movement in conservative Protestantism in America that arose in the 1940s and 1950s, emphasizing scholarship, an accommodation to evolutionary theory, and a repudiation of ecclesiastical separation as practiced by fundamentalists. More generally, the term has been used to describe any nonfundamentalist evangelical. Fundamentalists are the only major group still using the term the *new evangelicalism*; most observers use simply the term **evangelical** (q.v.) as the general designation.

Pentecostalism: An early twentieth-century form of US Protestant Christianity that holds to the restoration of New Testament spiritual gifts. The most notable of these gifts is speaking in tongues as a sign of the baptism of the Holy Spirit. See also **charismatic movement.**

personal separation: The practice of individual sanctification in refusing to follow the world's philosophy in thought and action.

positional sanctification: See **sanctification.**

postmillennialism: The belief that the Holy Spirit will work through the church until the gospel spreads throughout the world. Then Jesus Himself will return for the final judgment. See also **premillennialism** and **Rapture.**

postmodernism: A philosophical system arising in the latter half of the twentieth century that denies the rationalist basis of the Enlightenment and argues that human reason does not lead to a single unified view of reality and that scientific study is not a sure means to truth. Postmodernism makes truth a matter of individual perception. ("There are no facts, only interpretations.")

premillennialism: The belief that there will be a great outpouring of God's wrath on the earth followed by Christ's return to establish a millennial (thousand-year) kingdom. See also **postmillennialism.**

progressive sanctification: See **sanctification.**

Rapture: Based on the idea that Christ's return comes in two stages, the Rapture is the coming of Christ for His people just before

God's wrath is poured out on the earth. This teaching is commonly, but not exclusively, associated with dispensationalism.

realistic theology: The name given to the form of *neo-orthodoxy* (q.v.) advocated by Reinhold and H. Richard Niebuhr.

sanctification: The "setting apart" of a Christian to God when he is converted. Positional sanctification is the Christian's status "in Christ" by which the righteousness of Christ is credited to the Christian so that God views him as holy. Progressive sanctification is the process of realizing positional sanctification through personal growth in faith and holiness of life.

schism: "Division in the true visible church about matters that are not sufficient to justify division or separation" (D. Martyn Lloyd-Jones, "'Consider Your Ways': The Outline of a New Strategy," in *Knowing the Times*, 186).

second-degree separation: As used by some Christians in reference to ecclesiastical separation, second-degree separation is refusing to have fellowship with someone who does not practice first-degree separation (separation from false teaching); it is also known as secondary separation. Many separatists do not recognize a distinction between second- and *first-degree separation* (q.v.).

separation: Biblical separation is the realization of progressive sanctification in a believer's life by striving to be free of the presence of sin. The term may also be used in connection with a church body's growth in purity (cf. 1 Cor. 5:7–8).

"signs and wonders" movement: See *third wave.*

social gospel: The teaching pioneered by Walter Rauschenbusch (1861–1918) that the gospel needs to be applied to social institutions. The social gospel downplays original sin and Christ's atonement to stress individual personal reform and bringing all social organizations under the law of Christ. The goal of the social gospel is to build the kingdom of God on earth by human effort. The term *social gospel* is generally used by conservatives to mean a system of social reform with little reference to individual redemption through the atonement of Jesus Christ.

soteriology: The study of the doctrines concerning salvation.

theology of crisis: See *neo-orthodoxy.*

third wave: Also known as the "signs and wonders" movement, the third wave is an outgrowth of the Pentecostal and charismatic movements dating from the 1980s. It supposedly follows Pentecostalism and the charismatic movement as the third wave of the Holy Spirit's blessing. Its adherents claim to be neither Pentecostal nor charismatic but seek the same kind of spiritual gifts. Supporters of this position claim that miraculous signs and wonders (healings, exorcisms, etc.) are necessary to proclaim the gospel.

three marks of a true church: A concept formulated by the Protestant reformers against the teaching of the Roman Catholic Church, this approach defined a true church as being characterized by the gospel rightly preached, the sacraments (ordinances) rightly administered, and church discipline rightly practiced.

tradition: A body of oral teaching that, according to Roman Catholicism, Christ gave to the apostles along with the written Scriptures. Catholics consider this tradition of equal authority with the Bible. Catholics recognize the Church, under the leadership of the pope and the bishops, as the authoritative interpreter of tradition. Tradition is allegedly expressed in the interpretations of the church fathers (ancient), church doctors (medieval), and popes.

Trent, Council of: Three meetings held from 1545 to 1563 to formulate the official Catholic response to the Protestant Reformation. The council specifically condemned Protestant teachings and demanded submission to the official teaching of the Catholic Church as newly defined by the church hierarchy.

Vatican II: More properly called the Second Vatican Council, this Roman Catholic assembly met from 1962 to 1965. The council enacted many reforms, such as replacing Latin in its services with the vernacular. It also adopted a much friendlier tone toward non-Catholics. The council did not, however, significantly narrow the gap between Catholic teaching and historic Protestant teaching.

worldliness: An attitude of friendship toward, a desire for, and a wish to be recognized by the world system. It is sometimes used of the behavior of people characterized by this inner attitude.

world system: The unregenerate people of this earth as organized and dominated by Satan (in contrast to the physical world).

SELECT BIBLIOGRAPHY

BOOKS AND PAMPHLETS

Abrams, Douglas Carl. *Selling the Old-Time Religion: American Fundamentalists and Mass Culture, 1920–1940*. Athens: University of Georgia Press, 2001.

Ashbrook, John. *Axioms of Separation*. Mentor, OH: Here I Stand Books, n.d.

———. *The New Neutralism II*. Mentor, OH: Here I Stand Books, 1992.

Bauder, Kevin, and Robert Delnay. *One in Hope and Doctrine: Origins of Baptist Fundamentalism 1870–1950*. Schaumburg, IL: Regular Baptist Books, 2014.

Beacham, Roy E., and Kevin T. Bauder, ed. *One Bible Only? Examining Exclusive Claims for the King James Bible*. Grand Rapids: Kregel Publications, 2001.

Beale, David O. *In Pursuit of Purity: American Fundamentalism Since 1850*. Greenville, SC: Unusual Publications, 1986.

Bratt, James D., ed. *Abraham Kuyper: A Centennial Reader*. Grand Rapids: Eerdmans, 1998.

Budgen, Victor. *The Charismatics and the Word of God*. Welwyn, England: Evangelical Press, 1985.

Burgess, Stanley M., and Eduard M. Van Der Maas, ed. *New International Dictionary of Pentecostal and Charismatic Movements*. Rev. ed., Grand Rapids: Zondervan, 2002.

Cairns, Alan. *Apostles of Error*. Greenville, SC: Faith Presbyterian Church, 1989.

Carnell, Edward John. *The Case for Orthodox Theology*. Philadelphia: Westminster Press, 1959.

Carpenter, Joel. *Revive Us Again: The Reawakening of American Fundamentalism*. New York: Oxford University Press, 1997.

Cohen, Gary G. *Biblical Separation Defended: A Biblical Critique of Ten New Evangelical Arguments*. Philadelphia: Presbyterian and Reformed, 1966.

Dollar, George. *A History of Fundamentalism in America*. Greenville, SC: Bob Jones University Press, 1973.

Erickson, Millard. *The Evangelical Left: Encountering Postconservative Evangelical Theology*. Grand Rapids: Baker, 1997.

———. *The New Evangelical Theology*. Westwood, NJ: Revell, 1968.

Falwell, Jerry, Ed Dobson, and Ed Hindson. *The Fundamentalist Phenomenon: The Resurgence of Conservative Christianity*. Garden City, NY: Doubleday-Galilee, 1981.

Ferm, Robert O. *Cooperative Evangelism: Is Billy Graham Right or Wrong?* Grand Rapids: Zondervan, 1958.

Geisler, Norman L., and Ralph E. MacKenzie. *Roman Catholics and Evangelicals: Agreements and Disagreements*. Grand Rapids: Baker, 1995.

Groothuis, Douglas. *Truth Decay: Defending Christianity Against the Challenges of Postmodernism.* Downers Grove, IL: InterVarsity Press, 2000.

Gundry, Stanley N., and Alan F. Johnson, ed. *Tensions in Contemporary Theology.* Chicago: Moody, 1976.

Henry, Carl F. H. *The Uneasy Conscience of Modern Fundamentalism.* Grand Rapids: Eerdmans, 1947.

Hordern, William. *The Case for a New Reformation Theology.* Philadelphia: Westminster Press, 1959.

———. *A Layman's Guide to Protestant Theology.* Rev. ed. 1968; reprint, Eugene, OR: Wipf and Stock, 2002.

Hunter, James Davison. *Evangelicalism: The Coming Generation.* Chicago: University of Chicago Press, 1987.

Janz, Jason. *Young Fundamentalists' Beliefs and Personal Life Survey Findings.* Fleetwood, PA: Right Ideas Inc., 2005.

Jones, Bob. *Scriptural Separation: "First and Second Degree."* Greenville, SC: Bob Jones University Press, 1971.

Leedy, Randy. *Love Not the World: Winning the War Against Worldliness.* Greenville, SC: Bob Jones University Press, 2012.

Lentfer, Nathan V. "A History of the World's Christian Fundamentals Association (1919–1952)." PhD diss., Bob Jones University, 2011.

Lindsell, Harold. *The Battle for the Bible.* Grand Rapids: Zondervan, 1976.

Lloyd-Jones, D. Martyn. *Knowing the Times: Addresses Delivered on Various Occasions 1942–1977.* Edinburgh: Banner of Truth, 1989.

MacArthur, John. *Charismatic Chaos.* Grand Rapids: Zondervan, 1992.

———. *Strange Fire: The Danger of Offending the Holy Spirit with Counterfeit Worship.* Nashville: Nelson, 2013.

Machen, J. Gresham. *Christianity and Liberalism.* 1923. Reprint, Grand Rapids: Eerdmans, 1981.

Mangum, R. Todd. *The Dispensational-Covenantal Rift: The Fissuring of American Evangelical Theology from 1936 to 1944.* Eugene, OR: Wipf and Stock, 2007.

Mangum, R. Todd, and Mark S. Sweetnam. *The Scofield Bible: Its History and Impact on the Evangelical Church.* Colorado Springs: Paternoster Publishing, 2009.

Marsden, George. *Fundamentalism and American Culture: The Shaping of Twentieth-Century Evangelicalism, 1870–1925.* 2nd ed. New York: Oxford University Press, 2006.

———. *Reforming Fundamentalism: Fuller Seminary and the New Evangelicalism.* Grand Rapids: Eerdmans, 1987.

———. *Understanding Fundamentalism and Evangelicalism.* Grand Rapids: Eerdmans, 1991.

Martin, William C. *Prophet with Honor: The Billy Graham Story.* New York: Morrow, 1991.

Marty, Martin E. *Modern American Religion*. 3 vols. Chicago: University of Chicago Press, 1986, 1991, 1996.

Marty, Martin E. and R. Scott Appleby, ed. *Fundamentalisms Observed*. Chicago: University of Chicago Press, 1991.

Masters, Peter. *Are We Fundamentalists?* London: Sword & Trowel 1995.

———. *Stand for the Truth*. London: Sword and Trowel, 1996.

McCarthy, James G. *The Gospel According to Rome: Comparing Catholic Tradition and the Word of God*. Eugene, OR: Harvest House, 1995.

McCune, Rolland D. *Ecclesiastical Separation*. Allen Park, MI: Detroit Baptist Theological Seminary, n.d. Available online as "An Inside Look at Ecclesiastical Separation" on the DBTS website.

———. *Promise Unfulfilled: The Failed Strategy of Modern Evangelicalism*. Greenville, SC: Ambassador International, 2004.

McGrath, Alister. *Evangelicalism and the Future of Christianity*. Downers Grove, IL: InterVarsity Press, 1995.

McLachlan, Douglas R. *Reclaiming Authentic Fundamentalism*. Independence, MO: American Association of Christian Schools, 1993.

Moore, Howard Edgar. "The Emergence of Moderate Fundamentalism: John R. Rice and 'The Sword of the Lord.'" PhD diss., George Washington University, 1990.

Moritz, Fred. *"Be Ye Holy": The Call to Christian Separation*. Greenville, SC: Bob Jones University Press, 1994.

Murray, Iain. *Evangelicalism Divided: A Record of Crucial Change in the Years 1950 to 2000*. Edinburgh: Banner of Truth, 2000.

———. *The Forgotten Spurgeon*. 2nd ed. Edinburgh: Banner of Truth, 1973.

———. *David Martyn Lloyd-Jones: The Fight of Faith*. Edinburgh: Banner of Truth, 1990.

Naselli, Andrew David and Collin Hansen, ed. *Four Views on the Spectrum of Evangelicalism*. Grand Rapids: Zondervan, 2011.

Nash, Ronald. *The New Evangelicalism*. Grand Rapids: Zondervan, 1963.

Pickering, Ernest D. *The Biblical Doctrine of Separation*. Clarks Summit, PA: Baptist Bible College, 1976.

———, and Myron J. Houghton. *Biblical Separation: The Struggle for a Pure Church*. 2nd ed. Schaumburg, IL: Regular Baptist Press, 2008.

———, and Myron J. Houghton. *Charismatic Confusion*. Rev. ed. Schaumburg, IL: Regular Baptist Press, 2006.

———. *The Tragedy of Compromise: The Origin and Impact of the New Evangelicalism*. Greenville, SC: Bob Jones University Press, 1994.

Quebedeaux, Richard. *The Worldly Evangelicals*. New York: Harper and Row, 1978.

———. *The Young Evangelicals: Revolution in Orthodoxy*. New York: Harper and Row, 1974.

Reymond, Robert L. *Introductory Studies in Contemporary Theology*. Philadelphia: Presbyterian and Reformed, 1968.

Rice, John R. *Come Out or Stay In*. Nashville: Thomas Nelson, 1974.

———. *Earnestly Contending for the Faith*. Murfreesboro, TN: Sword of the Lord, 1965.

Rosell, Garth M. *The Surprising Work of God: Harold John Ockenga, Billy Graham, and the Rebirth of Evangelicalism*. Grand Rapids: Baker, 2008.

Ryrie, Charles Caldwell. *Neo-Orthodoxy*. Chicago: Moody Press, 1956.

Sandeen, Ernest. *The Roots of Fundamentalism: British and American Millenarianism, 1800–1930*. 1970. Reprint, Grand Rapids: Baker, 1978.

Sheehan, R. J. *C. H. Spurgeon and the Modern Church*. London: Grace Publications, 1985.

Smith, David L. *A Handbook of Contemporary Theology*. Wheaton: BridgePoint, 1992.

Spence, O. Talmadge. *Charismatism, Awakening or Apostasy?* Greenville, SC: Bob Jones University Press, 1978.

———. *Pentecostalism: Purity or Peril?* Greenville, SC: Unusual Publications, 1989.

Sproul, R. C. *Faith Alone: The Evangelical Doctrine of Justification*. Grand Rapids: Baker, 1995.

Torrey, R. A., A. C. Dixon, et al. *The Fundamentals: A Testimony to the Truth*. 4 vols. 1917. Reprint, Grand Rapids: Baker, 1988.

Tulga, Chester. *The Doctrine of Separation in These Times*. Chicago: Conservative Baptist Fellowship, 1952.

Van Til, Cornelius. *The New Modernism: An Appraisal of the Theology of Barth and Brunner*. 3rd ed. N.p.: Presbyterian and Reformed, 1973.

Veith, Jr., Gene Edward. *Postmodern Times: A Christian Guide to Contemporary Thought and Culture*. Wheaton: Crossway Books, 1994.

Wesley, John. *A Plain Account of Christian Perfection*. Louisville: Pentecostal Publishing, n.d.

Williams, J. B., ed. *From the Mind of God to the Mind of Man: A Layman's Guide to How We Got Our Bible*. Greenville, SC: Ambassador-Emerald International, 1999.

Woodbridge, Charles. *Bible Separation*. Halifax: The Peoples Gospel Hour Press, 1971.

Woodbridge, John D. *Biblical Authority*. Grand Rapids: Zondervan, 1982.

ARTICLES

Barnhouse, Donald Grey. "One Church." *Eternity*, July 1958, 17–23.

———. "Thanksgiving and Warning." *Eternity*, September 1957, 9, 44–45.

Bell, L. Nelson. "On 'Separation.'" *Christianity Today*, 8 October 1971, 26–27.

Eenigenburg, Elton M. "Separatism Is Not Scriptural." *Eternity*, August 1963, 16, 18–22.

Fea, John. "Understanding the Changing Facade of Twentieth-Century American Protestant Fundamentalism: Toward a Historical Definition." *Trinity Journal* 15 (1994): 181–99.

Graham, Billy. "The Lost Chord of Evangelism." *Christianity Today*, 1 April 1957, 26.

Grounds, Vernon. "Separation Yes, Schism No." *Eternity*, August 1963, 17–22.

Horton, Robert Lon. "The Christian's Role in Society." *Biblical Viewpoint* 15 (1981): 130–37.

Huffman, Jerry. "Separation—The Big 'S' Word." *Frontline*, January–February 1992, 5.

"Is Evangelical Theology Changing?" *Christian Life*, March 1956, 16–19.

Jones, Bob. "Pseudo-Fundamentalists: The New Breed in Sheep's Clothing." *Faith for the Family*, January 1978, 7, 16.

Jones III, Bob. "The Moral Majority." *Faith for the Family*, September 1980, 3, 27–28.

———. "The Ultimate Ecumenism." *Faith for the Family*, September 1985, 3, 9–10.

Leedy, Randy. "The Ethic of Love." *Biblical Viewpoint* 30, no. 1 (1996): 5–14.

Lightner, Robert. "A Biblical Perspective on False Doctrine." *Bibliotheca Sacra* 142 (1985): 16–22.

Martin, Walter R. "Love, Doctrine, and Fellowship: How Can We Put Them Together?" *Eternity*, November 1960, 20–22, 56–57.

———. "When Is Separation Necessary?" *Eternity*, January 1961, 30–31.

McCune, Rolland D. "The Self-Identity of Fundamentalism." *Detroit Baptist Theological Seminary Journal* 1 (1996): 9–34.

———. "Separation: An Important Benchmark of True Fundamentalism." *Frontline*, May–June 1993, 15–17.

McIntire, C. T. "Fundamentalism." In *Evangelical Dictionary of Theology*. Ed. Walter Elwell. Grand Rapids: Baker, 1984, 433–36.

Naselli, Andrew David. "Keswick Theology: A Survey and Analysis of the Doctrine of Sanctification in the Early Keswick Movement." *Detroit Baptist Seminary Journal* 13 (2008): 17–67.

Nutz, Earl. "Important Lessons: I John 2." *Biblical Viewpoint* 27, no. 1 (1993): 31–37.

Rosner, Brian S. "'Drive Out the Wicked Person': A Biblical Theology of Exclusion." *Evangelical Quarterly* 71 (1999): 25–26.

Runia, Klaas. "When Is Separation a Christian Duty?" *Christianity Today*, 23 June 1967, 3–5; 7 July 1967, 6–8.

Sanderson, John W. "Fundamentalism and Its Critics." *Sunday School Times*, 21 January 1961, 58–59, 66.

———. "Fundamentalism and Neo-Evangelicalism—Whither?" *Sunday School Times*, 4 February 1961, 90–91, 101–2.

———. "Neo-Evangelicalism and Its Critics." *Sunday School Times*, 28 January 1961, 74, 82.

———. "Purity of Testimony—or Opportunity?" *Sunday School Times*, 11 February 1961, 110–11.

Shumate, David R. "Separation Versus Limited Participation: Is There a Difference?" *Frontline*, May/June 2009, 12–16.

Sidwell, Mark. "Call to Separation and Unity: D. Martyn Lloyd-Jones and 'Evangelical Unity.'" *Detroit Baptist Seminary Journal* 3 (1998): 35–62.

Straub, Jeffrey P. "Fundamentalism and the King James Version: How a Venerable English Translation Became a Litmus Test for Orthodoxy." *Southern Baptist Journal of Theology* 15, no. 4 (2011): 44–62.

Sweeney, Douglas. "Fundamentalism and the Neo-Evangelicals." *Fides et Historia* 24, no. 1 (1992): 81–96.

Woodbridge, John D. "Is Biblical Inerrancy a Fundamentalist Doctrine?" *Bibliotheca Sacra* 142 (1985): 292–305.

———. "A Neoorthodox Historiography Under Siege." *Bibliotheca Sacra* 142 (1985): 3–15.

———. "The Rogers and McKim Proposal in the Balance." *Bibliotheca Sacra* 142 (1985): 99–113.

SCRIPTURE INDEX

SUBJECT INDEX